PREVENTION'S
Quick and Healthy
LOW-FAT COOKING™

FEATURING

CUISINES

FROM THE

MEDITERRANEAN

EDITED BY JEAN ROGERS, FOOD EDITOR, **PREVENTION** MAGAZINE HEALTH BOOKS

RODALE PRESS, EMMAUS, PENNSYLVANIA

Copyright © 1994 by Rodale Press, Inc.
Illustrations copyright © 1994 by Judy Reed
Photographs copyright © 1994 by Angelo Caggiano

Prevention is a registered trademark of Rodale Press, Inc.

Printed in the United States of America on acid-free ∞ , recycled paper containing a minimum of 10% post-consumer waste ♻

Front Cover: A typical *salade niçoise*, this one featuring grilled fresh tuna. See the box on page 99.
Cover Photographer: Angelo Caggiano
Food Stylist: Mariann Sauvion

ISBN 0–87596–192–4 hardcover
ISSN 1064–7503

2 4 6 8 10 9 7 5 3 1 hardcover

OUR MISSION

We publish books that empower people's lives.

RODALE ❧ BOOKS

Prevention's Quick and Healthy Low-Fat Cooking Staff

Editor: Jean Rogers

Executive Editor: Debora A. Tkac

Writers: Matthew Hoffman (Chapter 1), Martha Capwell (Chapter 2)

Book and Cover Designer: Debra Sfetsios

Book Layout: Ayers/Johanek Publication Design

Illustrator: Judy Reed

Photographers: Angelo Caggiano, Jerry Simpson, Alan Richardson

Photo Editor: Diane Buss

Food Stylist: Mariann Sauvion

Recipe Development: Laura Barton, Erin Bause-Landry, Anne Beal, Hugh Carpenter, Mary Carroll, Joanne D'Agostino, Dieter Dopplefeld, Barbara Fritz, Jean-Marc Fullsack, Victor Gielisse, Aliza Green, Matthew Hoffman, Judith Benn Hurley, Keith Keogh, August Mrozowski, Tom Ney, Judith Olney, Caprial Pence, Raymond Potter, Jean Rogers, Linda Rosensweig, Miriam Rubin, Marie Simmons

Home Economist, Rodale Food Center: JoAnn Brader

Nutritional Consultants: Arlene Dym, M.S., R.D.; Linda Yoakam, M.S., R.D.

Research Chief: Ann Gossy Yermish

Research Associate: Christine Dreisbach

Copy Editor: Rachelle Vander Schaaf

Editor in Chief: Bill Gottlieb

Editor, **Prevention** _Magazine:_ Mark Bricklin

Contents

Introduction

If you were creating the ideal recipe for a wonderful life, you'd toss together equal parts excellent health and longevity, then stir in an abundance of the simple pleasures. To make your recipe work, however, you'd probably need a little help from an entire culture centuries old.

This recipe, in essence, embodies the traditional Mediterranean way of life. People have intuitively recognized its health-giving powers for many years. Today, a growing body of research is adding scientific weight to the folklore and pushing this lifestyle into the spotlight.

The countries along the Mediterranean—including France, Italy, Greece and more—offer evidence that diet and lifestyle can truly play a vital role in the prevention of chronic diseases. Research has shown that locals who follow the traditional ways generally enjoy longer life spans and lower rates of heart disease and certain cancers than people in northern Europe and the United States.

In this book, we've delved into the proven scientific benefits of the Mediterranean diet. And then we've given you more than 200 recipes that draw inspiration from the ingredients and cooking methods typical of the area.

In keeping with the American desire to get meals on the table fast, a large portion of the recipes can be ready in 30 minutes or less. Many dishes can be made ahead to save you even more time. This symbol lets you know which ones those are. In addition, we've provided plenty of microwave shortcuts, chef's tips and timesaving secrets so you can cook healthy foods fast.

You need only look at the beautiful photos scattered throughout the book to see just how appealing Mediterranean-type cooking is. We hope they'll inspire you to put a taste of the Mediterranean on *your* table—often!

JEAN ROGERS
Food Editor, *Prevention* Magazine Health Books

CHAPTER 1

THE
WORLD'S
HEALTHIEST
CUISINE

THE MEDITERRANEAN DIET

According to Samuel Johnson, the great eighteenth-century writer and lexicographer, tourists who fail to visit Italy miss one of the greatest spectacles the world has to offer. "The grand object of traveling," said Dr. Johnson, "is to see the shores of the Mediterranean."

Indeed, there is much about this vast, fertile region that stirs the imagination like few other places on earth. It's home to many exotic cultures, among them Spain, Portugal, Italy, France, Turkey and a dozen more. Every one of these countries has its own customs and languages.

And each has its own cuisine.

Stop in the south of France and you'll find *salade niçoise*, a wonderfully fresh (and filling) salad that typically includes tuna, potatoes, anchovies, tomatoes and olives. Swing by Morocco for *harira*, a hearty soup thick with beans and vegetables. Drop by Spain for *arroz a la marinera*, a deliciously rich saffron-flavored rice dish made with squid, shrimp and monkfish. And that's only the beginning.

As you can see, the food is as varied as the countries it comes from. But there is a Mediterranean *style* that permeates it all. And it's wonderfully eclectic, easy to prepare and fabulously tasty.

Chefs (and happy diners) aren't the only ones with an interest in the Mediterranean. Doctors and researchers worldwide are also taking notice. In fact, more than 200 of the world's top scientists and food writers met in Cambridge, Massachusetts, for a three-day conference devoted solely to this ancient cuisine.

Why? Because the Mediterranean diet is more than just delicious. Experts say it's also one of the healthiest cuisines in the world.

AHEAD OF THEIR TIME

For nearly 50 years, researchers have noted that people living in Mediterranean countries seem uncommonly healthy. Heart disease, America's number one killer, is rare in the Mediterranean. So, too, are diabetes, gallstones, high cholesterol and many other serious health problems.

From the beginning, researchers suspected that there must be something—a very *healthy* something—in the Mediterranean diet that accounts for all of this robust good health.

As it turns out, there are many things. If you take a close look at the foods eaten in the Mediterranean every day—legumes, whole grains and fresh fruits and vegetables—you'll see that this diet is almost identical to that recommended by the U.S. Department of Agriculture in its official dietary guidelines.

Of course, the Mediterraneans were eating that way long before scientists came along with the good-food seal of approval. "This isn't a recent phenomenon," says Walter Willett, M.D., Dr.P.H., a professor of epidemiology and nutrition at Harvard's School of Public Health. "It was discovered thousands of years ago by the Mediterranean people themselves."

A GOOD-EATING PLAN

Before we set sail on our Mediterranean journey, let's take a look at what our government recommends we eat every day as part of a well-rounded, healthy diet.

HOW DO WE COMPARE?

*A*re you curious about how the current American diet stacks up against a traditional Mediterranean diet?

What Mediterraneans and most Americans eat is dramatically different. Traditional Mediterraneans eat seven times more bread and over twice as much fruits and vegetables as we do. On the other hand, we typically consume 3½ times as much red meat as they do. Whenever we wolf down two quarter-pound burgers for dinner, we're eating about as much beef as a Greek farmer might have in a whole week.

The fat in Mediterranean diets is nearly 75 percent heart-healthy monounsaturates and only 20 percent worrisome saturates. Most of the fat that Mediterraneans eat comes from olive oil. Our diet is composed of approximately 38 percent monos and 35 percent saturates.

When it comes to refined sugar, Mediterraneans eat very little. We, however, get nearly one out of every ten calories from the white stuff. How sweet it isn't!

The latest official guidelines come in the form of the Food Guide Pyramid. Like its Egyptian namesake, the government's pyramid is broad at the base and narrow at the top. That makes it possible to see at a glance which foods we should be eating and in what proportions.

The bottom tier of the pyramid, for example, represents grains: wheat, rye, rice and so on. Grains are literally the foundation of any healthy diet. According to the guidelines, we should be eating six to eleven servings of bread, cereal, rice or other grains every day. That sounds like a lot. But as you'll notice by looking at the recipes in this book, it's almost impossible *not* to get enough grains when you cook the Mediterranean way.

The next, somewhat smaller level of the pyramid represents fruits and vegetables: a combined total of five to nine servings a day. Higher up come protein sources such as meat, fish, beans and dairy products, with a recommended combined total of four to six servings a day. At the very pinnacle are fats, oils and sweets.

These are accompanied by the government's caution to "use them sparingly."

By now, you're probably wondering how you're going to count every morsel of food that passes your lips. And, more to the point, whether it's possible to eat all the servings recommended. Those are fair questions. In fact, experts agree that going by the numbers *can* be difficult. "I know as much about the health benefits of fruit and vegetables as anyone, and I don't always eat the minimum recommended five servings a day," confesses Gladys Block, Ph.D., a professor of public health nutrition and epidemiology in the school of public health at the University of California, Berkeley.

THE MEDITERRANEAN SECRET

The wonderful thing about cooking the Mediterranean way is that it's almost impossible *not* to eat a proper diet. Virtually every meal represents a healthy, delicious balance of grains, legumes, vegetables and fruit. "We won't change our diets just by hearing about it," adds Dr. Block. "We need to incorporate these changes in all parts of our lives."

That's easy. Although there are more than a dozen Mediterranean countries with many different cooking styles, they tend to use the same basic ingredients. Let's take a look at these foods one by one.

■ Fresh fruits and vegetables are a part of almost every meal. You might have something as simple as a salad of sliced cucumbers and tomatoes or as rich and aromatic as an appetizer of stuffed grape leaves. Fruit, of course, is always served: fresh figs, peaches, apricots, melons and much more show up at every meal and are used for snacks.

Besides being high in fiber, fresh fruits and green vegetables are rich in vitamin E, an important nutrient that has been found to help lower cholesterol, blood pressure and the risk for heart disease, says Dr. Block. In addition, "raw and fresh vegetables are almost universally associated with a reduced risk of cancer," adds John D. Potter, M.D., Ph.D., a professor of epidemiology at the University of Minnesota School of Public Health.

■ A little meat goes a long way. People in Mediterranean countries typically eat meat—usually chicken, pork or lamb—no more than once or twice a week. Even when they do have meat with their meals, it's generally included more for flavor than as the main event.

From a health point of view, this pays off because red meats are high in saturated fat, which is a major culprit in causing high cholesterol, high blood pressure, heart disease and possibly even cancer. In the Mediterranean, the small amount of red meat almost certainly contributes to the low rate of heart disease, says Dr. Willett.

■ Fresh fish abounds. Because every country in this region is touched by the Mediterranean sea, most people eat fresh seafood frequently. As a result, they get heart-healthy amounts of omega-3 fatty acids. Studies have shown that diets rich in omega-3s help lower cholesterol, blood pressure and the risk for heart disease.

■ Mediterraneans adore fresh bread, everything from Turkish *lavas* to French *baguettes*. And when they're not eating bread, they may be filling up on pasta, polenta, couscous, bulgur or other wonderful grain foods. In the Mediterranean, grains and other complex carbohydrates supply about 50 percent of daily calories. (In the United States, by contrast, only about 25 percent of our calories come from complex carbs.) Experts are unanimous in their assertion that whole grains, which provide lots of energy and are very low in fat, are among the healthiest foods you can eat.

■ Olive oil is used in generous amounts throughout the region and may in fact be *the* key to the health-boosting power of Mediterranean cuisine. "If there is one ingredient that really defines this diet," says Dimitrios Trichopoulos, M.D., chairman of the department of epidemiology at Harvard School of Public Health, "it is olive oil."

The Heart of Mediterranean Health

Olive oil is such an important part of Mediterranean cooking that it deserves some extra attention. Although Mediterraneans typically eat little meat or other foods high in saturated fat, their consumption of olive oil (a monounsaturated fat) can be prodigious. In some countries, somewhere around 40 percent of calories come from fat, mainly olive oil, Dr. Willett says.

Wait a minute. Haven't nutritionists been warning us to eat *less* fat? Don't they say that the 41 percent level we hover near in this country is too high? Hasn't the American Heart Association been preaching that we should lower our fat consumption to 30 percent of calories—or even less? Yet here are these Mediterraneans pouring olive oil on everything and thriving. What gives?

As it turns out, their "paradoxical" diet may in fact make a lot of sense. Studies have shown that some of the factors that determine a person's risk of heart disease—for example, weight and blood pressure—are about the same in people who eat large amounts of fat as they are in those who follow low-fat diets, says Dr. Willett.

What sets olive oil apart is that it doesn't appear to raise cholesterol the way saturated fat does. And since high blood cholesterol has been linked to strokes, heart attacks and other cardiovascular problems, it just makes sense to keep your cholesterol as low as possible.

In one study involving 4,903 men and women, Italian researchers found that people who took in large amounts of saturated fat (mostly in the form of butter) tended to have high cholesterol levels and high blood pressure. Those who reported using lots of olive oil, on the other hand, had much healthier cholesterol and blood pressure readings.

Another benefit of olive oil is that it's rich in vitamin E. Like vitamin C, beta-carotene and other important nutrients called antioxidants, vitamin E has been found to help reduce the risk of cancer, cataracts, heart disease and other serious diseases.

GOOD CHOLESTEROL, BAD CHOLESTEROL

Olive oil has some unique—and positive—effects on the body's cholesterol. In large amounts, it appears to raise levels of a protective kind of cholesterol while leaving a harmful kind unchanged. And that shift in balance can be very beneficial. Here's why.

It's standard advice by now that all of us would benefit from lowering our total cholesterol readings—ideally, to a level of less than 200. Study after study has shown that as cholesterol falls, so does the risk for heart disease. But in recent years, researchers have found that this equation is a bit more complicated than it seems on the surface. Two very different types of blood cholesterol exist, and they affect the arteries in totally different ways, says Lilian Cheung, D.Sc., R.D., director of the Nutrition and Fitness Project at Harvard School of Public Health.

One type of cholesterol is called low-density lipoproteins (or LDLs). This is the "bad" cholesterol that can lead to heart disease, says Dr. Cheung. Another type is called high-density lipoproteins (HDLs). This is "good" cholesterol that actually helps protect the arteries.

What usually happens when people go on low-fat diets to lower their cholesterol is that they reduce both types. A better solution is to lower LDLs without affecting HDLs.

That is where olive oil shines. "There is an increase in HDL when you put some olive oil in your diet, but total cholesterol stays about the same," says Martijn B. Katan, Ph.D., an associate professor of human nutrition at Wageningen Agricultural University in the Netherlands.

Moderation Is the Key

Following a Mediterranean-style diet—using olive oil as the primary fat, small amounts of meat and an abundance of fruits, grains, beans and vegetables—can put you on the road to better health. And because the food *tastes* so good, it's also a diet you can enjoy.

That is important because people are far more likely to stick with a healthy diet if they enjoy it. That may seem obvious to you, but people often forget about the pleasure factor when they try to change their eating habits. As Dr. Willett says, it's better to include some olive oil in your meals and be able to live with the diet than to cut out fat altogether and end up with a diet that's so unpalatable you give up on it.

Of course, some experts, including Dean Ornish, M.D., director of the Preventive Medicine Research Institute in Sausalito, California, worry that recommending *any* fat—even one as heart-healthy as olive oil—sends the wrong message. They're concerned that people will take the advice to eat more olive oil as carte blanche to eat all they want while still consuming a diet high in saturated fat.

Margo Denke, M.D., an assistant professor of internal medicine in the Center for Human Nutrition at the University of Texas Southwestern Medical Center in Dallas, seconds this caution. "Olive oil is not a magic bullet," she says. "Your goal should be to replace saturated fats in your diet—not to have olive oil *and* saturated fats."

Rooting Out Fat

As Dr. Denke is quick to point out, Mediterranean cooking isn't healthy only because fresh, nutritious ingredients go into it—it's also wonderful because of what comes out.

No matter what Mediterranean fare you're eating—spinach fettuccine, chick-peas with bulgur, tomato-and-basil salads—you'll

THE SOUL OF THE MEDITERRANEAN

Olive oil is *the* cooking oil of the Mediterranean. Countries in that area, such as Greece, Italy, Spain and Tunisia, produce about 95 percent of the world's supply of this fruity, rich-tasting, heart-healthy oil.

There are dozens of varieties of olive oil to choose from, each with its own aroma and its own special taste. "I still haven't tried them all," admits Linda Russo, a representative for the International Olive Oil Council in the United States.

You should know before you begin your quest that there are several distinctly different types of oil, which vary considerably in price and taste. They are:

Extra virgin. This is the crème de la crème, which is made only from top-quality olives. The olives are harvested by hand, then washed and pressed to extract the oil. Because no heat is used, the process is called cold-pressing. By law, an oil labeled extra virgin must contain less than 1 percent free oleic acid. Too much of this fatty acid can have an adverse effect on the oil's flavor.

rarely find large amounts of meat, butter, whole milk or other foods high in saturated fat.

But Americans are brought up on fatty foods, says R. Curtis Ellison, M.D., chief of the preventive medicine and epidemiology section at Boston University School of Medicine. "This is something we have to start moving away from."

And the sooner we change our habits, the better. New research is showing that the unhealthy foods we ate when we were younger may return to haunt us later. In a study lasting more than 30 years, researchers at Johns Hopkins University School of Medicine found that people with high cholesterol early in life were more likely to experience serious health problems, including heart disease, later on.

That isn't a uniquely American problem, of course. Diets are changing worldwide, and usually not for the better. Even in the Mediterranean, people are starting to adopt an American style of eating—with predictably unhealthy results.

According to the World Health Organization, diet-related diseases are becoming a serious problem throughout the world as

Extra virgin oil can vary in color from greenish gold to a pale gold with a slight greenish hue. In taste, it can range from robust to delicate. Because of its high quality (and often high price), it's used more as a flavoring agent in salad dressings and for drizzling over cooked food than as a cooking oil.

Virgin. Oil that would otherwise qualify for the extra virgin label but is not quite up to par for one reason or another may simply be called virgin. It's used in the same ways as extra virgin oil.

Olive oil. This is the official name for oils not good enough to be termed extra virgin or virgin. This oil is an economical choice for cooking.

Light. Don't let this one fool you—it's not lower in fat or calories than other olive oils. It is simply light in flavor and color. It is basically refined olive oil that contains a *very* small amount of virgin and is highly filtered. Use as you would any other vegetable oil.

people "abandon traditionally healthy diets in favor of 'affluent' foods" high in saturated fat, sugar and salt.

THE HEART-HEALTHY WAY

Saturated fat does more than set up camp on unsuspecting hips. Studies also show it can be *the* villain behind stroke, heart disease, high blood pressure and other long-term problems. In fact, says Dr. Denke, if you look at the amount of saturated fat in the diet, you'll come up with a better predictor of heart disease than if you concentrate only on total fat.

Consider Glasgow. In this seaport city in southern Scotland, residents like to boast about how little fruit—and how much fat—they typically eat. They stop boasting when chest pains start, which happens remarkably often. Glasgow has the highest death rate from heart attacks in the world—about 380 per 100,000.

Let's contrast this with France, where, as in other Mediterranean countries, people eat an abundance of fruit and vegetables and relatively little saturated fat. Their rate of heart disease is about 79 per 100,000—about one-fifth that of Glasgow's!

For years, experts have been telling us Americans to lower our cholesterol levels in order to reduce our risk for stroke, heart attacks, high blood pressure and other problems. The easiest, quickest way to succeed is to cut saturated fat.

That was convincingly demonstrated in a study at Columbia University College of Physicians and Surgeons, where students were given either an "average" American diet with an abundance of fat or one of two different lower-fat diets.

Not surprisingly, students on the high-fat fare had about the same cholesterol levels at the end of the study as they had at the beginning. Students on one lower-fat diet, which was still high in saturated fat, also showed little benefit. Only the third group, whose diet was lower in *both* total fat and saturated fat, achieved a meaningful drop in cholesterol.

So the prime targets in the cholesterol war are red meats, full-fat dairy products and other foods high in saturated fat. "You have to get *saturated* fat as low as possible," says Frank Sacks, M.D., an associate professor of medicine and nutrition at Harvard School of Public Health.

THE CANCER CONNECTION

Here's yet another reason to follow the Mediterranean example and cut back on saturated fat: There is increasing evidence that some cancers—of the breast, colon and prostate gland, for example—may be affected by saturated fat in the diet. For proof, researchers point to countries such as Japan, where the rate of cancer is rising now that people are following our example and eating more fatty foods.

In a large Canadian study, 56,837 women were asked to fill out detailed questionnaires about their diets, lifestyles and medical histories. Five years later, the same women were contacted for follow-up assessments. Researchers found that the women who developed breast cancer often were the very ones who had previously reported consuming the most fat.

Once again, the Mediterranean diet seems to be a winner. "Southern European countries have the lowest breast cancer rates," says José Martin-Moreno, M.D., Ph.D., Dr.P.H., chairman of the department of epidemiology at Escuela Nacional de Sanidad in Madrid. Diet may not be the only explanation, he adds, but clearly it plays a protective role.

Best of all, modifying our diets is something we can do for ourselves without delay. From a health perspective, following a Mediterranean-style diet—small amounts of meat, moderate intake of olive oil and lots of grains, vegetables and legumes—just makes good sense. And for our taste buds, it's a real treat. So let's put on our chef's toques and begin!

An International Cuisine

There was a time when "healthy food" meant tofu, raw carrots and unadorned brown rice. Sure, it was good for you . . . if you ate it. Most people didn't—at least, not for long.

Mediterranean cooking most assuredly is good for you, but it's anything but dull. In fact, it's a rich, vibrant cuisine, packed with flavor and virtually infinite in variety. Good health is just one reason to go Mediterranean. "The other part is poetry," says Nancy Harmon Jenkins, who is herself working on a Mediterranean cookbook.

"I think food should be a positive experience," adds Lillian Sonnenberg, D.Sc., R.D., a dietitian and manager of outpatient nutrition services at Massachusetts General Hospital in Boston. "You need to have a diet you can live with—and stick with—the rest of your life."

You can't get bored in the Mediterranean. This truly is an international cuisine, with recipes drawn from Italy, France, Morocco and wherever else your taste buds lead you. That's the beauty of setting a Mediterranean table, says Dr. Willett. "There are so many wonderful foods we can enjoy!"

Mediterranean Basics

Best of all, many Mediterranean recipes are marvelously easy to shop for and prepare. You may already have most of the ingredients necessary to get started. All you really need, after all, is a grain, a bean and a green.

Let's start with the greens—and the reds, yellows and oranges! Vegetables, fruits and fresh produce are featured players on the Mediterranean stage. Have you ever had baked sweet potatoes with honey and ginger? How about broccoli rabe with a sprinkle of Parmesan? Sun-kissed tomatoes with fresh basil and balsamic vinegar? Garlic-scented mashed potatoes? Sure, they sound (and taste) exotic, but each of these recipes is quick, easy and very good!

And as we've seen, fresh fruits and vegetables are gold mines of fiber and important nutrients such as vitamin C, vitamin E and beta-carotene—the so-called antioxidants. "The presence of substances known as oxidants may have a lot to do with what we call aging," says Jeffrey Blumberg, Ph.D., chief of the Antioxidants Research Laboratory at Tufts University. By eating produce and vegetables rich in antioxidants, "we can really talk about slowing down the aging process," he says.

In fact, studies have shown that people who get abundant amounts of antioxidants may have less risk of such divergent problems as cataracts and arthritis. And in a Scottish study, men eating large amounts of antioxidants had the lowest rate of heart disease. With antioxidants, says Dr. Blumberg, "we can advance the goal of dying young—as late as possible."

MARKET RESEARCH

Variety is the key to Mediterranean cuisine. So the next time you're at the market, Jenkins advises, "slow down. Look at what's available, and be ready to try new things."

Let us look at lettuce. Why stop with boring iceberg? Try such colorful greens as arugula, radicchio and watercress, and use them in varied ways. Fashion a zesty spring salad from arugula dressed with a touch of olive oil and a splash of balsamic vinegar. Or try more elaborate creations, mixing and matching greens, olives, tomatoes, cucumbers—whatever you have. With a little creativity, you can make a ho-hum salad come alive.

"I tell my students to try as many different combinations as they can," says David Smythe, a chef and instructor at the Culinary Institute of America in Hyde Park, New York. "If one doesn't work, you'll know better next time." Chances are, though, you'll love your creations.

Chances are, too, that you can whip up a delicious meal using what you've already got in your pantry and refrigerator. How about lasagna swirls stuffed with spinach and ricotta? Peppers filled with a savory blend of corn, rice and carrots? You can try a polenta casserole made with cornmeal, beans and pasta.

"Cooking this way doesn't have to be a big production," Jenkins says. "You can sauté a few onions and peppers for an easy side dish or slice cucumbers for a salad. We're talking about real people in real life. Italian mothers don't spend hours in the kitchen!"

KNOWING BEANS

Since meat plays such a small role in Mediterranean cooking, legumes—better known as tasty, inexpensive and wonderfully easy-to-prepare beans—are served with virtually every meal. For protein, they are the backbone of Mediterranean cuisine.

Beans come in all hues, shapes and flavors. You'll find that many Mediterranean recipes call for lentils, chick-peas and fava beans. But you should feel free to substitute personal favorites—say, navy beans, black beans or kidney beans.

Beans are extremely low in fat and packed with protein, fiber and other important nutrients. On a cold winter day, what could be more satisfying and warming than a bowl of steamy lentils topped with spicy vegetables? Add a green vegetable and a crisp salad, and you have the fixings for a hearty, delectable meal you can prepare with almost no work. And, of course, no one leaves a Mediterranean table hungry.

Despite their admirable health benefits, beans have a way of causing, well, an awkward social problem. But it's possible, experts say, to take the social sting from beans. Here's what they recommend:

- Rinse dried beans in cold water, removing any foreign particles and wizened or broken beans.
- Soak them overnight in plenty of new water. This can help reduce the amounts of gas-causing compounds that cause trouble.
- The next day, drain off the old water and replace it with fresh. Then cook the beans, covered, for about half an hour. Drain, and add new water. Continue cooking until the beans are soft to the bite. Exact timing will depend on the variety.

FRESH FROM THE SEA

The Mediterranean sea washes up on many coasts, among them Spain, France, Italy, Portugal and Greece. As a result, most Mediterraneans eat seafood at least once a week.

Once touted as brain food, this finny fare is among the smartest food choices you can make. Fish is lower in saturated fat than most meats and high in important nutrients such as magnesium, potassium and zinc. What's more, most fish are packed with omega-3 fatty acids, powerful allies for healthy hearts.

OF AVOCADOS AND ALMONDS

*N*ow that olive oil has been inducted into the Nutritionally Correct Hall of Fame, researchers are taking a second look at some other foods high in heart-healthy monounsaturates.

That's led them to such fare as avocados and almonds. And it's made them do an about-face on their stand concerning these foods. Not so long ago, nutritionists pretty much declared these high-fat foods off-limits, or at least off everyday menus. New evidence, however, is emerging that may bring these dietary outcasts back into the fold.

In one study, Australian researchers put people on a high-avocado diet, feeding them anywhere from ½ to 1½ of the pear-shaped fruits a day. Three weeks into the study, the people's cholesterol levels had dropped significantly, from an average of 236 to 217. What's more, their protective HDL cholesterol remained steady, while their undesirable LDLs dropped nearly 14 percent. Score one for the avocados.

Nuts also have been getting a second look. In one study, for example, researchers found that when people ate 3½ ounces of almonds a day, their cholesterol dropped 20 points, despite the fact that their total intake of dietary fat rocketed. Again, the drop in cholesterol came from the nasty LDL side of the equation, with the helpful HDLs remaining steady.

Does all this mean it's time to abandon our low-fat diets? Not at all, researchers say. What it does mean is that we can add a few select, delicious, high-fat foods such as avocados and almonds to our diets without worrying about the consequences.

Studies have shown that eating foods rich in omega-3s can help lower blood pressure, cut cholesterol and reduce the risk for heart attack. There is some evidence that fish oils can help relieve inflammatory conditions such as arthritis and psoriasis as well.

In one study, people with painful rheumatoid arthritis were given fish-oil supplements for 24 weeks. Before the study, all had been taking steroids or other anti-inflammatory drugs. Twelve weeks into the study, researchers noted a significant decrease in swollen joints. After 18 weeks, many of the patients also had a stronger hand grip and less morning pain and stiffness.

Twenty years ago, it was almost impossible to enjoy fresh fish unless you lived near a lake or ocean. Today, many fish are raised in man-made lakes and ponds. This, combined with improved interstate transportation, means you can have the "catch of the day" every day.

Just as there are many varieties of fish, so are there dozens, *hundreds* of ways to prepare them, says Smythe. "About the easiest thing you can do is put a fillet on the grill and brush it with a little olive oil," he suggests. For some Mediterranean zest, you can jazz it up with a little garlic and lemon juice, he adds.

If you're feeling a bit more ambitious, cook up some seafood risotto—which can actually be quite effortless if you do it in your microwave. Or try a quick entrée of linguine and clam sauce.

THE STAFF OF LIFE

Perhaps no other ingredients are enjoyed so often or in so many shapes, textures and flavors as grains. Virtually every town in the Mediterranean has its own bakery. A meal without bread—whether it's plain French bread, olive-and-rosemary focaccia, onion cornbread or any of the myriad other varieties—is thought to be slim pickings indeed.

Of course, grains are used for more than just bread. There's pasta for sure—and *it* comes in an infinite array of colors, shapes, textures and sizes. (You can even try black pasta, which is colored with squid ink.) And then there are the rice, bulgur, couscous, quinoa and cornmeal dishes.

As we've seen from the Food Guide Pyramid, grains are the foundation of any healthy diet. There's no question that eating several servings a day of bread, pasta, rice or other whole grains can reduce cholesterol, lower blood pressure and maybe knock a few pounds off the hips, too.

For that matter, some people with diabetes can control their blood-sugar swings just by sticking to a low-fat, high-grain diet. "I'll always try changing the diet before using drugs for diabetes," says Terry Shintani, M.D., director of preventive medicine at the Waianae Coast Comprehensive Health Center.

In studies at his clinic in Hawaii, Dr. Shintani has treated overweight patients with diabetes by putting them on diets low in fat and high in complex carbohydrates, without calorie restriction. "With this diet, I even got some people who had type II (adult-onset) diabetes to decrease their insulin," he says.

A SPICE FOR LIFE

Garlic isn't really one of the main food groups, but it's used so often in the Mediterranean that it at least deserves honorary mention. "I can't think of a single recipe that you can't add garlic to," says Catherine Cremaldi, owner of Cremaldi's, an Italian food store in Cambridge, Massachusetts. "It's wonderful on everything!" Well, maybe not apple pie or rice pudding . . . but certainly, any savory dish would be enhanced by this versatile aromatic.

Some ideas? Sprinkle crushed garlic on sliced tomatoes. Sauté a little with sweet peppers. Mix some in with whatever sauce you're using on your pasta. True garlic aficionados often crush several cloves and stir in a little olive oil, then drizzle it on thick slices of toasted Italian bread.

But garlic is much more than just another pretty, pungent face. This powerful herb, of the genus *Allium*, has been a standby in medicine for thousands of years. It was used for everything from sterilizing wounds to relieving coughs and treating snakebites. Even today, it's a commonly used folklore medicine in Europe.

Studies have shown that garlic can "thin" the blood and lower cholesterol. Eaten in large amounts, it may help prevent cancer as well. According to Dr. Potter, "there are a wide variety of compounds in garlic that may be helpful in their anticancer properties." So don't delay—eat more garlic today!

The more researchers learn about Mediterranean cuisine, the more convinced they are that it can work as well today for us as it has for the Mediterranean people over thousands of years.

You might say this is the opposite of a fad diet. It's passed the test of time. And it's practiced every day by real people—hardworking people who aren't about to leave the table hungry. They eat well, they live well—and they live longer. Theirs is a diet we can all live with!

As you'll discover when you try the recipes in this book, Mediterranean cuisine is incredibly rich and varied. That's especially important because good food, like life itself, should be an adventure. The more varied the menu, the more excitement you can look forward to. This is one journey that can last a lifetime.

CHAPTER 2

A HEALTH-
WATCHER'S
GUIDE TO
LOW-FAT
FOOD
SHOPPING

NAVIGATING THE SUPERMARKET

These days, markets are full of lower-fat versions of many of your favorite foods. So if you're serious about cutting fat and eating better, you're in luck—all the low-fat, high-fiber, high-nutrition foods you want are at your favorite store. You just have to know where to look and how to read labels. Following is a "low-fat tour" of a typical grocery store.

THE PRODUCE DEPARTMENT

Fruits and vegetables have little or no fat (avocados are the big exception). In addition, they have no cholesterol and are generally pretty cheap, so load up your cart here. But don't fall for some of the tempting blandishments savvy market managers pad their produce sections with, such as gourmet salad dressings and croutons. They're pricey and loaded with fat; you'll find cheaper, healthier alternatives a few aisles away.

If your budget allows, broaden your culinary horizons with one new fruit or veggie each week—many markets offer suggestions for preparing new as well as familiar produce. Items like broccoflower, broccoli rabe, arugula, radicchio, exotic mushrooms, okra, yellow potatoes, mangoes, blackberries and persimmons are tasty alternatives to your produce selections. Give them a chance to become new favorites.

THE DAIRY CASE

Unless you have kids under age two, bypass the whole milk and opt for 1 percent or 2 percent low-fat milk. Better still, choose skim. If your family drinks only the "real" thing, try mixing half whole milk and half lower-fat milk. They'll never know the difference. And try cooking with evaporated skim milk—it has a nice creamy texture and no fat.

Nonfat plain yogurt is a great—and inexpensive—substitute for sour cream. Nonfat flavored yogurts make great desserts, too. If you really prefer the flavor of sour cream, the new reduced-calorie and nonfat sour creams are worth trying. They taste very close to the real thing at a fraction of the fat cost.

Despite what the labels say, there really is no such thing as low-fat margarine. Some brands have *less* fat and fewer calories per tablespoon than others, but that's because they are whipped or have water added to them. All the calories in *all* margarines come from fat.

Still, some margarines are better choices than others. Whipped and water-added tub spreads are difficult to cook and bake with because you can't simply substitute an equal amount for what's listed in a recipe. However, you can use them as spreads and on vegetables and other foods. Squeeze-bottle brands whose first ingredient is "liquid vegetable oil" are more versatile because you *can* cook with them. Some people particularly like liquid margarine because it's so easy to spread thinly on toast, muffins and other baked goods.

The new reduced-fat cheeses are a mixed bag. Some of the nonfat and reduced-fat ricottas are as good as whole-milk versions.

Many of the "light" hard and processed cheeses are quite tasty; however, hardly any have less than five grams of fat per ounce, so they really don't qualify as low-fat foods. Some brands of cheese that truly are low in fat don't have much taste, while others are fine. Trial and error is in order here.

THE FISH COUNTER

Not every market has a fresh-fish counter, but you can almost always find unbreaded, no-fat-added fillets in the freezer. Any fish is a good choice for the fat-conscious, as long as it's naked. Most processed fish sticks, croquettes and cakes have added fat and salt you don't want. If you are trying to introduce fish to your family, start with firm, meaty types like swordfish, monkfish and halibut, which can be broiled or grilled.

Over in the canned-fish aisle is another fat-cutter's friend: tuna packed in water. You may even find reduced-salt brands, but if not, don't worry—you pour off a lot of the sodium when you drain the tuna.

THE CEREAL AISLE

If you have kids, sugar in cereal is probably a bigger issue than fat. But there are some brands, like old favorites Cheerios and Wheaties, that combine the best of both worlds: low fat and low sugar. Check labels, and look for brands that have three grams or less of fat per ounce—and at least two grams of fiber. Bear in mind, though, that the serving size listed on most cereal boxes may be smaller than what many of us eat. A realistic serving size is two or three ounces, so multiply accordingly if needed.

THE SOUP AISLE

The shelves that used to be solid red and white are now a rainbow of labels that all seem to bear the word *healthy* somewhere. But the plain fact is that most soup never was high in fat, except for cream soups, chowders and some of the "chunky" varieties. What canned soup had, and in many cases still does, is a lot of sodium. Here's where it's time to read labels.

On the label, you'll find information on a soup's calories, fat and sodium per serving. Choose on the basis of how much you eat—the serving is usually half of the total yield. So if you normally eat the whole can, double all the numbers.

Beans, Rice and Pasta

Little do most of us realize what a nutritional bonanza humble beans, in their plain plastic bags and simple cans, offer.

Beans are probably your best buy in the whole market. They're cheap, high in protein, rich in fiber and virtually fat-free. Best of all, they can replace meat in any number of dishes. Buy a bag or a can, and make chili or a hearty bean soup. Your family will love it, and their hearts will, too.

One of the best things to appear in the supermarket lately is quick-cooking brown rice. Although white rice is certainly a fat-fighter's friend, brown rice has more flavor and healthy fiber. With the quick versions at your disposal, you get those benefits in about one-quarter of the time it used to take.

Pasta is another nutritional champ, full of B vitamins and complex carbohydrates. This may come as a surprise, but it's not the pasta itself that's fatty—it's what you top it with. Cheese, butter, cream and heavy oil-based sauces are obvious "bad boys," but don't forget about the less recognizable fat in commercial spaghetti sauces and meat sauces. Some seemingly "harmless" tomato-based toppers contain more than six grams of fat per serving. Read those labels.

The Bread Aisle

This is a veritable health-food department. Full of fiber and low in fat, whole-grain breads are one of your best buys. The dark, hearty slices are more expensive than bland white loaves, but whole-grain bread offers a painless, nutritious and tasty way to add complex carbohydrates to your daily diet. It's certainly suitable for everything from breakfast toast and lunch sandwiches to dinner rolls.

Cookies, Crackers and Snacks

It's sad, but true: This aisle is pretty much a mine field for the fat-conscious shopper. Here's where you will find some nonfat snack cakes and "lite" chips, but they don't offer much in the way of nutrients.

There are a few safe spots, though, like rice, corn and popcorn cakes. These have virtually no fat, and the flavored versions make a good substitute for crackers and cookies. Graham crackers and fig bars are also fairly low-fat treats.

Imported whole-grain crackers such as Ry-Krisp are a bit of an acquired taste but a good choice. Low in fat, they make a tasty base for sandwiches or dips. And when broken up, they can substitute for high-fat croutons in salads.

Pretzels have very little fat, and if sodium is a concern, you can usually find no-salt versions. Here's where you'll find popcorn for your air-popper, too. Skip the microwave brands, though—most of them have added fat, even the "light" versions.

MAYO AND SALAD DRESSINGS

Here's another department that is bigger than it used to be. Nonfat mayonnaise is available from various manufacturers. Some are better than others, so taste-test until you find one you like.

Some salad dressings also have no fat. Again, experiment with different brands. You can also try the reduced-fat versions—they usually have about half the fat (two or three grams per tablespoon) of regular. Here, of course, it's important to watch how much you pour on—most people find a tablespoon a pretty skimpy serving. So if you use more, realize that you'll eat more fat.

THE POULTRY AND MEAT COUNTER

Poultry is the low-fat, low-price champ of the meat department, and cut-up turkey parts and ground turkey are as common as chicken in most markets. Boneless turkey and chicken breasts are quick-cooking, easy to use in many dishes and very low in fat.

Beef has a lot less fat than it used to, though it still doesn't compare with poultry in terms of either fat or cholesterol. Loin and round cuts are lowest in fat; look for the "select" label, which is the USDA's designation for lower-fat cuts.

Many stores now label their ground beef for fat, but read carefully! Often the numbers are for just one ounce, while you probably use three to five ounces to make a burger. Except for the brands that have carrageenan or other extenders added, you're not likely to find hamburger that has less than 10 percent fat (by weight).

Even hot dogs have slimmed down a bit. There are chicken and turkey franks, but they are often only a little "lighter" than the old classic wieners. A better (and tastier) choice is franks labeled 90 percent fat-free; they pack just five grams of fat per dog.

THE FREEZER CASE

Frozen entrées have come a long way since the early days of the TV dinner—many are now low in fat, sodium and calories. What they aren't low in, though, is price. So unless convenience is your highest priority, you probably won't resort to these very often.

But frozen vegetables can be a mainstay for a fat-cutting cook. Plain frozen vegetables are best; besides being cheapest, they have no added fat. Do, however, read the labels on "medleys," "international vegetables" and boil-in bags—they often *are* high in fat and sodium.

One of the sweetest things to happen to fat-watchers was the invention of nonfat frozen yogurt and other treats like fruit ices and sorbets. Nonfat yogurt gives you the calcium goodness of ice cream with minimal fat (less than one-half gram per four-ounce serving). Sugar in these products does add calories, though, so these sweets should still remain occasional treats. And though fruit ices are low in fat and calories, they don't pack the fiber and vitamin punch of a piece of fresh fruit.

Now take your low-fat, nutrient-laden selections to the checkout counter. We bet you'll go home with great food—maybe even a fuller wallet, too.

WINNING FOODS

If you were handing out awards for the best, most nutritious, wisest-choice foods on the planet, the selections below would top your list. In each group, the food listed first is the overall winner, followed in descending order by a handful of runners-up. Although the rankings are somewhat arbitrary, they were arrived at through a complicated rating system that determined which nutrients are especially important for each food group and how much of those nutrients individual foods contain. (Vitamin C, for instance, is very important in fruits, so it was weighted heavily in that category. Dairy has no vitamin C but plenty of calcium, so that mineral figured prominently in those ratings. When negatives like fat or cholesterol were present, foods with the least amount got the best scores.)

Vegetables. Nobody can contest broccoli's right to the trophy in this category. While second-place sweet potato has broccoli outclassed in terms of cancer-preventing beta-carotene, the green giant is loaded with fiber and is a runaway champ when it comes to vitamin C. All of the foods on this list have laudable amounts of potassium, a mineral that can help regulate blood pressure.

- broccoli
- sweet potato
- hubbard squash
- artichoke
- butternut squash
- cauliflower
- carrot
- asparagus
- beets
- eggplant

Leafy greens. Chicory chalks up its victory thanks to its stores of potassium, beta-carotene, fiber, vitamin C and folate, a B vitamin that's important for healthy blood cells. But the also-rans are no slouches, either, and score well in many of these same areas.

- chicory
- spinach
- beet greens
- brussels sprouts
- turnip greens
- mustard greens
- romaine lettuce
- red cabbage
- collard greens

Fruit. Cantaloupe came in first due to its plentiful supplies of beta-carotene and potassium (even more potassium than bananas, which are an excellent source). Blackberries outshine most other fruits in terms of dietary fiber. And papaya earned its spot by beating out oranges in the vitamin C department.

- cantaloupe
- blackberries
- papaya
- raspberries
- mango
- strawberries
- orange
- kumquats
- blueberries
- pear
- banana
- apple

Dairy. In the dairy division, nonfat yogurt beat skim milk in a closely contended match. Both are equally low in cholesterol and fat, but the yogurt earned extra points because it's got more calcium. All of the items on our list are smart dairy choices.

- nonfat yogurt
- skim milk
- low-fat yogurt
- 1 percent low-fat milk
- buttermilk
- 2 percent low-fat milk
- nonfat or part-skim mozzarella cheese
- nonfat or part-skim ricotta cheese

Shellfish. Each of these items has earned its boasting rights. Oysters have the highest amount of heart-healthy omega-3 fatty acids, and they're overflowing with zinc, which is so important for wound healing and immune-system function. Clams put other shellfish to shame in the blood-building vitamin B_{12} category. Although not nearly as high in B_{12}, mussels are also a good source. And crab and shrimp garner honors for their exceptionally low fat content.

- eastern oysters
- clams
- Alaskan crab
- blue crab
- blue mussels
- shrimp

Finfish. All of these fish are excellent choices. Some, like herring, are quite high in omega-3s. Others, such as halibut, are very low in fat. All are decent sources of some B vitamins, including B_6 and B_{12}.

- bluefin tuna
- coho salmon
- halibut
- snapper
- herring
- mackerel
- sockeye salmon
- Atlantic cod

Beans. All beans are outstanding sources of fiber. And many pack hefty amounts of potassium, folate and iron. They're all low in fat— even chick-peas, which do have more fat than most other varieties.

- baby lima beans
- pinto beans
- large lima beans
- lentils
- navy beans
- black beans
- black-eyed peas
- white beans
- fava beans
- chick-peas

Grains. In the grain department, bulgur muscled its way to the top with its overpowering fiber content. With almost three grams more per cup of cooked grain than its nearest competitor—whole-wheat spaghetti—bulgur makes an outstanding addition to your diet.

- bulgur
- whole-wheat spaghetti
- oatmeal
- brown rice
- white rice
- spaghetti
- couscous

Poultry. To reach the top in the poultry division, a competitor had to be lean and mean. And that's exactly the description of turkey breast. In fact, turkey breast is considerably lower in fat than the next-best poultry meat, chicken breast. But all the items on this list merit a place because of their iron, zinc and vitamin B_{12} content. As is always the case with poultry, these cuts should be consumed without their fatty skin.

- turkey breast
- chicken breast
- turkey leg
- chicken drumstick
- chicken leg
- chicken thigh

Meats. When it comes to meat, there are only two words that really count: *fat* and *cholesterol*. And in both cases, top-of-the-list eye round has rock-bottom stats. It's even leaner than pork tenderloin, which is considered a very lean meat. Naturally, red meat is high in blood-building iron and vitamin B_{12}.

- beef eye round
- beef tip round
- beef bottom round
- beef top sirloin
- beef tenderloin
- pork tenderloin
- lamb leg shank
- lamb arm
- lamb leg sirloin
- lamb loin

CHAPTER 3

DIPS,
DRINKS
AND EASY
APPETIZERS

$\mathscr{S}$IMPLE STARTERS

The companionship of family and friends is an important concept in Mediterranean countries. And the fellowship shared at both large and small gatherings may be an immeasurable contributor to the health of people in that part of the world. Resolve now to spend a little more of your time relaxing with those you love. And help them stay healthy by serving low-fat—but great-tasting—food at your get-togethers. Fun items like mini pizzas will make a big hit; so will such easy fare as crab beignets, chicken nuggets, turkey canapés and shrimp fritters. Set out an assortment of lean dips, whip up some out-of-the-ordinary fruit drinks, and have yourself a grand old time.

MIDDLE EASTERN CHICK-PEA DIP

MAKES ABOUT 2 CUPS

*C*hick-pea dip, also known as hummus, is a favorite in Middle Eastern countries. Serve it with warm pita wedges that you can use to scoop up the dip. This particular version is the creation of Sharon Stocker, a research editor with *Prevention* magazine.

1   can (16 ounces) chick-peas, rinsed and drained
½   cup nonfat yogurt
¼   cup minced scallions
¼   cup packed finely minced fresh parsley
    Juice of 2 lemons
5   teaspoons tahini
3   cloves garlic, minced
⅛   teaspoon ground black pepper
    Dash of low-sodium soy sauce
    Pinch of ground red pepper

In a food processor, process the chick-peas until smooth, stopping to scrape down the sides of the container as necessary.

Add the yogurt, scallions, parsley, lemon juice, tahini, garlic, black pepper, soy sauce and red pepper. Process until smooth and creamy. (If necessary, add a small amount of water to achieve the proper consistency.)

Spread in an even layer on a large shallow platter. If not serving immediately, cover and chill. Let warm to room temperature for best flavor.

Preparation time: 10 minutes

Per ¼ cup: 63 calories, 1.7 g. fat (25% of calories), 2.1 g. dietary fiber, no cholesterol, 171 mg. sodium.

SPINACH DIP WITH PITA WEDGES

SERVES 8

Spinach, yogurt, garlic and pita breads are popular in many different Mediterranean countries. This dip is particularly easy. But do allow at least 30 minutes for the yogurt to drain so the dip will be nice and thick. This recipe comes from Matthew Hoffman, a health and fitness writer who loves experimenting with food from many different cultures. Garlic is a particular favorite of his. If you're not quite as fond of it, use only one or two cloves. You may serve the dip warm or at room temperature.

   2 *cups nonfat yogurt*
   1 *tablespoon olive oil*
   4 *cloves garlic, minced*
   1 *cup packed fresh spinach, finely chopped*
   ¼ *teaspoon lemon juice*
   ⅛ *teaspoon ground black pepper*
   8 *mini pita breads, warmed and cut into wedges*

Spoon the yogurt into a yogurt cheese funnel or a sieve lined with cheesecloth. Place over a bowl and allow to drain for 30 minutes.

In a large no-stick frying pan over medium heat, warm the oil. Add the garlic and cook, stirring constantly, for 1 minute. Add the spinach. Cook, stirring, for 2 minutes, or until wilted. Remove from the heat.

Stir in the yogurt, lemon juice and pepper. Transfer to a shallow serving dish. Serve with the pita wedges.

Preparation time: 30 minutes
Cooking time: 5 minutes

Per serving: 103 calories, 2.1 g. fat (18% of calories), 0.5 g. dietary fiber, 1 mg. cholesterol, 157 mg. sodium.

A Traditional Provençal Dipping Sauce

R ouille is a spicy sauce that's great as a dip for crisp raw vegetables. Because the sauce is so hot, you'll want to use just a little at a time on your vegetables of choice. That's all to the good, since this dip is composed mostly of oil—albeit healthy olive oil. You can also use the sauce to give extra flavor to soups and fish stews. Just stir a small amount into your individual bowl. The sauce keeps very well in the refrigerator. It will have a tendency to separate upon standing, so whisk it well before using.

ROUILLE

MAKES ½ CUP

1   hot red pepper, seeds removed (wear
     plastic gloves when handling)
3   cloves garlic, chopped
2   slices firm bread, crusts removed
⅓   cup olive oil
     Ground black pepper

Chop the red pepper. Using a mini food processor, blend the peppers and garlic into a paste.

Hold the bread under cold running water. When it is soaked, squeeze out the moisture. Add the bread to the food processor and blend well.

Slowly blend in the oil to form a sauce of medium consistency. Add black pepper to taste.

Preparation time: 5 minutes

Chef's note: If you don't have a small food processor, grind the red pepper and garlic with a mortar and pestle, then mash in the bread and black pepper. Start blending in the oil, a little at a time. If the mortar gets too full, transfer the mixture to a bowl and add the remaining oil.

Per teaspoon: 32 calories, 3.1 g. fat (87% of calories), trace dietary fiber, no cholesterol, 10 mg. sodium.

FIESTA DIP

*S*weet red peppers and shredded cucumbers add crunch to this low-fat offering that features several Mediterranean favorite foods: red peppers, garlic and thyme. Serve it with pita wedges, low-fat crackers or crisp raw vegetables.

½   *cup shredded cucumbers*
1   *cup nonfat sour cream*
½   *cup minced sweet red peppers*
1   *clove garlic, minced*
½   *teaspoon dried thyme*

Squeeze all excess moisture from the cucumbers. Place the cucumbers in a small bowl. Stir in the sour cream, peppers, garlic and thyme. Transfer to a serving bowl and chill until needed.

Preparation time: 5 minutes

Per 2 tablespoons: 15 calories, trace fat (3% of calories), trace dietary fiber, no cholesterol, 14 mg. sodium.

BASIL AND SUN-DRIED TOMATOES DIP

un-dried tomatoes originated in Italy, where they were a means of preserving an abundant harvest. As you would expect, the dry-pack variety is much lower in fat than those preserved in oil. If you're using the oil-packed tomatoes, blot them well with paper towels to remove most of the excess fat. Then chop and blend with the other ingredients as directed. Serve this dip with carrot sticks, blanched snow peas, thinly sliced sweet peppers, blanched broccoli florets or other vegetables.

6	*sun-dried tomato halves*
½	*cup boiling water*
2	*cups low-fat cottage cheese*
¼	*cup thinly sliced scallions*
¼	*cup chopped fresh basil*
1	*tablespoon lemon juice*
½	*teaspoon ground black pepper*

In a small bowl, combine the tomatoes and water. Let stand for 5 minutes to soften the tomatoes. Drain well and chop finely.

Place the cottage cheese in a food processor. Add the tomatoes, scallions, basil, lemon juice and pepper. Process with on/off turns until well mixed and somewhat smooth.

Preparation time: 10 minutes

Per 2 tablespoons: 32 calories, 0.3 g. fat (9% of calories), 0.3 g. dietary fiber, 1 mg. cholesterol, 119 mg. sodium.

FRUIT WITH CREAMY GINGER DIP

SERVES 6

*N*onfat mayonnaise and sour cream are a real boon to those who love dips but can do without the fat and calories regular versions deliver. You can use any type of fruit for this lightly sweet dip. We particularly like the combination of Italian favorites used below.

½	cup nonfat sour cream
½	cup nonfat mayonnaise
	Grated rind of 1 lime
1	tablespoon lime juice
1	tablespoon honey
1	tablespoon grated fresh ginger
1½	cups cantaloupe cubes
1½	cups honeydew melon cubes
12	large apricots, quartered
6	medium fresh figs, halved

In a small bowl, whisk together the sour cream, mayonnaise, lime rind, lime juice, honey and ginger. Chill for at least 20 minutes.

Transfer to a decorative serving bowl. Place the bowl in the center of a large platter and surround with the cantaloupe, honeydew, apricots and figs. Provide decorative food picks for spearing and dipping the fruit.

Preparation time: 10 minutes plus chilling time

Chef's note: It's much easier to grate the rind from citrus fruits, such as limes, lemons and oranges, while they're still whole than after they've been cut or juiced. Use a metal grater with fine holes or a special hand-held zester.

Per serving: 149 calories, 0.6 g. fat (3% of calories), 5.3 g. dietary fiber, no cholesterol, 296 mg. sodium.

STRAWBERRIES WITH ALMOND AND YOGURT DIP

SERVES 6

*W*hat could be simpler? For variety, substitute any other flavor of yogurt. If you can buy strawberries that still have long stems attached, you'll have a prettier dish for a buffet table.

> 1 cup nonfat vanilla yogurt
> 3 tablespoons blanched almonds, toasted and finely chopped
> 1 teaspoon grated lemon rind
> 3 cups fresh strawberries

In a small bowl, mix the yogurt, almonds and lemon rind. Chill for at least 20 minutes.

Transfer to a decorative serving bowl. Place the bowl in the center of a large platter and surround with the strawberries. Provide decorative food picks for spearing and dipping the fruit.

Preparation time: 5 minutes plus chilling time

Per serving: 76 calories, 2.4 g. fat (26% of calories), 2.3 g. dietary fiber, 1 mg. cholesterol, 25 mg. sodium.

RUBYBURST WARM-UPS

*E*ven many Mediterranean countries experience cold spells. In his book *A Year in Provence,* author Peter Mayle details just how chilly that southern France locale can become. Both there and here, this hot mulled drink would be just the ticket to warm up revelers at midwinter festivities. But you can also enjoy this brew when the weather warms up—simply chill the mixture after simmering it, then serve it over ice.

3   *cups cranberry-apple juice*
2   *cups cranberry-raspberry juice*
1   *cup orange juice*
4   *strips orange rind*
8   *whole cloves*
2   *cinnamon sticks*

In a 3-quart saucepan, combine the cranberry-apple juice, cranberry-raspberry juice, orange juice, orange rind, cloves and cinnamon sticks. Bring to a boil over medium heat, then reduce the heat to low and simmer for 20 minutes to bring out the flavor of the spices. Discard the rind and spices. Ladle into warm mugs.

Preparation time: 5 minutes
Cooking time: 20 minutes

Chef's note: To make an individual serving, combine ½ cup *each* of the two cranberry juices, 2 tablespoons orange juice, a small piece of orange rind, 1 whole clove and a sprinkle of ground cinnamon or a small piece of cinnamon stick in a microwave-safe mug. Microwave on high for 2 minutes. Let stand a few minutes for the spices to release their flavorings.

Per serving: 111 calories, 0.1 g. fat (1% of calories), trace dietary fiber, no cholesterol, 3 mg. sodium.

STRAWBERRY AND PEACH COOLERS

*S*erve these creamy shakes when the weather is warm. They're also good for a quick, nutritious breakfast. If desired, serve over crushed ice.

2 cups sliced strawberries
2 ripe bananas, sliced
2 peaches, peeled and sliced
1 cup nonfat vanilla yogurt
1 cup apple juice
1 cup sparkling water

Place 1 cup strawberries, half of the bananas, half of the peaches, ½ cup yogurt, ½ cup apple juice and ½ cup sparkling water in a blender. Process until smooth. Pour into tall glasses.

Repeat with the remaining ingredients.

Preparation time: 10 minutes

Chef's note: To peel fresh peaches, bring enough water to a boil in a medium saucepan to allow you to submerge the peaches. Place in the boiling water and let stand for about 20 seconds. (Exact timing will depend upon the ripeness and temperature of the peaches.) Remove with a slotted spoon, rinse with cold water, and use a paring knife to remove the loosened skin. If the skin doesn't come off easily, return the peaches to the water for a few seconds longer.

Per serving: 97 calories, 0.3 g. fat (2% of calories), 1.2 g. dietary fiber, 1 mg. cholesterol, 26 mg. sodium.

MANGO SMOOTHIES

SERVES 4

Mangoes and bananas have a rich, creamy texture but only the barest trace of fat. That makes them good choices for low-fat shakes. Mangoes are available from January through August. Buy fruit that's got a yellow or reddish-yellow skin.

1 can (8 ounces) juice-packed pineapple
    chunks
1 large ripe mango, peeled and chopped
1 ripe banana, sliced
1 cup nonfat frozen vanilla yogurt
    Crushed or cracked ice

In a blender, combine the pineapple (with juice), mangoes and bananas. Process until smooth. Add the frozen yogurt. Blend well.

With the blender running, gradually drop in enough ice to bring the level up to 4 cups. Blend until the ice is pureed.

Preparation time: 10 minutes

Chef's note: Because mangoes are quite juicy, they're a bit messy to peel. They also have a large pit in the center that makes cutting them a little tricky. Marion Gorman, author of *Cooking with Fruit*, has lived in the tropics, where mangoes are plentiful. She offers these tips for success: Use a sharp knife to cut the flesh away from both sides of the large flat pit. Then use a knife and fork to cut the flesh from the skin.

Per serving: 142 calories, 0.3 g. fat (2% of calories), 2.1 g. dietary fiber, no cholesterol, 37 mg. sodium.

ORANGE-APPLE SPARKLERS

SERVES 4

*T*his very simple drink is refreshing on a hot summer's eve. You can easily double or triple the recipe to serve a crowd.

½ cup orange juice concentrate
2 cups sparkling cider
2 cups sparkling water
Crushed or cracked ice
Orange slices

Place the juice concentrate in a pitcher (if it's still frozen, stir until liquefied). Stir in the cider and sparkling water.

Fill tall glasses with the ice. Add the cider mixture. Garnish with the orange slices.

Preparation time: 5 minutes

Per serving: 98 calories, 0.1 g. fat (1% of calories), 0.2 g. dietary fiber, no cholesterol, 34 mg. sodium.

CREAMY SMOOTH ORANGE DRINKS

SERVES 4

*U*sing frozen yogurt makes these frosty drinks extra easy. Oranges are abundant in Mediterranean countries, and they appear in most every type of dish, from appetizers and drinks like this to main courses and baked goods.

3   *cups orange juice*
2   *cups nonfat frozen vanilla yogurt*
2   *tablespoons all-fruit orange marmalade*
6   *ice cubes, cracked*
    Mint leaves

In a blender, combine the orange juice, frozen yogurt, marmalade and ice cubes. Process until smooth. Pour into tall glasses. Garnish with the mint.

Preparation time: 5 minutes

Per serving: 205 calories, 0.4 g. fat (2% of calories), 1.5 g. dietary fiber, no cholesterol, 72 mg. sodium.

Smooth-as-Silk Cantaloupe Coolers

SERVES 6

*T*his nutritious drink is as welcome for breakfast as it is at a party. Melons are a favorite in Italy; in fact, cantaloupes take their name from the town of Cantalupo, near Rome.

4 *cups cantaloupe cubes*
2 *ripe bananas, sliced*
1 *cup nonfat vanilla yogurt*
1 *cup orange juice*
8 *ice cubes, cracked*

Combine 2 cups cantaloupe, half of the bananas, ½ cup yogurt, ½ cup orange juice and 4 ice cubes in a blender. Process until smooth. Pour into tall glasses.

Repeat with the remaining ingredients.

Preparation time: 10 minutes

Per serving: 121 calories, 0.6 g. fat (4% of calories), 1.8 g. dietary fiber, 1 mg. cholesterol, 34 mg. sodium.

MINT EYE-OPENERS

SERVES 4

resh herbs are a hallmark of Mediterranean cuisines from Spain and Morocco to Turkey and Greece. This refreshing drink uses fresh mint and combines it with two kinds of vitamin C–rich juices. Use whatever variety of mint you prefer, whether it's peppermint, spearmint, apple mint, lemon mint or another type.

½	cup chopped fresh mint
½	cup water
1½	tablespoons honey
2	cups orange juice
2	cups pink grapefruit juice
1	teaspoon grenadine (optional)
	Ice cubes

In a 1-quart saucepan over medium-high heat, bring the mint, water and honey to a boil. Reduce the heat and simmer, stirring occasionally, for 5 minutes. Remove from the heat and allow to steep for 20 minutes. Strain into a pitcher.

Stir in the orange juice, grapefruit juice and grenadine. Serve over ice in tall glasses.

Preparation time: 5 minutes plus standing time
Cooking time: 5 minutes

Chef's note: Grenadine is a sweet red syrup flavored with pomegranate juice. It's used to give color and flavor to drinks and desserts.

For a nice presentation, serve this drink over mint ice cubes. Half fill the sections of an ice-cube tray and place a mint leaf in each compartment. Freeze for about 30 minutes, or until the water is solid enough to hold the leaves in place. Carefully cover with more water and freeze until solid.

Per serving: 128 calories, 0.5 g. fat (4% of calories), 1.3 g. dietary fiber, no cholesterol, 3 mg. sodium.

BROCCOLI AND SHRIMP FRITTERS

MAKES 18

These easy little pancakes make nice finger food for a party. They look especially appealing arranged on a platter lined with bright leafy greens, such as kale or ornamental cabbage. Decorate the platter with blanched snow peas or snap peas and cherry tomatoes, which can be eaten along with the fritters. You may make the fritters ahead and reheat them at a low temperature in the oven or for a short period in the microwave.

> 4 *egg whites*
> ½ *cup finely chopped broccoli*
> ½ *cup finely chopped mushrooms*
> ½ *cup small cooked shrimp, chopped*
> ½ *cup diced sweet red peppers*
> ⅓ *cup bean sprouts, chopped*

In a medium bowl, beat the egg whites with a fork until frothy. Add the broccoli, mushrooms, shrimp, peppers and sprouts.

Coat a large no-stick frying pan with no-stick spray. Let warm over medium heat for 2 minutes. Drop small rounded tablespoons of the egg mixture into the pan and cook for 2 minutes, or until browned underneath. Flip and cook on the other side for 2 to 3 minutes, or until just set.

Preparation time: 10 minutes
Cooking time: 15 minutes

Per fritter: 11 calories, <0.1 g. fat (6% of calories), 0.2 g. dietary fiber, 9 mg. cholesterol, 24 mg. sodium.

CRAB AND CORN BEIGNETS

MAKES 18

Don't be intimidated by the name. *Beignet* is simply a fancy French word for a fritter. This version features some good old American ingredients, crab and corn, in a low-fat batter. Serve as an appetizer or as hors d'oeuvres.

¼ cup fat-free egg substitute
¼ cup skim milk
2 tablespoons unbleached flour
1 teaspoon olive oil
1 teaspoon honey
1 teaspoon Dijon mustard
½ teaspoon baking powder
½ teaspoon ground black pepper
1 cup flaked crab
1 cup corn
1 tablespoon minced fresh tarragon or parsley

In a medium bowl, whisk together the egg, milk, flour, oil, honey, mustard, baking powder and pepper until smooth. Stir in the crab, corn and tarragon or parsley.

Coat a large no-stick frying pan with no-stick spray. Let warm over medium heat for 2 minutes. Drop scant tablespoons of the crab mixture into the pan; flatten lightly with the back of the spoon to form beignets that are about 2" in diameter.

Cook for 2 to 3 minutes per side, or until golden. If necessary, reduce the heat to keep the beignets from getting too dark before they're cooked through.

Preparation time: 10 minutes
Cooking time: 15 minutes

Per beignet: 27 calories, 0.4 g. fat (14% of calories), 0.2 g. dietary fiber, 5 mg. cholesterol, 118 mg. sodium.

Turkey-Potato Frittata

MAKES 12 WEDGES

A frittata is an Italian omelet. Unlike French omelets, frittatas have their filling mixed right in with the eggs. This version is a good way to use up a leftover baked potato. Serve warm or at room temperature.

1	*medium baked potato, diced*
1	*medium onion, diced*
⅓	*cup diced smoked turkey breast*
2	*teaspoons olive oil*
1	*cup fat-free egg substitute*
3	*tablespoons crumbled peppercorn feta cheese*
2	*tablespoons minced fresh parsley*
2	*tablespoons minced fresh thyme*

Coat a large no-stick frying pan with no-stick spray. Let warm over medium heat for 2 minutes. Add the potatoes, onions, turkey and oil. Sauté for 5 minutes, or until the potatoes are lightly browned. Spread the mixture evenly across the pan.

Pour in the eggs. Do not stir. Sprinkle with the feta, parsley and thyme. Cover, reduce the heat to medium-low and cook for 5 minutes, or until the eggs are set on top and are nicely browned underneath.

Carefully loosen with a spatula and slide onto a serving platter or cutting board. Cut into wedges.

Preparation time: 10 minutes
Cooking time: 10 minutes

Chef's note: If your supermarket does not carry peppercorn feta cheese, use regular feta. Sprinkle about ½ teaspoon coarsely ground black pepper over the feta.

Per wedge: 40 calories, 1.3 g. fat (28% of calories), 0.5 g. dietary fiber, 3 mg. cholesterol, 78 mg. sodium.

SCALLOPED OYSTERS

*S*eafood is abundant in Mediterranean countries. This light first course features oysters that are sprinkled with bread crumbs and baked until just cooked through. For an attractive presentation, make the oysters in scallop shells, which are available in cookware and gourmet shops as well as in many large department stores. The shells will be hot when they come out of the oven, so place them on small doily-lined plates for serving. Although the percent of calories from fat in this recipe is high, both the total calories and grams of fat per serving are nicely low.

24   *small shucked oysters, well drained*
 1   *cup fresh bread crumbs*
 2   *tablespoons olive oil*
½   *teaspoon minced garlic*
      Pinch of ground red pepper
¼   *cup evaporated skim milk*
 3   *tablespoons minced fresh parsley*
 8   *lemon wedges*

Coat 8 medium (4") scallop shells or small ramekins with no-stick spray. Place on a baking sheet. Place 3 oysters, in a single layer, in each shell or dish.

In a small bowl, mix the bread crumbs, oil, garlic and pepper until the oil is evenly distributed. Sprinkle the mixture over the oysters. Drizzle with the milk.

Bake at 400° for 15 minutes, or until the edges of the oysters curl. Sprinkle with the parsley. Serve with the lemon wedges.

Preparation time: 10 minutes
Baking time: 15 minutes

Per serving: 83 calories, 4.7 g. fat (51% of calories), 0.3 g. dietary fiber, 24 mg. cholesterol, 86 mg. sodium.

Marinated Mushroom Brochettes

SERVES 4

$\mathcal{M}$ushrooms have a meaty taste and texture, which makes them quite satisfying as an appetizer or hors d'oeuvre. In this recipe, they pick up rich flavor from the marinade ingredients. Threading the mushrooms onto skewers through their sides allows them to sit flat on the broiler rack so they cook evenly. To make turning them easier, you might want to use two skewers, parallel to each other, for each brochette. If you're cooking outdoors, you can also do these brochettes on the grill.

1   *pound large mushrooms, stems removed*
2   *tablespoons ketchup*
2   *teaspoons Worcestershire sauce*
1   *teaspoon low-sodium soy sauce*
2   *cloves garlic, minced*

Blanch the mushrooms in boiling water for about 3 minutes. Drain and pat dry.

In a medium bowl, combine the ketchup, Worcestershire sauce, soy sauce and garlic. Add the mushrooms and toss well to coat. Let marinate for at least 30 minutes.

Thread the mushrooms through their sides onto thin, flat skewers. Set them on a broiler rack. Broil 5" from the heat for about 4 minutes per side.

Preparation time: 5 minutes plus marinating time
Cooking time: 10 minutes

Per serving: 41 calories, 0.5 g. fat (9% of calories), 1.5 g. dietary fiber, no cholesterol, 162 mg. sodium.

ARTICHOKE MINI PIZZAS

---

*P*izza makes a hit at any party, and mini versions are particularly easy to prepare and serve. This recipe uses store-bought biscuit dough, available in tubes in the refrigerator case. Be sure to look for dough that has only one gram or less of fat per biscuit. The only drawback to this type of dough is that it's high in sodium. If you are on a low-sodium diet, use a salt-free homemade crust.

> 1 *tube (7.5 ounces) refrigerated biscuit dough (10 biscuits)*
> ⅓ *cup diced green peppers*
> ⅓ *cup tomato sauce*
> *Dried oregano*
> *Red-pepper flakes*
> ⅔ *cup chopped artichoke hearts*
> 5 *large black olives, pitted and sliced*
> ⅔ *cup shredded low-fat mozzarella cheese*

Coat a large baking sheet with no-stick spray. Press or roll each biscuit into a 3½" round and place on the sheet.

Place the green peppers in a custard cup and microwave on high for 1 minute, or until softened.

Divide the tomato sauce among the biscuits, using about 1½ teaspoons for each pizza. Spread to within ¼" of the edges. Sprinkle with the oregano and pepper flakes. Sprinkle with the artichokes, olives and green peppers. Top with the mozzarella.

Bake at 400° for 10 minutes, or until the cheese has melted and the biscuits are browned on the bottom.

Preparation time: 20 minutes
Baking time: 10 minutes

Per pizza: 77 calories, 1.9 g. fat (22% of calories), 0.2 g. dietary fiber, 2 mg. cholesterol, 258 mg. sodium.

TURKEY-APPLE CANAPÉS

*F*inger food is welcome at any type of party. The spread used on these little canapés combines lean cooked turkey breast with fiber-rich apples. The inspiration for these tidbits comes from Jean Holmes, owner of Jean Elizabeth's Lavender 'n' Lace Tea Room in Emmaus, Pennsylvania. She uses a very similar filling for her lovely tea sandwiches. If smoked turkey is too high in sodium for your diet, replace it with roasted or poached turkey breast.

¾	*cup diced smoked turkey breast*
¾	*cup diced red apples*
⅓	*cup shredded reduced-fat Cheddar cheese*
⅓	*cup nonfat mayonnaise*
1	*teaspoon Dijon mustard*
10	*mini bagels, split*
¼	*cup minced fresh parsley*

Place the turkey, apples and Cheddar in a food processor. Finely chop using on/off turns. Spoon in the mayonnaise and mustard. Mix in, using a few more on/off turns.

If desired, lightly toast the bagel halves. Spread about 1 tablespoon of the filling on each half. Sprinkle lightly with the parsley.

Preparation time: 10 minutes

Chef's note: For variety, you may replace the bagels with melba toast or party-size rye bread slices. If using the party rye, lightly toast it and let the slices cool before adding the spread.

Per canapé: 68 calories, 1.6 g. fat (22% of calories), 0.4 g. dietary fiber, 6 mg. cholesterol, 203 mg. sodium.

HERB-SEASONED CHICKEN NUGGETS

SERVES 8

*F*orget frying! You can turn out a batch of crispy little hors d'oeuvres without the aid of a deep fryer. Baking achieves the same effect and doesn't contribute any extra fat or calories. Serve these morsels with a lean dipping sauce, such as plain honey or a mixture of Dijon mustard, honey and nonfat yogurt.

> 1 *pound boneless, skinless chicken breasts*
> ¼ *cup fat-free egg substitute*
> 1 *tablespoon water*
> ½ *cup plain dry bread crumbs*
> ¼ *cup wheat germ*
> 1 *teaspoon dried parsley*
> 1 *teaspoon dried basil*
> 1 *teaspoon dried marjoram*
> ½ *teaspoon dried thyme*
> ½ *teaspoon ground black pepper*
> *Pinch of ground red pepper*
> 1 *tablespoon olive oil*

Trim all visible fat from the chicken. Cut the meat into 1" cubes.

In a medium bowl, mix the egg and water. Add the chicken and stir to coat well.

In a small bowl, mix the bread crumbs, wheat germ, parsley, basil, marjoram, thyme, black pepper and red pepper. With a fork, stir in the oil and mix well to distribute it evenly. Transfer the crumbs to a plastic or paper bag.

Working in batches, add the chicken to the bag and shake well to coat all the pieces evenly with the crumbs.

Coat a jelly-roll pan or a large baking sheet with no-stick spray. Add the chicken pieces in a single layer, leaving a little space between them. Bake at 425° for 10 minutes. Turn the pieces over and bake for 5 minutes, or until lightly browned and crisp.

Preparation time: 15 minutes
Baking time: 15 minutes

Chef's note: You may prepare your own bread crumbs. Use whole-wheat, oat or white bread. Tear several slices into pieces and pulverize them in a food processor or blender. Spread evenly in a large shallow baking pan and let dry in a 200° oven.

Per serving: 114 calories, 3 g. total fat (24% of calories), trace dietary fiber, 33 mg. cholesterol, 93 mg. sodium.

STRAWBERRY TEA SANDWICHES

SERVES 8

For those occasions when you want fancy little finger sandwiches, try these berry easy ones.

4   *ounces nonfat cream cheese, softened*
1   *cup chopped strawberries*
8   *slices whole-wheat or oat bread*
     Watercress leaves

In a small bowl, mix the cream cheese and strawberries.

If desired, cut the crusts from the bread. Divide the strawberry mixture among 4 of the slices, spreading it evenly to the edges. Cover with watercress leaves and top with the remaining 4 slices of bread. Cut the sandwiches into quarters, triangles or thin fingers.

Preparation time: 10 minutes

Per serving: 87 calories, 1.3 g. fat (13% of calories), 3.7 g. dietary fiber, 3 mg. cholesterol, 264 mg. sodium.

CHAPTER 4

FROM HOT
AND
HEARTY TO
COOL AND
CREAMY

SOUP DU JOUR

ou just can't go wrong with a bowl of soup. No matter how pressed for time you are, you can spare a few moments to heat up a bowlful and savor its rich combination of vitamin-packed ingredients. (And on really hot days, you can pull some ready-made cold soup from the refrigerator for an instant lunch or light dinner.) Part of the beauty of soups is that they *can* be made ahead. Many types actually improve in flavor as the herbs, spices and vegetables they contain mellow during storage. But even when you've neglected to plan ahead, the soups in this chapter are so easy to prepare that you can have a really satisfying meal on the table in practically no time at all.

SQUASH AND CHESTNUT SOUP

*W*e often think of chestnuts as an American specialty, but they're abundant in Europe. In fact, Mount Olympus was said to have many chestnut trees.

4	*stalks celery, coarsely chopped*
4	*leeks (white part only), chopped*
2	*teaspoons canola oil*
5½	*cups defatted chicken stock*
1½	*cups unsweetened canned chestnuts*
2	*boxes (12 ounces each) frozen cooked squash, thawed*
2	*tablespoons minced fresh ginger*
1	*tablespoon minced fresh thyme*
2	*teaspoons ground mace*
¼	*teaspoon ground black pepper*
1⅓	*cups nonfat sour cream*

In a 3-quart saucepan over medium heat, sauté the celery and leeks in the oil and ½ cup of the stock for 10 minutes, or until the vegetables are soft and translucent. Reserve 2 chestnuts. Stir in the remaining chestnuts, squash, ginger, thyme, mace and pepper.

Transfer the mixture to a food processor or blender and process until smooth. Return the mixture to the pan. Stir in the remaining 5 cups stock. Bring to a boil over high heat, then reduce the heat to medium-low and let simmer for 7 minutes. Ladle into individual bowls and top each with a generous dollop of the sour cream. Thinly slice the reserved chestnuts and use as a garnish.

Preparation time: 10 minutes
Cooking time: 20 minutes

Per serving: 137 calories, 2.7 g. fat (18% of calories), 1.5 g. dietary fiber, no cholesterol, 107 mg. sodium.

PROVENÇAL EGGPLANT SOUP

SERVES 6

*T*his stew combines the traditional ingredients of ratatouille, a flavorful mixture of eggplant, tomatoes, peppers and zucchini. The bread cubes used here help thicken the soup and are often found in peasant-type soups.

1	*medium eggplant, peeled and diced*
1	*small zucchini, halved and thinly sliced*
1	*onion, thinly sliced*
1	*sweet red pepper, diced*
1	*tablespoon olive oil*
1	*clove garlic, minced*
4	*cups defatted chicken stock*
2	*tomatoes, seeded and diced*
1	*cup slightly stale French bread cubes*
½	*teaspoon dried oregano*
½	*teaspoon ground black pepper*
2	*tablespoons minced fresh parsley*
2	*tablespoons grated Parmesan cheese*

Place the eggplant in a 3-quart casserole. Cover with vented plastic wrap and microwave on high for 5 minutes, or until softened.

Meanwhile, in a 4-quart pot over medium heat, sauté the zucchini, onions and red peppers in the oil for 5 minutes, or until softened and lightly browned. Stir in the eggplant and garlic. Sauté for 5 minutes.

Add the stock, tomatoes, bread, oregano and black pepper. Bring to a boil. Cover, reduce the heat and simmer for 15 minutes, or until the vegetables are tender and the flavors have blended. Ladle into individual bowls and sprinkle with the parsley and Parmesan.

Preparation time: 10 minutes
Cooking time: 25 minutes

Per serving: 78 calories, 3.4 g. fat (37% of calories), 1.3 g. dietary fiber, 2 mg. cholesterol, 651 mg. sodium.

TARRAGON-FLAVORED BROCCOLI SOUP

SERVES 4

*B*roccoli is a vegetable superstar, overflowing with vitamins. And it's a member of the cruciferous family of cancer-preventing vegetables.

- ½ cup diced onions
- 2 teaspoons olive oil
- 1 clove garlic, minced
- 3 cups defatted chicken stock
- 2 cups chopped broccoli florets
- 1 small red potato, peeled and diced
- 2 tablespoons minced fresh parsley
- ½ teaspoon dried tarragon
- ¼ cup nonfat sour cream

In a 2-quart saucepan over medium heat, sauté the onions in the oil for 5 minutes, or until tender. Add the garlic and stir for 1 minute.

Add the stock, broccoli, potatoes, parsley and tarragon. Bring to a boil over medium-high heat. Reduce the heat to medium and simmer for 10 minutes, or until the vegetables are tender. Remove from the heat and stir in the sour cream.

Preparation time: 10 minutes
Cooking time: 15 minutes

Per serving: 87 calories, 2.6 g. fat (25% of calories), 2.7 g. dietary fiber, no cholesterol, 700 mg. sodium.

CREAMY MUSHROOM SOUP

SERVES 4

*N*onfat sour cream helps keep fat and calories down in this silken soup. And mashed potatoes—use leftovers or whip up some instant potatoes—contribute body usually provided by a butter-and-cream sauce. If you make this soup ahead, reheat it over low heat. Or place an individual serving in a 2-cup glass measure and microwave until hot. Try to avoid boiling the soup so it doesn't curdle.

1	*large onion, minced*
8	*ounces mushrooms, finely chopped*
1	*tablespoon olive oil*
2	*cups defatted chicken stock*
1	*tablespoon butter-flavored sprinkles*
½	*teaspoon ground black pepper*
½	*teaspoon dried savory or tarragon*
	Pinch of ground red pepper
¾	*cup mashed potatoes*
½	*cup nonfat sour cream*

In a 3-quart saucepan over medium heat, sauté the onions and mushrooms in the oil for 10 minutes, or until the liquid exuded from the mushrooms evaporates.

Stir in the stock, sprinkles, black pepper, savory or tarragon and red pepper. Bring to a boil.

If the potatoes are cold, place them in a medium bowl and stir to break them up. Whisk into the pan. Cover and cook for 5 minutes. Remove from the heat and whisk in the sour cream.

Preparation time: 10 minutes
Cooking time: 15 minutes

Chef's note: The easiest way to chop the mushrooms is in a food processor. Clean the mushrooms by wiping with a damp paper towel. Halve or quarter so the pieces are somewhat uniform. Place in a food processor and chop with on/off turns until fine but not pureed.

Per serving: 126 calories, 3.9 g. fat (27% of calories), 1.7 g. dietary fiber, 1 mg. cholesterol, 608 mg. sodium.

FRESH PEA SOUP

SERVES 4

*T*here's nothing to compare with the flavor of fresh peas in the spring. If they're out of season, use a box of frozen petite peas, the tender tiny variety. If desired, you may serve this soup chilled.

½ cup minced onions
1 teaspoon olive oil
1 cup defatted chicken stock
1 cup peas
2 leaves romaine or Boston lettuce, shredded
¼ cup minced fresh parsley
2 tablespoons minced fresh mint
1 cup 1% low-fat milk

In a 2-quart saucepan over medium heat, sauté the onions in the oil for 5 minutes, or until tender. Stir in the stock, peas, lettuce, parsley and mint. Bring to a boil. Cover and cook for 5 minutes, or until the peas are tender.

Transfer to a blender. Add the milk. Blend until smooth. Return to the saucepan and reheat briefly.

Preparation time: 10 minutes
Cooking time: 10 minutes

Per serving: 82 calories, 2 g. fat (21% of calories), 0.6 g. dietary fiber, 3 mg. cholesterol, 252 mg. sodium.

SPANISH ROASTED RED PEPPER SOUP

SERVES 6

*R*oasted red peppers make an appearance in many types of Mediterranean dishes. Here they're the backbone of a savory soup. If you don't want to take the time to prepare the peppers, buy a large jar of roasted red peppers or pimentos. Drain them well. If they're packed in oil, blot off the excess with paper towels.

6	*sweet red peppers, halved lengthwise*
1	*large onion, diced*
1	*tablespoon olive oil*
5	*cups defatted chicken stock*
1	*large baking potato, peeled and diced*
3	*cloves garlic, minced*
½	*teaspoon ground black pepper*
3	*tablespoons chopped fresh coriander*

Place the red peppers, cut side down, on a baking sheet lined with foil. Broil about 4" from the heat until the skins are black, about 10 minutes. Remove from the oven, enclose the peppers in the foil and let stand for about 5 minutes, or until cool enough to handle.

Meanwhile, in a 3-quart saucepan over medium heat, sauté the onions in the oil for 5 minutes, or until translucent. Add the stock, potatoes, garlic and black pepper. Bring to a boil. Cover, reduce the heat and simmer for 10 minutes, or until the potatoes are tender.

Remove the blackened skin from the peppers. Roughly chop the flesh and add to the saucepan. Working in batches, transfer the mixture to a blender and process until smooth. Serve sprinkled with the coriander.

Preparation time: 10 minutes
Broiling time: 10 minutes
Cooking time: 15 minutes

Per serving: 80 calories, 2.5 g. fat (26% of calories), 2 g. dietary fiber, no cholesterol, 729 mg. sodium.

Left to right: Strawberry and Peach Cooler (page 35), Mint Eye-Opener (page 40)
and Orange-Apple Sparkler (page 37)

Scalloped Oysters (page 44)

Artichoke Mini Pizzas (page 46)

59

South-of-France Vegetable Soup (page 68)

Portuguese Mussel Soup (page 76)

Squash and Chestnut Soup (page 51)

Turkey and Rice Salad with Apples and Almonds (page 108)

Warm Lentil and Chicory Vinaigrette (page 92)

BUTTERNUT-CORN CHOWDER

SERVES 6

*T*his savory vegetable chowder won a prize for Noel Marie Kelton of San Francisco in the second annual *Prevention* Cooking for Health recipe contest.

2	large butternut squash
1¼	cups defatted chicken stock
1¼	cups water
1	teaspoon olive oil
1	green pepper, diced
1	onion, diced
1	carrot, diced
3	cloves garlic, minced
1	jalapeño pepper, minced (wear plastic gloves when handling)
¼	cup chopped fresh coriander
	Juice of 1 lime
½	teaspoon ground red pepper
½	teaspoon ground cinnamon
¼	teaspoon ground black pepper
½	cup corn

Using a paring knife, peel the squash. Halve them and scoop out the seeds. Cut the flesh into ½" cubes. Place in a Dutch oven.

Add the stock and water. Bring to a boil over medium heat. Cover and simmer for 10 minutes.

Meanwhile, in a large no-stick frying pan over medium heat, warm the oil. Add the green peppers, onions, carrots and garlic. Sauté for 8 minutes, or until soft. Add to the Dutch oven.

Stir in the jalapeño peppers, coriander, lime juice, red pepper, cinnamon and black pepper. Simmer for 10 minutes, or until the squash is tender. Stir in the corn and cook briefly.

(continued)

Preparation time: 15 minutes
Cooking time: 20 minutes

Per serving: 139 calories, 2.1 g. fat (12% of calories), 6.1 g. dietary fiber, no cholesterol, 38 mg. sodium.

SPICY TOMATO AND PEPPER SOUP

SERVES 4

Serve this piquant soup with cornbread or a rustic Italian bread such as focaccia. Most of the sodium in this soup comes from the stock. If you need to reduce your sodium consumption, look for a brand that's low in sodium.

1	*large onion, minced*
2	*cups finely chopped sweet red or yellow peppers*
1	*clove garlic, minced*
2	*teaspoons oil*
2	*teaspoons chili powder*
1	*teaspoon dried oregano*
1/8	*teaspoon ground red pepper*
1/4	*teaspoon ground black pepper*
4	*cups defatted chicken stock*
2	*cups diced tomatoes*

In a 3-quart saucepan over medium heat, sauté the onions, peppers and garlic in the oil for 5 minutes, or until softened. Stir in the chili powder, oregano, red pepper and black pepper. Sauté for 1 minute. Add the stock and tomatoes. Bring to a boil. Cover and simmer for 20 minutes. Transfer about half of the soup to a blender and puree; pour back into the pan.

Preparation time: 10 minutes
Cooking time: 30 minutes

Per serving: 83 calories, 3 g. fat (29% of calories), 2.7 g. dietary fiber, no cholesterol, 890 mg. sodium.

CREAMY POTATO AND SQUASH SOUP

SERVES 6

*U*sing frozen mashed squash saves time when making this pureed soup. It also adds a nice amount of cancer-preventing beta-carotene to this dish.

1	onion, diced
1	teaspoon olive oil
2½	cups defatted chicken stock
1	tart apple, peeled and diced
1	baking potato, peeled and diced
½	teaspoon dried thyme
¼	teaspoon dried marjoram
¼	teaspoon ground black pepper
	Pinch of ground red pepper
1	box (12 ounces) frozen cooked squash
½	cup skim or evaporated skim milk

In a 3-quart saucepan over medium heat, sauté the onions in the oil for 5 minutes, or until softened. Add the stock, apples, potatoes, thyme, marjoram, black pepper and red pepper. Bring to a boil.

Add the frozen block of squash. Cover and simmer for 10 minutes, or until the squash has thawed and the vegetables are soft.

Working in batches, transfer the mixture to a blender and puree. Return to the pot. Stir in the milk. Heat briefly.

Preparation time: 10 minutes
Cooking time: 20 minutes

Per serving: 82 calories, 1.3 g. fat (14% of calories), 3.1 g. dietary fiber, <1 mg. cholesterol, 86 mg. sodium.

South-of-France Vegetable Soup

A soup like this is most often served with a bowl of pistou—the French version of pesto sauce. Diners spoon the sauce into their individual bowls.

> 5 *cups defatted chicken stock*
> 1 *cup rinsed and drained canned white beans*
> 1 *cup diced potatoes*
> 1 *cup chopped tomatoes*
> ½ *cup thinly sliced carrots*
> ½ *cup thinly sliced onions*
> ½ *cup thinly sliced leeks*
> ½ *small zucchini, thinly sliced*
> ½ *cup halved green beans*
> ½ *cup cubed butternut squash or pumpkin*
> 2 *tablespoons chopped fresh parsley*
> 1 *teaspoon dried thyme*
> 1 *clove garlic, minced*
> ½ *teaspoon ground black pepper*
> 1 *ounce angel hair pasta, broken*

In a 4-quart pot, combine stock, white beans, potatoes, tomatoes, carrots, onions, leeks, zucchini, green beans, squash or pumpkin, parsley, thyme, garlic and pepper. Bring to a boil over high heat.

Cover, reduce the heat to medium and simmer for 20 minutes, or until the vegetables are tender. Stir in the pasta. Cook, uncovered, for 5 minutes, or until the pasta is tender.

Preparation time: 20 minutes
Cooking time: 30 minutes

Per serving: 182 calories, 0.8 g. fat (4% of calories), 3 g. dietary fiber, 6 mg. cholesterol, 1,202 mg. sodium.

A Classic French Basil Sauce

*P*istou is the French version of pesto sauce. It's an excellent way to preserve a bumper basil crop. The French particularly like to use this sauce to add an extra fillip of flavor to all sorts of soups, including vegetable blends and fish stews. They add a spoonful of the sauce to a bowl of soup and swirl it in a decorative pattern.

You can use the sauce in myriad other ways: Spoon some over a plateful of thick, ripe tomato slices and eat them as a salad. Drizzle it over fresh goat cheese to spread on crusty bread. Add to a plateful of hot pasta for a main dish. You can also use pistou as a dip for crisp vegetables, such as green beans, zucchini, peppers and broccoli.

Store pistou in the refrigerator, where it will keep for a month. The sauce will separate during storage. Simply stir it well before using.

PISTOU

MAKES 1¼ CUPS

2   *cups loosely packed basil leaves*
3–4   *cloves garlic, minced*
2   *tablespoons pine nuts*
¼   *cup olive oil*
½   *cup grated Parmesan or finely shredded Gruyère cheese*

In a food processor, combine the basil, garlic and pine nuts. Process with on/off turns until finely chopped. (Add a little oil as necessary to make blending easier.)

Transfer to a bowl. Thoroughly stir in the oil and Parmesan or Gruyère to form a creamy sauce with the consistency of thick gravy.

Preparation time: 5 minutes

Per tablespoon: 43 calories, 4 g. fat (84% of calories), 0.1 g. dietary fiber, 2 mg. cholesterol, 47 mg. sodium.

ITALIAN MINESTRONE

*T*his no-cholesterol soup is quite light on calories, especially when you consider that it's virtually a meal in itself. All you need to round out the meal is some crusty whole-grain bread and a green salad with low-fat dressing. Orzo is a type of small pasta that resembles grains of rice.

½	cup diced onions
½	cup diced celery
½	cup diced carrots
1	tablespoon olive oil
1	clove garlic, minced
5	cups defatted chicken stock
1	can (14 ounces) chopped tomatoes
1	can (16 ounces) canned red kidney beans, rinsed and drained
1	cup packed chopped escarole
¼	cup orzo
1	cup sliced (½" pieces) green beans
½	cup diced zucchini

In a 3-quart saucepan over medium heat, sauté the onions, celery and carrots in the oil for 5 minutes, or until lightly browned. Add the garlic and stir for a few seconds.

Add the stock, tomatoes (with juice), kidney beans, escarole and orzo. Bring to a boil over high heat. Reduce the heat to medium and simmer for 10 minutes.

Add the green beans and zucchini. Cover and simmer for 5 minutes, or until the beans are tender.

Preparation time: 15 minutes
Cooking time: 20 minutes

Per serving: 159 calories, 4 g. fat (23% of calories), 5.8 g. dietary fiber, no cholesterol, 249 mg. sodium.

ESCAROLE AND SQUASH BISQUE

SERVES 6

*E*scarole is one of the deep-colored leafy greens that's part of the endive family. It's a favorite in Italy, where this soup is also beloved. This recipe is the creation of Chef Aliza Green, who was introduced to the concept by the well-known cooking teacher Marcella Hazan.

> 4 *cups defatted chicken stock*
> 1 *large baking potato, peeled and diced*
> 1 *onion, diced*
> 2 *small turnips, diced*
> 1 *cup thinly sliced carrots*
> 1 *box (12 ounces) frozen cooked squash*
> 1 *tablespoon minced fresh thyme*
> *Pinch of grated nutmeg*
> *Pinch of ground black pepper*
> 1 *cup thinly shredded escarole*

In a 3-quart saucepan, combine the stock, potatoes, onions, turnips, carrots and squash. Bring to a boil over high heat. Cover, reduce the heat to medium and simmer, stirring occasionally, for 15 minutes, or until the vegetables are tender. Stir in the thyme.

Working in batches, puree the soup in a blender or food processor. Return the mixture to the pot and bring to a boil. Season with the nutmeg and pepper. Add the escarole and cook for 5 minutes.

Preparation time: 15 minutes
Cooking time: 20 minutes

Per serving: 81 calories, 1.2 g. fat (12% of calories), 2 g. dietary fiber, no cholesterol, 67 mg. sodium.

GAZPACHO WITH AN ORIENTAL ACCENT

SERVES 4

Gazpacho is a very traditional cold soup from northern Spain. It usually combines tomatoes, cucumbers, lemon juice and other regional ingredients. This version gives gazpacho an unexpected Far Eastern flair. It's a specialty of Hugh Carpenter, a chef from California who was a founder of Chopstix restaurant in Los Angeles and now has his own cooking school in the Napa Valley area. Hugh sometimes garnishes the soup with cooked baby shrimp or crab.

1½	*pounds tomatoes*
2	*cups defatted chicken stock*
2	*tablespoons chopped fresh coriander*
1	*tablespoon low-sodium soy sauce*
4	*scallions, chopped*
4	*thin slices fresh ginger*
1	*teaspoon sherry extract*
¼	*teaspoon Chinese chili sauce (optional)*
2	*limes*

Cut the tomatoes in half crosswise and squeeze gently to remove the seeds and excess juice. Dice and place in a 2- or 3-quart saucepan. Add the stock, coriander, soy sauce, scallions and ginger. Over low heat, bring to a simmer and cook for 20 minutes.

Working in batches, puree in a food processor or blender. Chill thoroughly. Stir in the sherry extract and chili sauce. Grate the rind from one of the limes and add it to the soup. Squeeze the juice from both limes and stir into the soup.

Preparation time: 10 minutes plus chilling time
Cooking time: 20 minutes

Per serving: 80 calories, 1.4 g. fat (16% of calories), 2.6 g. dietary fiber, no cholesterol, 209 mg. sodium.

CREAMY TOMATO SOUP

SERVES 4

*T*his is a good soup to make in winter because it uses canned tomatoes. You may replace them in the summer with about three cups of peeled, seeded and chopped vine-ripe tomatoes. Plum tomatoes are especially good.

4	*shallots, minced*
1	*clove garlic, minced*
1	*teaspoon olive oil*
1	*tablespoon unbleached flour*
1	*can (28 ounces) plum tomatoes, drained and chopped*
2	*cups defatted chicken stock*
½	*teaspoon dried basil*
½	*teaspoon ground black pepper*
½	*cup nonfat sour cream*
2	*tablespoons minced fresh parsley*

In a 3-quart saucepan over medium-low heat, sauté the shallots and garlic in the oil for 5 minutes, or until tender. Stir in the flour and mix well.

Add the tomatoes, stock, basil and pepper. Bring to a boil. Cover, reduce the heat and simmer for 15 minutes. Working in batches, process in a blender until smooth. Return to the pan. Whisk in the sour cream; heat very briefly but do not allow to boil. Ladle into individual bowls and sprinkle with the parsley.

Preparation time: 10 minutes
Cooking time: 20 minutes

Per serving: 101 calories, 1.7 g. fat (14% of calories), 1.8 g. dietary fiber, no cholesterol, 811 mg. sodium.

Turnip Soup

*N*ot many people think about using turnips when making soup. But these root vegetables have a mild taste when cooked. So do their relatives the rutabagas, which you could also use in this soup. If you make this soup ahead, reheat it over medium-low heat to avoid scorching it.

1	onion, diced
1	teaspoon olive oil
½	teaspoon ground black pepper
¼	teaspoon dried sage
	Pinch of grated nutmeg
6	turnips, diced
3	cups defatted chicken stock
1	cup evaporated skim milk
1	tablespoon butter-flavored sprinkles

In a 3-quart saucepan over medium heat, sauté the onions in the oil for 5 minutes, or until tender. Stir in the pepper, sage and nutmeg. Stir for 1 minute.

Add the turnips and stock. Bring to a boil. Cover, reduce the heat and simmer for 10 to 15 minutes, or until the turnips are tender.

Working in batches, process in a blender until smooth. Return the mixture to the pan. Stir in the milk and sprinkles; heat briefly.

Preparation time: 10 minutes
Cooking time: 20 minutes

Per serving: 74 calories, 1 g. fat (11% of calories), 2.6 g. dietary fiber, 2 mg. cholesterol, 537 mg. sodium.

QUICK OYSTER STEW

SERVES 4

Oysters are good sources of important minerals, including iron and zinc. They even contain a fair share of copper, which helps regulate cholesterol metabolism. For those reasons alone, they would rate a place in your diet. But they're also delicious and make a wonderful chowder.

1	onion, minced
1	stalk celery, minced
1	tablespoon olive oil
1	clove garlic
½	teaspoon dried savory
1	baking potato, diced
1½	cups defatted chicken stock
½	cup bottled clam juice
½	cup corn
1½	cups small oysters, drained
1½	cups 1% low-fat milk
¼	cup minced fresh parsley

In a 3-quart saucepan over medium heat, sauté the onions and celery in the oil for 5 minutes, or until tender. Add the garlic and savory; stir for 30 seconds.

Add the potatoes, stock and clam juice. Bring to a boil. Cover, reduce the heat and simmer for 15 minutes, or until the potatoes are tender.

Stir in the corn and oysters. Simmer over low heat for 5 minutes, or until the oysters are just cooked through and their edges have begun to curl. Add the milk and parsley; heat briefly.

Preparation time: 10 minutes
Cooking time: 20 minutes

Per serving: 266 calories, 9.1 g. fat (31% of calories), 1.9 g. dietary fiber, 105 mg. cholesterol, 631 mg. sodium.

PORTUGUESE MUSSEL SOUP

Mineral-rich mussels are a great seafood that people often overlook in favor of the more popular clams, shrimp and oysters. But there's good reason to include mussels in your diet. They have iron for protection against anemia, potassium to help keep blood pressure on an even keel and even some zinc for proper wound healing. This soup is best served fresh, but you may prepare it ahead and reheat it. Rewarm it over medium-low heat to keep the milk from curdling.

2	pounds mussels in the shell
¾	cup defatted chicken stock
1	bay leaf
1	clove garlic, crushed
1	sprig parsley
1	scallion, chopped
1	large baking potato, diced
1	carrot, diced
½	teaspoon ground turmeric
2½	cups 1% low-fat milk
¼	cup diced tomatoes
2	tablespoons minced fresh parsley
¼	teaspoon dried thyme
¼	teaspoon ground black pepper

Discard any mussels with shells that are cracked or won't close tightly when you gently tap them with your finger. Place the remainder in a large bowl of cold water and let stand for 10 minutes. Drain. Cut off the beards and scrub the shells with a brush.

Place in a 4-quart pot. Add the stock, bay leaf, garlic, parsley sprig and scallions. Cover, bring to a boil and cook for 5 minutes, or until the mussels open.

Using tongs, transfer the mussels to a platter; reserve the cooking liquid. Discard any mussels that haven't opened. Remove the mussels from their shells and set aside.

Line a sieve with a double thickness of cheesecloth and set it over a bowl. Use it to strain the broth left in the pan. If necessary, add water to equal ¾ cup.

In a 3-quart saucepan over medium heat, combine the potatoes, carrots, turmeric and the reserved mussel liquid. Bring to a boil, cover and cook, stirring often, until the vegetables are very tender, about 10 minutes.

Add the milk, tomatoes, parsley, thyme and pepper. Stir in the reserved mussels. Heat, stirring, over low heat just until hot; do not boil.

Preparation time: 15 minutes
Cooking time: 20 minutes

Per serving: 176 calories, 3.5 g. fat (18% of calories), 2 g. dietary fiber, 46 mg. cholesterol, 317 mg. sodium.

GARLIC STOCK

*G*arlic is one of the favored foods in Mediterranean countries. In France, for instance, it's used in most every type of dish except sweets. And garlic is considered a restorative, as good for the body as it is for the soul. The French often make a garlic tonic that they sip slowly and savor.

The tonic is equally good as a very flavorful, easy stock for all kinds of soup. To make about 1 quart of stock, peel and slice 6 to 10 cloves of garlic. Place them in a 2-quart saucepan along with 4 cups of water, 2 bay leaves, 1 tablespoon of olive oil and 4 fresh sage leaves. Bring to a boil and simmer for 15 minutes. Strain before using.

FENNEL AND FISH CHOWDER

SERVES 4

*F*ennel is an unusual vegetable that's used often in Mediterranean countries. It somewhat resembles celery but has a large bulbous base and feathery leaves. Its mild anise flavor becomes even more mellow when cooked.

1	*large fennel bulb, halved and very thinly sliced*
1	*onion, diced*
2	*teaspoons olive oil*
3	*cups defatted chicken stock*
1	*cup thinly sliced carrots*
¼	*teaspoon dried thyme*
	Pinch of ground red pepper
4	*ounces halibut, cut into ½" cubes*
½	*cup evaporated skim milk*

In a 3-quart saucepan over medium heat, sauté the fennel and onions in the oil for 5 minutes, or until wilted. Add the stock, carrots, thyme and pepper. Bring to a boil. Cover, reduce the heat and simmer for 15 minutes, or until the vegetables are tender. Add the halibut. Cook for 5 minutes. Stir in the milk.

Preparation time: 10 minutes
Cooking time: 25 minutes

Chef's note: Fennel is available most of the year, starting in August and going until the next May. When buying fennel, look for bulbs that are crisp and solid with bright green leaves. To use, trim off and discard woody stalks to within an inch of the bulb. Cut the bulb in half or into quarters lengthwise, then thinly slice crosswise.

Per serving: 113 calories, 3.2 g. fat (25% of calories), 1.6 g. dietary fiber, 10 mg. cholesterol, 742 mg. sodium.

CURRIED FISH SOUP

SERVES 4

*A*lthough curry is not a flavor generally associated with Mediterranean cooking, the other ingredients in this easy soup are favorites in that region. You can make the soup spicy or mild, depending on the strength of your curry powder.

3	*cups defatted chicken stock*
1	*cup thinly sliced carrots*
1	*onion, thinly sliced*
½	*cup corn*
½	*cup quick-cooking brown rice*
½	*teaspoon curry powder*
¼	*teaspoon dried thyme*
¼	*teaspoon ground black pepper*
6	*ounces flounder, cut into cubes*

In a 3-quart saucepan, combine the stock, carrots, onions, corn, rice, curry powder, thyme and pepper. Bring to a boil over medium-high heat.

Cover, reduce the heat to medium and simmer for 10 minutes, or until the carrots are tender. Stir in the flounder. Cook for 3 minutes, or until the flounder is cooked through; do not overcook.

Preparation time: 10 minutes
Cooking time: 15 minutes

Chef's note: For variety, replace the flounder with chopped cooked chicken, flaked crab or peeled, deveined and chopped shrimp.

Per serving: 171 calories, 1.3 g. fat (7% of calories), 2.1 g. dietary fiber, 20 mg. cholesterol, 696 mg. sodium.

SPICY BEAN AND CORN STEW

SERVES 4

This filling stew has an international flavor, blending beans and vegetables prominent in Italian cooking with peppers and spices often associated with Mexican cuisine. Serve the stew over rice or with a generous slice of cornbread. You can easily make this dish ahead and reheat it just before serving. If the stew thickens too much after being refrigerated, add a little more stock or some water.

1	cup diced onions
1	cup thinly sliced carrots
½	cup diced celery
2	teaspoons olive oil
¼	cup diced canned jalapeño peppers (wear rubber gloves when handling)
1	teaspoon ground cumin
1	teaspoon ground coriander
1	teaspoon chili powder
2	cups defatted chicken stock
2	cups corn
1	can (19 ounces) cannellini beans, rinsed and drained
3	tablespoons chopped fresh coriander

In a 3-quart saucepan over medium heat, sauté the onions, carrots and celery in the oil for 5 minutes, or until softened. Add the peppers, cumin, coriander and chili powder; stir well.

Add the stock and corn. Cover and simmer for 15 minutes. Add the beans and heat through. Sprinkle with the coriander before serving.

Preparation time: 10 minutes
Cooking time: 25 minutes

Per serving: 198 calories, 4.6 g. fat (19% of calories), 7.1 g. dietary fiber, no cholesterol, 610 mg. sodium.

BLACK BEAN SOUP

*C*anned beans make any type of bean soup very quick and easy. For best results—and less sodium—put the beans in a strainer and rinse well with cold water before adding to the soup. In the case of black beans, rinsing will also remove some of the black color that would discolor the soup.

1	*sweet red pepper, diced*
1	*onion, diced*
1	*teaspoon olive oil*
2	*cloves garlic, minced*
1	*teaspoon dried oregano*
½	*teaspoon ground cumin*
½	*teaspoon ground black pepper*
2	*cans (16 ounces each) black beans, rinsed and drained*
2	*cups defatted chicken stock*
4	*ounces medium shrimp, peeled, deveined and coarsely chopped*
½	*cup chopped fresh coriander*

In a 3-quart saucepan over medium heat, sauté the red peppers and onions in the oil for 5 minutes, or until tender. Stir in the garlic, oregano, cumin and black pepper; cook for 1 minute.

Add the beans and stock. Bring to a boil over medium-high heat. Cover, reduce the heat to medium and simmer for 10 minutes.

Stir in the shrimp and coriander. Cook for 2 minutes. Do not overcook.

Preparation time: 10 minutes
Cooking time: 20 minutes

Per serving: 365 calories, 2.9 g. fat (7% of calories), 10.5 g. dietary fiber, 44 mg. cholesterol, 491 mg. sodium.

BEAN AND TURKEY SOUP

SERVES 6

A good way to use up leftover cooked turkey breast is in a soup like this. Navy beans contribute lots of fiber. Fresh basil gives the soup a south-of-France flavor.

- 1 onion, thinly sliced
- 2 tablespoons minced smoked turkey breast
- 2 teaspoons olive oil
- 2 cloves garlic, minced
- 4 cups defatted chicken stock
- 2 cups diced cooked turkey breast
- 2 cups rinsed and drained canned navy beans
  Pinch of ground red pepper
- ¼ cup minced fresh basil
- 2 tablespoons grated Parmesan cheese

In a 3-quart saucepan over medium heat, sauté the onions and smoked turkey in the oil for 5 minutes, or until lightly browned. Add the garlic and stir for 1 minute.

Add the stock, diced turkey, beans and pepper. Bring to a boil. Cover, reduce the heat and simmer for 10 minutes. Stir in the basil. Ladle into individual bowls and sprinkle with the Parmesan.

Preparation time: 10 minutes
Cooking time: 20 minutes

Per serving: 195 calories, 3 g. fat (14% of calories), 0.4 g. dietary fiber, 34 mg. cholesterol, 853 mg. sodium.

VIBRANT CHICKEN AND RICE SOUP

SERVES 6

*T*his recipe was the Grand Prize winner in *Prevention*'s first annual Cooking for Health recipe contest. Its creator, Melani Juhl-Chandler, is a free-lance artist living in Palo Alto, California. She's used ingredients typical of Mediterranean countries, such as chicken, rice, tomatoes and avocado, to come up with this filling soup.

4	cups water
2	cups defatted chicken stock
1	onion, diced
3	carrots, thinly sliced
3	boneless, skinless chicken breast halves, cubed
2½	cups cooked white rice
1	small avocado, cubed
2	tomatoes, cubed
3	tablespoons minced fresh coriander
3	tablespoons lime juice
⅛	teaspoon ground red pepper
4	ounces farmer's cheese, crumbled or cubed

In a 4-quart pot over medium heat, bring the water, stock, onions and carrots to a boil. Reduce the heat and simmer for 10 minutes. Add the chicken and simmer for 10 minutes, or until the chicken is cooked through and the carrots are tender.

Stir in the rice, avocados, tomatoes, coriander, lime juice and pepper. Heat for 3 to 5 minutes, but don't boil. Ladle into individual bowls and sprinkle with the farmer's cheese.

Preparation time: 10 minutes
Cooking time: 25 minutes

Per serving: 273 calories, 7.4 g. fat (24% of calories), 2.4 g. dietary fiber, 43 mg. cholesterol, 104 mg. sodium.

SWEET POTATO, SAUSAGE AND APPLE STEW

SERVES 8

*H*ere's an easy stew that's lower in fat than most other dishes made with sausage. That's because we've used turkey sausage in place of regular pork sausage, and we've drained it well after browning to get rid of any fat. This dish was created by Susan Zarrow, a former *Prevention* editor, and is a slimmed-down version of an old family favorite.

8 *ounces turkey sausage*

2 *Granny Smith apples, diced*

1 *can (35 ounces) whole sweet potatoes, drained and cubed*

2 *tablespoons unbleached flour*

1 *cup defatted chicken stock*

½ *cup apple juice*

1 *tablespoon maple syrup*

½ *teaspoon ground cinnamon*

If the sausage is in casings, remove them. Crumble the meat into a large no-stick frying pan. Brown over medium heat, breaking up the pieces with a wooden spoon. Transfer to a large plate lined with a triple thickness of paper towels. Blot with additional towels to remove all fat.

Transfer to a 2-quart casserole. Add the apples and sweet potatoes; toss to combine well.

Place the flour in a small bowl. Gradually whisk in the stock. Add the apple juice, maple syrup and cinnamon. Pour over the sausage mixture.

Cover and bake at 350° for 30 minutes, or until the ingredients are hot and the liquid has thickened slightly.

Preparation time: 10 minutes
Cooking time: 30 minutes

Per serving: 295 calories, 7.2 g. fat (22% of calories), 5 g. dietary fiber, 33 mg. cholesterol, 357 mg. sodium.

SUNNY PEACH SOUP

SERVES 4

*T*his is a perfect soup to serve on lazy summer days. It's ready in no time and is quite refreshing. Buttermilk lends a creamy texture without adding a lot of fat or cholesterol.

4	*large peaches, peeled and chopped*
2	*cups cantaloupe chunks*
¼	*cup buttermilk*
¼	*cup orange juice*
1	*teaspoon honey*
⅛	*teaspoon grated nutmeg*
4	*sprigs fresh mint*

In a blender or food processor, combine the peaches, cantaloupe, buttermilk, orange juice, honey and nutmeg. Process until very smooth and thick.

Pour into a large bowl and chill for 30 minutes. Ladle into individual bowls and garnish with the mint.

Preparation time: 10 minutes

Chef's note: To peel the peaches, drop them into boiling water and let stand for about 20 seconds. Remove with a slotted spoon and run under cold water. Use a paring knife to remove the loosened peel. If fresh peaches are out of season, use frozen peaches. Thaw them until just pliable.

For variety, you may replace the peaches with nectarines or your choice of berries.

For a dairy-free soup, replace the buttermilk with tofu.

Per serving: 85 calories, trace fat (<1% of calories), 2.1 g. dietary fiber, trace cholesterol, 23 mg. sodium.

CHAPTER 5

MUCH
MORE
THAN
RABBIT
FOOD

SALADS TO SAVOR

In Italy, France and other Mediterranean countries, salads have an honored place on the table. They're more than an afterthought fashioned from a few lettuce leaves and some heavy bottled dressing—they're a celebration of all the beautiful fresh fruits and vegetables available in those regions. And quite often they become the centerpiece of an entire meal with the addition of pasta, beans, grains, poultry, seafood or some other protein-rich food. Salads are so important to the Mediterranean lifestyle that we've made this chapter the largest one in the book. And we've rounded it out with a selection of delicious low-fat dressings that you can use to spruce up your own creations.

Black Bean and Tomato Salad

SERVES 8

*B*eans are prevalent in Mediterranean salads. They add lots of soluble fiber (the kind that can help lower cholesterol) to meals. And they turn side-dish salads into main courses. This salad is particularly nice for warm-weather luncheons or light dinners.

3 cans (19 ounces each) black beans, rinsed and drained

2 cups diced tomatoes

½ cup corn

½ cup thinly sliced scallions

¼ cup diced green peppers

¼ cup olive oil

2 tablespoons lime juice

2 tablespoons minced fresh coriander

1 teaspoon minced fresh jalapeño peppers

1 teaspoon ground cumin

1 clove garlic, minced

In a large bowl, toss together the beans, tomatoes, corn, scallions and green peppers.

In a small bowl, mix the oil, lime juice, coriander, jalapeño peppers, cumin and garlic. Pour over the bean mixture and toss to mix well.

Preparation time: 15 minutes

Chef's note: Canned beans are high in sodium. Rinsing them well with cold water will help remove some of it. Be sure to drain the beans thoroughly before incorporating them into the salad. If you're on a very-low-sodium diet, you'll be better off soaking and cooking dried beans. You can do that ahead and store the beans in the refrigerator or even the freezer.

Per serving: 280 calories, 7.9 g. fat (25% of calories), 12.9 g. dietary fiber, no cholesterol, 333 mg. sodium.

KIDNEY BEANS AND RICE

SERVES 8

*I*f you grow your own kidney beans or live in an area where fresh ones are available, use them in this salad. Steam them until tender, then proceed with the recipe directions.

2   *cups cold cooked brown rice*
2   *sweet red peppers, diced*
2   *cups rinsed and drained canned kidney beans*
1   *cup thinly sliced scallions*
1   *stalk celery, diced*
½   *cup minced fresh parsley*
1   *tablespoon grated lemon rind*
¼   *cup cider vinegar*
2   *tablespoons lemon juice*
2   *tablespoons olive oil*
1   *teaspoon sesame oil*
1   *teaspoon low-sodium soy sauce*
⅛   *teaspoon ground red pepper*

In a large bowl, toss together the rice, red peppers, beans, scallions, celery, parsley and lemon rind.

In a small bowl, whisk together the vinegar, lemon juice, olive oil, sesame oil, soy sauce and ground pepper. Pour over the rice mixture and toss to mix well.

Preparation time: 15 minutes

Chef's note: If you don't have any rice already cooked, stir 1½ cups of quick-cooking brown rice into a saucepan containing 1¼ cups of boiling water. Cover and simmer for 5 minutes. Remove from the heat and let stand 5 minutes. Fluff with a fork and either chill the rice or proceed with the recipe using warm rice.

Per serving: 158 calories, 4.7 g. fat (26% of calories), 4.8 g. dietary fiber, no cholesterol, 240 mg. sodium.

THREE-BEAN SALAD

SERVES 6

*T*his is a fresher form of the traditional three-bean salad that you can buy in cans. Because the wax beans and green beans are freshly cooked, they have a crisper texture and retain their color.

12	*ounces fresh wax beans*
12	*ounces fresh green beans*
2	*cans (19 ounces each) kidney beans, rinsed and drained*
⅔	*cup diced cucumbers*
¼	*cup minced fresh parsley*
¼	*cup white wine vinegar*
3	*tablespoons olive oil*
1	*clove garlic, minced*
¼	*teaspoon ground black pepper*

Cut the wax beans and green beans into 1" pieces. Steam for 5 minutes, or until tender. Transfer to a large bowl. Add the kidney beans, cucumbers and parsley.

In a cup, stir together the vinegar, oil, garlic and pepper. Pour over the bean mixture and toss to mix well.

Preparation time: 15 minutes

Per serving: 270 calories, 7.6 g. fat (24% of calories), 7.1 g. dietary fiber, no cholesterol, 148 mg. sodium.

FRESH HERB AND BEAN SALAD

SERVES 4

This is the type of dish you might find in many Mediterranean countries, where people grow the ingredients they use in their salads. Fresh soybeans and limas, for instance, are easy to grow in a home garden. So are cherry tomatoes, herbs and leaf lettuce.

1½ *cups fresh soybeans*
1½ *cups fresh baby lima beans*
12 *red or yellow cherry tomatoes*
1 *tablespoon olive oil*
2 *tablespoons lemon juice*
2 *tablespoons minced fresh mint*
1 *clove garlic, minced*
8 *thin slices French bread*
2 *teaspoons parsley flakes*
1 *teaspoon garlic powder*
2 *cups leaf lettuce*

Steam the soybeans and limas for 5 minutes, or until tender. Place in a large bowl. Add the tomatoes and toss well.

In a small bowl, whisk together the oil, lemon juice, mint and minced garlic. Pour over the beans and toss to mix well.

Lightly coat both sides of each bread slice with no-stick spray. Sprinkle with the parsley and garlic powder. Arrange in a single layer on a baking sheet. Toast under the broiler until lightly browned on both sides. Let cool slightly, then cut into cubes.

Serve the salad over the lettuce and sprinkle with the bread cubes.

Preparation time: 15 minutes
Broiling time: 5 minutes

Per serving: 373 calories, 11.9 g. fat (29% of calories), 6.6 g. dietary fiber, no cholesterol, 202 mg. sodium.

PASTA AND BEAN SALAD WITH MUSTARD DRESSING

SERVES 6

You can use most any types of beans and pasta for this hearty salad. You may also vary the herbs according to what's fresh. Even in winter, many markets often have such fresh herbs as basil, rosemary and coriander.

1	cup cut (1″ pieces) fresh green beans
2	cups rinsed and drained canned chick-peas
1	cup cooked small shells
½	cup thawed frozen peas
½	cup thinly sliced scallions
2	tablespoons minced fresh parsley
2	tablespoons minced fresh basil
2	tablespoons lemon juice
2	tablespoons olive oil
2	teaspoons Dijon mustard
½	teaspoon ground black pepper

Steam the beans for 5 minutes, or until just tender. Rinse with cold water and drain well. Transfer to a large plate and spread in a thin layer. Place in the freezer for 5 minutes, or until cold.

Transfer to a large bowl. Add the chick-peas, shells, peas, scallions, parsley and basil. Toss to mix well.

In a small bowl, mix the lemon juice, oil, mustard and pepper. Pour over the bean mixture and toss to mix well.

Preparation time: 15 minutes
Cooking time: 5 minutes

Chef's note: This salad is a good way to use up leftover cooked pasta. If you do not have any on hand, cook about ½ cup of dried pasta in a pot of boiling water for 10 minutes, or until tender. Pour into a colander and rinse with cold water.

Per serving: 170 calories, 6.3 g. fat (33% of calories), 5 g. dietary fiber, no cholesterol, 167 mg. sodium.

WARM LENTIL AND CHICORY VINAIGRETTE

SERVES 4

*C*ompared with most other dried legumes, lentils cook quickly. They come in various sizes and colors. Brown and green ones are larger than the reddish-orange variety and hold their shape better for use in a salad. Cook the lentils until just tender to the bite. If you can't find green lentils, substitute the brown ones and cook them for less time.

1⅓ *cups green lentils, sorted and rinsed*
1 *carrot, diced*
1 *stalk celery, diced*
1 *bay leaf*
1 *tablespoon red wine vinegar*
½ *teaspoon ground black pepper*
2 *tablespoons olive oil*
½ *cup diced onions*
2 *ounces lean smoked ham, cut into 1″ × ¼″ slivers*
1 *pound chicory, thinly sliced*
¼ *cup defatted chicken stock*

In a 3-quart saucepan, combine the lentils, carrots, celery and bay leaf. Add cold water to cover by about 2″. Bring to a boil over high heat. Reduce the heat to medium and simmer for 20 minutes, or until the lentils are just tender. Drain; discard the bay leaf. Return the mixture to the pan.

In a cup, mix the vinegar, pepper and 1 tablespoon oil. Drizzle over the lentils and toss lightly to mix. Set aside.

Meanwhile, in a large no-stick frying pan over medium heat, warm the remaining 1 tablespoon oil. Add the onions and ham. Cook, stirring often, for 5 minutes, or until the onions are tender. Add the chicory and stock. Cover and cook for 5 minutes, or until the chicory is wilted. Add the lentils and toss lightly to mix.

Preparation time: 15 minutes
Cooking time: 20 minutes

Per serving: 327 calories, 8.4 g. fat (22% of calories), 10.6 g. dietary fiber, 6 mg. cholesterol, 247 mg. sodium.

BLACK-EYED PEAS AND CARROTS

SERVES 4

*H*ere's another main-dish salad that you can toss together in a hurry. The peas give you plenty of protein, but you could toss in leftover cooked shrimp, bay scallops, other seafood, poultry or meat for a little extra.

¼	*cup white wine vinegar*
4	*teaspoons olive oil*
1	*teaspoon dry mustard*
1	*teaspoon dried tarragon*
2	*cups rinsed and drained canned black-eyed peas*
1	*cup shredded carrots*
½	*cup minced onions*
4	*cups shredded kale*

In a large bowl, whisk together the vinegar, oil, mustard and tarragon. Add the black-eyed peas, carrots and onions. Toss well. Serve on a bed of kale.

Preparation time: 10 minutes

Per serving: 196 calories, 6 g. fat (28% of calories), 7.7 g. dietary fiber, no cholesterol, 400 mg. sodium.

CHICKEN, MUSHROOM AND BARLEY SALAD

SERVES 6

*B*arley is a delicious substitute for rice in grain-based salads. Cook it up ahead of time and chill until needed. The quick-cooking variety is particularly handy and ready in about 10 minutes.

3	*cups shredded cooked chicken breast*
1½	*cups cooked barley*
¼	*cup diced canned pimentos, well drained*
4	*large mushrooms, thinly sliced*
2	*tablespoons snipped chives*
1	*tablespoon minced fresh basil*
3	*tablespoons balsamic vinegar*
2	*tablespoons olive oil*
2	*teaspoons Dijon mustard*

In a large bowl, toss together the chicken, barley, pimentos, mushrooms, chives and basil.

In a cup, mix the vinegar, oil and mustard. Pour over the chicken mixture and toss to mix well.

Preparation time: 15 minutes

Chef's note: If you don't have cooked chicken on hand, poach 4 boneless, skinless chicken breast halves in stock or water for about 15 minutes, or until cooked through. Drain and let stand until cool enough to handle. Cut the meat into bite-size pieces or shred it with your fingers.

Per serving: 196 calories, 6.9 g. fat (28% of calories), 2.3 g. dietary fiber, 48 mg. cholesterol, 74 mg. sodium.

Balsamic Vinegar

*N*ot so long ago, you practically had to be an heiress to get hold of a good bottle of balsamic vinegar. It was sold almost exclusively in gourmet stores—and even then, diligent searching was required. So was a well-endowed pocketbook.

But over the past few years, this specially aged seasoning has become America's favorite flavored vinegar, and a sizable good-quality bottle can be had for a reasonable price in local supermarkets. In terms of flavor, balsamic vinegar is a bargain. Just a little bit lends an elegant, complex sweet-and-sour taste to a wide variety of foods, without adding a drop of fat.

Balsamic vinegar is still aged in wooden casks in Italy the way it has been for hundreds of years. But thanks to technological improvements, only about four years are needed for a good result instead of the ten or more traditionally required. The vinegar is aged with skins from grapes used to make red wine, which gives it its winelike sweetness (although the vinegar is alcohol-free). Naturally, the longer the vinegar is aged, the more mellow it becomes, so check labels.

Here are some ways to use this super flavor enhancer.

- Sprinkle it on salads. Balsamic is mellow enough to stand on its own as a salad dressing.

- Pour it over fresh strawberries or a melon-ball salad. The fruit's sweetness, combined with the wine flavor and vinegary tang, make an incredible eating experience.

- Marinate vegetables or chicken in a combo of balsamic vinegar, a little olive oil, garlic and basil. It's a great marinade for mushrooms, too.

- When replacing regular vinegar with balsamic, you can use a lot less of the balsamic because it's so flavorful.

SPICY SHRIMP AND RICE SALAD

SERVES 4

Marjorie Farr of Rockville, Maryland, garnered a prize in *Prevention*'s second annual Cooking for Health recipe contest with this rice salad. Although it's got an Indonesian feel, the salad combines rice, seafood, vegetables and fruit—foods also prominent in Mediterranean dishes.

1¼	cups water
1½	teaspoons curry powder
1	teaspoon powdered ginger
1½	cups quick-cooking brown rice
8	ounces small peeled shrimp, cooked
½	cup chopped scallions
½	cup chopped sweet red peppers
½	cup raisins
½	cup mango chutney
1	tablespoon lime juice
1	tablespoon low-sodium soy sauce
2	teaspoons canola oil
¼	teaspoon crushed red-pepper flakes
1	tablespoon chopped roasted peanuts

In a 2-quart saucepan over high heat, bring the water, curry powder and ginger to a boil. Add the rice. Cover, reduce the heat to medium and simmer for 5 minutes. Remove from the heat and let stand for 5 minutes, or until all the liquid has been absorbed. Fluff with a fork and place in a large bowl.

Add the shrimp, scallions, red peppers and raisins. Toss to mix well.

In a food processor, puree the chutney, lime juice, soy sauce, oil and pepper flakes. Transfer to a 1-quart saucepan and warm over low heat.

Divide the rice mixture among individual plates. Drizzle with the warm dressing. Sprinkle with the peanuts.

Preparation time: 20 minutes
Cooking time: 5 minutes

Per serving: 332 calories, 4.3 g. fat (12% of calories), 5.8 g. dietary fiber, 111 mg. cholesterol, 315 mg. sodium.

CURRIED CHICKEN AND FRUIT SALAD

SERVES 4

This is a quick salad to prepare when you've got leftover cooked chicken breast to use up.

1½	*cups chopped cooked chicken breast*
½	*cup sliced celery*
½	*cup halved green seedless grapes*
2	*tablespoons raisins*
2	*tablespoons chopped roasted peanuts*
½	*cup nonfat mayonnaise*
½	*cup nonfat sour cream*
1	*tablespoon lemon juice*
1	*teaspoon Dijon mustard*
1	*teaspoon curry powder*

In a large bowl, toss together the chicken, celery, grapes, raisins and peanuts.

In a small bowl, whisk together the mayonnaise, sour cream, lemon juice, mustard and curry powder. Pour over the chicken mixture and toss to mix well.

Preparation time: 15 minutes

Per serving: 178 calories, 4 g. fat (20% of calories), 0.8 g. dietary fiber, 36 mg. cholesterol, 533 mg. sodium.

GREEK SCALLOP SALAD

*S*callops are low in calories and cook very quickly. They're particularly good in this dish, which won a prize for Alex Fotopoulos of Cresskill, New Jersey, in the first annual *Prevention* Cooking for Health recipe contest. This is a good way to use up leftover cooked rice.

16	medium sea scallops
2	tablespoons lemon juice
1	teaspoon water
½	tablespoon garlic powder
3	cups chopped romaine lettuce
2	tomatoes, chopped
1	cucumber, thinly sliced
1	cup cooked rice
2	tablespoons crumbled feta cheese
¼	cup red wine vinegar
1	tablespoon olive oil
1½	tablespoons minced fresh parsley
1	teaspoon dried basil
¼	teaspoon dried oregano
⅛	teaspoon ground black pepper
1	cup canned crushed tomatoes
¼	cup diced onions

Coat a large no-stick frying pan with no-stick spray. Place over medium heat for 2 minutes. Add the scallops and sauté for 3 minutes. Add the lemon juice, water and garlic powder. Cook for 2 minutes, or until the scallops are opaque.

In a large bowl, toss together the lettuce, tomatoes and cucumbers. Cover with the rice, then the scallops. Sprinkle with the feta.

In a large bowl, whisk together the vinegar, oil, parsley, basil, oregano and pepper. Mix in the tomatoes and onions. Pour over the scallop mixture and toss well.

Preparation time: 15 minutes
Cooking time: 5 minutes

Per serving: 208 calories, 6 g. fat (25% of calories), 3.9 g. dietary fiber, 19 mg. cholesterol, 162 mg. sodium.

SALADE NIÇOISE

No trip to the Mediterranean region of France would be complete without a *salade niçoise*, that hearty salad that shares some of the same elements as an Italian antipasto.

One hallmark of food from the area around Nice is the combination of tomatoes, black olives, garlic and often anchovies. *Salade niçoise* is almost guaranteed to contain those items, no matter where you get it. Typical embellishments might include cooked green beans, fresh herbs, hard-cooked eggs, onions, tuna, leaf lettuce, capers, cooked artichoke hearts, steamed baby potatoes or even potato salad. The final mix is pretty well up to the cook.

The most authentic recipes call for canned tuna. And even Julia Child says she prefers her *salade niçoise* that way. But with fresh tuna steaks so readily available, you can modify *your* version to include it. Lightly brush some steaks (about 3 ounces per person) with olive oil, and broil or grill them for 5 minutes per side. Cut the fish into strips about 1" wide. Arrange with the other ingredients on a platter or dinner plates.

Drizzle the salad with vinaigrette. Use a low-fat commercial version, or make your own reduced-fat dressing the way the experts at the Culinary Institute of America do. For 1 cup of dressing, dissolve 1 teaspoon arrowroot in 1 tablespoon water. Place in a small saucepan and whisk in ½ cup defatted chicken stock. Simmer for 2 minutes, or until thick. Cool completely and transfer to a blender. With the machine running, slowly add ¼ cup wine vinegar and ¼ cup olive oil to form a thick emulsion. Season to taste with cracked pepper, minced garlic, herbs, Dijon mustard or other flavorings.

COUSCOUS SALAD

SERVES 4

Couscous is a pasta product that resembles uncooked bulgur in texture. It's especially popular among the cultures of North Africa, where it's often used in place of rice as a base for vegetable and meat stews or as a salad grain.

1½ cups defatted chicken stock
¼ teaspoon crumbled saffron threads
1½ cups couscous
1 cup thinly shredded arugula or lettuce
⅔ cup currants
½ cup finely chopped celery
½ cup finely chopped sweet red peppers
¼ cup finely chopped red onions
2 tablespoons pine nuts, toasted
5 tablespoons lemon juice
2 tablespoons olive oil
1 tablespoon water
¼ teaspoon ground cinnamon
1 large tomato, diced

In a 2-quart saucepan over high heat, bring the stock and saffron to a boil. Remove from the heat. Stir in the couscous. Cover and let stand for 5 minutes, or until all the liquid has been absorbed. Fluff with a fork, transfer to a large bowl and let cool for 5 minutes.

Add the arugula or lettuce, currants, celery, peppers, onions and pine nuts. Toss lightly.

In a small bowl, whisk together the lemon juice, oil, water and cinnamon. Pour over the couscous mixture and toss to mix well. Sprinkle with the tomatoes.

Preparation time: 20 minutes

Per serving: 448 calories, 10.5 g. fat (21% of calories), 12.1 g. dietary fiber, no cholesterol, 56 mg. sodium.

FRESH BEAN AND BARLEY SALAD

SERVES 4

Here's another bean-and-grain combo. This salad is an excellent source of hunger-appeasing complex carbohydrates. The small amount of anchovy used is characteristic of many Mediterranean salads. This dish is a good way to use up leftover cooked barley.

2	cups cold cooked barley
2	cups thawed frozen wax beans
1½	cups thawed frozen baby lima beans
1	cup diced celery
½	cup diced sweet yellow peppers
⅓	cup red wine vinegar
2	tablespoons olive oil
2	teaspoons Dijon mustard
1	clove garlic, minced
1	teaspoon mashed anchovies or anchovy paste

Fluff the barley with a fork and place in a large bowl. Add the wax beans, lima beans, celery and peppers. Toss to mix well.

In a small bowl, whisk together the vinegar, oil, mustard, garlic and anchovies or anchovy paste. Pour over the barley mixture and toss to mix well.

Preparation time: 15 minutes

Per serving: 295 calories, 7.9 g. fat (24% of calories), 10.7 g. dietary fiber, 1 mg. cholesterol, 133 mg. sodium.

HERBED QUINOA SALAD

SERVES 4

Quinoa is a grain of South American origin. It was prized by the ancient Incans and is today valued for its high protein content. Combining the quinoa with goat cheese and fresh herbs gives this New World food some Old World flavor.

2	*cups water*
1	*cup quinoa*
1½	*cups thawed frozen snap peas*
½	*cup crumbled low-fat goat cheese*
⅓	*cup chopped fresh parsley*
⅓	*cup chopped fresh tarragon*
⅓	*cup snipped fresh chives*
⅓	*cup lemon juice*
1	*tablespoon extra virgin olive oil*

In a 2-quart saucepan over high heat, bring the water to a boil. Add the quinoa. Reduce the heat to low, cover the pan and cook for 15 minutes, or until the quinoa is tender but not mushy. Drain off any remaining liquid. Fluff with a fork to separate the grains. Spread in a thin layer on a large platter. Place in the freezer for 5 minutes, or until cooled. Transfer to a large bowl.

Add the peas, goat cheese, parsley, tarragon and chives. Toss lightly to mix well.

In a cup, combine the lemon juice and oil. Pour over the quinoa mixture and toss to mix well.

Preparation time: 25 minutes
Cooking time: 15 minutes

Per serving: 321 calories, 7.9 g. fat (22% of calories), 5.4 g. dietary fiber, 7 mg. cholesterol, 100 mg. sodium.

Bulgur, Tomato and Corn Salad

SERVES 4

*B*ulgur is a very fast-cooking grain that's the mainstay of many Middle Eastern salads, including tabbouleh. Here it's combined with vegetables and fresh herbs. If you've got red or yellow cherry tomatoes, use them in place of the chopped tomatoes. And if corn is in season, lightly steam an ear, then slice off the kernels.

1	*cup defatted chicken stock*
1	*cup bulgur*
2	*cups diced tomatoes*
1	*cup thawed frozen corn*
1	*cup diced cucumbers*
½	*cup chopped fresh coriander*
¼	*cup thinly sliced scallions*
2	*tablespoons chopped fresh mint*
1	*small jalapeño pepper, minced (wear plastic gloves when handling)*
3	*tablespoons lime juice*
1½	*tablespoons olive oil*
1	*clove garlic, minced*

In a 1-quart saucepan over high heat, bring the stock to a boil. Stir in the bulgur. Remove from the heat, cover and let stand for 15 minutes, or until the bulgur is tender and the liquid has been absorbed. Fluff with a fork and transfer to a large bowl.

Add the tomatoes, corn, cucumbers, coriander, scallions, mint and peppers. Toss lightly.

In a cup, whisk together the lime juice, oil and garlic. Pour over the bulgur mixture and toss to mix well.

Preparation time: 25 minutes

Per serving: 222 calories, 5.8 g. fat (24% of calories), 8.5 g. dietary fiber, no cholesterol, 17 mg. sodium.

COLD SPAGHETTI AND ASPARAGUS SALAD

*T*his salad has a dressing made with tahini, the sesame seed paste popular in Middle Eastern dishes such as hummus. If you don't have any handy, substitute peanut butter or another nut butter.

1	*pound asparagus, cut diagonally into 1″ pieces*
10	*ounces thin spaghetti, broken into 2″ lengths*
1	*cup shredded romaine lettuce*
1	*sweet red pepper, julienned*
½	*cup minced scallions*
¼	*cup tahini*
¼	*cup lemon juice*
1	*tablespoon honey*
1	*clove garlic, minced*
¾	*cup defatted chicken stock*

Bring a large pot of water to a boil. Drop in the asparagus and cook for 3 minutes, or until crisp-tender. Use a slotted spoon to remove the asparagus. Place on a platter lined with a double thickness of paper towels. Set aside.

Add the spaghetti to the water and cook for 6 minutes, or until just tender. Do not overcook. Drain in a colander and rinse with cold water. Allow to drain well.

In a large bowl, toss together the asparagus, spaghetti, lettuce, peppers and scallions.

In a small bowl, whisk together the tahini, lemon juice, honey and garlic until smooth. Gradually whisk in the stock. Pour over the spaghetti mixture and toss to mix well.

Preparation time: 20 minutes
Cooking time: 10 minutes

Per serving: 273 calories, 8.1 g. fat (27% of calories), 2.8 g. dietary fiber, no cholesterol, 169 mg. sodium.

MACARONI AND FAVA BEAN SALAD

*F*ava beans are a favorite in Italy, and you can sometimes buy them fresh here. Shell and cook until tender. Or use the canned ones, as we have in this recipe.

- ¾ *cup ridged elbow macaroni*
- 2 *medium plum tomatoes, quartered lengthwise and thinly sliced*
- ½ *cucumber, peeled, halved lengthwise and thinly sliced*
- 1 *large yellow pepper, thinly sliced*
- ½ *cup minced fresh parsley*
- 1 *can (19 ounces) fava beans, rinsed and drained*
- ½ *cup defatted chicken stock*
- 2 *tablespoons lemon juice*
- 2 *tablespoons Dijon mustard*
- 1 *clove garlic, minced*
- 8 *leaves romaine lettuce, thinly sliced*

Cook the macaroni in a large pot of boiling water for 10 minutes, or until tender. Pour into a colander, rinse with cold water and drain well. Place in a large bowl. Add the tomatoes, cucumbers, peppers, parsley and beans. Toss to mix well.

In a 1-quart saucepan, whisk together the stock, lemon juice, mustard and garlic. Bring to a boil over high heat. Pour over the macaroni mixture and toss to mix well. Serve warm or cold on a bed of lettuce.

Preparation time: 15 minutes
Cooking time: 10 minutes

Per serving: 136 calories, 1 g. fat (7% of calories), 4.3 g. dietary fiber, no cholesterol, 135 mg. sodium.

FRENCH DUCK SALAD

SERVES 4

*D*uck contains lots of blood-building iron, so it's worth including in your diet. Although roast duck can be very high in fat, skinless breast meat is considerably leaner. Here it's combined with cooked beans for a salad version of cassoulet, a classic French casserole.

2½ *tablespoons olive oil*

2 *boneless, skinless duck breast halves (about 7 ounces each)*

2 *cans (19 ounces each) Great Northern beans, rinsed and drained*

1 *cup thinly sliced red onions*

½ *cup finely chopped fresh parsley*

2 *tablespoons white wine vinegar*

1 *teaspoon Dijon mustard*

1 *clove garlic, minced*

2 *teaspoons minced fresh thyme*

Arugula or leaf lettuce

1 *pint cherry tomatoes, halved*

Place a no-stick frying pan over medium-high heat and let stand for 3 minutes. Add ½ tablespoon oil and swirl the pan to distribute it. Add the duck. Cook for 10 minutes. Reduce the heat to medium, flip the pieces and cook for 5 minutes, or until just cooked through. Set aside.

Meanwhile, in a large bowl, toss together the beans, onions and parsley.

In a cup, whisk together the vinegar, mustard, garlic, thyme and the remaining 2 tablespoons oil. Pour over the bean mixture and toss to mix well.

Line individual plates with the arugula or lettuce. Top with the salad and the tomatoes.

Cut the duck into thin crosswise slices. Divide among the plates.

Preparation time: 20 minutes
Cooking time: 15 minutes

Per serving: 382 calories, 10.9 g. fat (25% of calories), 10.4 g. dietary fiber, 77 mg. cholesterol, 123 mg. sodium.

BOW-TIES WITH ROSEMARY VINAIGRETTE

SERVES 4

A small amount of tofu added to the pasta gives this entrée extra protein.

1	*cup firm tofu, cut into ½" cubes*
½	*cup lemon juice*
4	*teaspoons olive oil*
2	*teaspoons Dijon mustard*
4	*scallions, minced*
1	*clove garlic, minced*
2	*teaspoons minced fresh rosemary*
½	*teaspoon ground black pepper*
	Pinch of ground red pepper
8	*ounces bow-tie noodles*
2	*cups shredded fresh spinach*

In a large bowl, mix the tofu, lemon juice, oil, mustard, scallions, garlic, rosemary, black pepper and red pepper. Set aside to marinate for at least 10 minutes and up to 8 hours.

Cook the bow-ties in a large pot of boiling water for 10 minutes, or until just tender. Drain and rinse with cold water. Add to the bowl, along with the spinach. Toss well.

Preparation time: 10 minutes plus marinating time
Cooking time: 10 minutes

Per serving: 441 calories, 11.5 g. fat (23% of calories), 4 g. dietary fiber, no cholesterol, 70 mg. sodium.

TURKEY AND RICE SALAD
WITH APPLES AND ALMONDS

SERVES 8

*H*ere's an excellent way to use up leftover turkey at Thanksgiving.

1¾   cups water
2¼   cups quick-cooking brown rice
1½   cups finely chopped cooked turkey
1   cup diced apples
1   cup chopped sweet red peppers
¼   cup chopped celery
2   tablespoons finely chopped smoked ham
2   tablespoons currants
⅓   cup lemon juice
⅓   cup apple juice
2   tablespoons olive oil
2   tablespoons slivered almonds, toasted

In a 2-quart saucepan over high heat, bring the water to a boil. Add the rice. Cover, reduce the heat to medium and simmer for 5 minutes. Remove from the heat and let stand for 5 minutes, or until all the liquid has been absorbed. Fluff with a fork and place in a large bowl.

Add the turkey, apples, peppers, celery, ham and currants. Toss well to combine.

In a small bowl, whisk together the lemon juice, apple juice and oil. Pour over the turkey mixture and toss to mix well. Sprinkle with the almonds.

Preparation time: 20 minutes
Cooking time: 5 minutes

Per serving: 229 calories, 6 g. fat (23% of calories), 4.1 g. dietary fiber, 20 mg. cholesterol, 64 mg. sodium.

FRUITED TURKEY SALAD

SERVES 6

*T*his salad is perfect for hot summer days. To keep it low in sodium, be sure to cook the pasta in unsalted water. If you buy ready-cooked turkey, read the label carefully— many brands are very high in sodium.

3	cups tricolor rotelle
1½	cups cubed cooked turkey breast
1	cup cantaloupe cubes
1	cup seedless grapes
½	cup drained crushed pineapple
2	tablespoons raisins
1	cup nonfat yogurt
1	tablespoon honey
1	tablespoon cider vinegar
¼	cup minced fresh mint
¼	cup minced fresh parsley
2	cups torn lettuce
2	tablespoons unsalted sunflower seeds

Cook the rotelle in a large pot of boiling water for 10 minutes, or until just tender. Drain and rinse with cold water. Place in a large bowl.

Add the turkey, cantaloupe, grapes, pineapple and raisins. Toss well.

In a small bowl, whisk together the yogurt, honey and vinegar. Stir in the mint and parsley. Pour over the salad and toss to mix well. Serve over the lettuce and sprinkle with the sunflower seeds.

Preparation time: 20 minutes
Cooking time: 10 minutes

Per serving: 344 calories, 3.7 g. fat (10% of calories), 2.2 g. dietary fiber, 25 mg. cholesterol, 64 mg. sodium.

Pork Tenderloin Salad

The tenderloin is the leanest cut of pork you can buy. To make this main-course salad, you first marinate the meat, then quickly bake it and very thinly slice it. Serve the meat over mixed bitter greens.

6	ounces pork tenderloin, trimmed of all visible fat
2	tablespoons orange juice
1	tablespoon soy sauce
1	tablespoon honey
½	tablespoon minced fresh ginger
1	teaspoon chopped fresh rosemary
1	clove garlic, minced
⅛	teaspoon ground black pepper
½	cup balsamic vinegar
1	tablespoon olive oil
2	teaspoons Dijon mustard
6	cups mixed bitter greens

Place the pork in a glass or ceramic dish just large enough to hold it. In a small bowl, whisk together the orange juice, soy sauce, honey, ginger, rosemary, garlic and pepper. Pour over the pork and turn it to coat all sides. Cover with plastic wrap, refrigerate and allow to marinate for at least 30 minutes and up to 12 hours; flip the piece occasionally during this time.

Remove the pork from its marinade and transfer it to a 9" pie plate; discard the marinade. Bake at 400° for 25 minutes, or until a meat thermometer inserted in the thickest part reads 160°.

Remove from the oven and transfer to a cutting board. Let stand about 10 minutes before carving into ¼" slices.

In a small bowl, whisk together the vinegar, oil and mustard.

Place the greens in a large bowl. Drizzle with the dressing and toss well. Divide among individual plates and top with the pork slices.

Preparation time: 20 minutes plus marinating time
Baking time: 25 minutes

Per serving: 130 calories, 4.6 g. fat (32% of calories), 1.3 g. dietary fiber, 28 mg. cholesterol, 218 mg. sodium.

PEANUT SLAW

SERVES 6

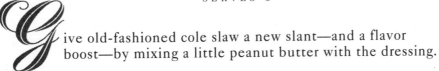ive old-fashioned cole slaw a new slant—and a flavor boost—by mixing a little peanut butter with the dressing.

2	cups shredded red or green cabbage
1	cup shredded carrots
¼	cup raisins
¼	cup minced onions
2	tablespoons peanut butter
2	tablespoons cider vinegar
1	tablespoon orange juice
½	cup nonfat mayonnaise
½	teaspoon ground black pepper
⅛	teaspoon celery seeds

In a large bowl, toss together the cabbage, carrots, raisins and onions.

In a small bowl, whisk together the peanut butter, vinegar and orange juice until creamy. Whisk in the mayonnaise, pepper and celery seeds. Pour over the salad and toss to mix well.

Preparation time: 15 minutes

Per serving: 83 calories, 3 g. fat (29% of calories), 2.1 g. dietary fiber, no cholesterol, 266 mg. sodium.

GARDEN SALAD WITH CANTALOUPE DRESSING

You can vary this dish according to what fruits and vegetables are at their peak. This salad was created by Walt Disney World Chef Keith Keogh and is a popular attraction on the menu at the Wonders of Life pavilion at Epcot Center.

Dressing

1½	*cups finely chopped cantaloupe*
2	*tablespoons water*
1	*tablespoon honey*
1	*tablespoon minced fresh ginger*
1	*tablespoon balsamic vinegar*

Salad

1	*cup small broccoli florets*
1	*cup snow peas*
1	*carrot, julienned*
1½	*cups cantaloupe cubes*
1½	*cups strawberry halves*
8	*red radishes, julienned*
2	*cups fresh spinach*

To make the dressing: In a blender, process the cantaloupe, water, honey, ginger and vinegar until smooth.

To make the salad: Steam the broccoli, snow peas and carrots for about 4 minutes, or until crisp-tender. Transfer to a large plate and spread out in a thin layer. Place in the freezer for 5 minutes, or until cold; do not let the vegetables freeze. Transfer to a large bowl.

Add the cantaloupe, strawberries and radishes; toss well. Divide the spinach among individual plates. Top with the salad. Drizzle with the dressing.

Preparation time: 20 minutes
Cooking time: 5 minutes

Per serving: 116 calories, 0.9 g. fat (7% of calories), 5.5 g. dietary fiber, no cholesterol, 51 mg. sodium.

CUCUMBER SALAD

SERVES 4

Old-fashioned cucumber salad has a full-fat sour-cream dressing. This recipe retains all the creamy flavor of the original but cuts back tremendously on the fat.

2	large cucumbers
3	tablespoons chopped fresh dill
2	tablespoons snipped chives
1	cup buttermilk
1	teaspoon white wine vinegar
½	teaspoon honey
1	clove garlic, minced
½	teaspoon ground black pepper

Peel the cucumbers and halve lengthwise. Scoop out the seeds using a small spoon; discard the seeds. Cut the cucumbers into paper-thin slices. Squeeze out excess moisture. Place in a large bowl and break up the clumps with a fork. Add the dill and chives. Toss to mix well.

In a small bowl, mix the buttermilk, vinegar, honey, garlic and pepper. Pour over the cucumber mixture and toss to mix well.

Preparation time: 15 minutes

Per serving: 51 calories, 0.5 g. fat (8% of calories), 1.1 g. dietary fiber, 2 mg. cholesterol, 64 mg. sodium.

Orange Moroccan Salad

SERVES 6

range salads are popular in Mediterranean countries, including Morocco. For this salad, Chef Aliza Green combines sweet-tart oranges with cantaloupe and carrots. All are good sources of health-building beta-carotene and vitamin C. Serve this salad with grilled chicken or a couscous-and-vegetables main dish.

3	*navel oranges, peeled and sliced crosswise*
½	*cantaloupe, thinly sliced*
8	*ounces carrots, shredded*
2	*tablespoons olive oil*
2	*tablespoons balsamic vinegar*
	Juice of ½ lemon
2	*teaspoons Dijon mustard*
¼	*teaspoon ground black pepper*
2	*tablespoons chopped fresh mint*

Divide the oranges, cantaloupe and carrots among individual salad plates.

In a small bowl, whisk together the oil, vinegar, lemon juice, mustard and pepper. Add the mint. Drizzle over the salads.

Preparation time: 15 minutes

Per serving: 111 calories, 4.8 g. fat (37% of calories), 3.1 g. dietary fiber, no cholesterol, 39 mg. sodium.

Bitter Greens with
Hot Vinaigrette Dressing

Bitter greens are used often in Italy and other Mediterranean countries. You may take your pick of the many types available, including arugula, curly endive, radicchio and dandelion. This recipe comes from Joanne D'Agostino, a healthy-cooking author from Pennsylvania who wanted a substitute for the hot bacon dressing popular in her part of the country.

1	*pound bitter greens, torn into bite-size pieces*
2	*strips turkey bacon*
½	*cup balsamic vinegar*
2	*teaspoons honey*
1	*teaspoon Dijon mustard*
2	*cloves garlic, minced*
½	*teaspoon dried tarragon*
⅛	*teaspoon coarsely ground black pepper*

Divide the greens among individual salad plates.

Broil the bacon until crisp. Drain on paper towels to remove as much fat as possible. Crumble the bacon and sprinkle it evenly over the greens.

In a 1-quart saucepan, whisk together the vinegar, honey, mustard, garlic, tarragon and pepper. Whisk over medium-low heat for 5 minutes, or until hot but not boiling. Spoon immediately over the greens.

Preparation time: 15 minutes
Cooking time: 5 minutes

Per serving: 114 calories, 2.3 g. fat (17% of calories), 1.1 g. dietary fiber, 5 mg. cholesterol, 212 mg. sodium.

GREEK SALATA

SERVES 4

*F*eta cheese is a hallmark of Greek salads. Here just a sprinkle of feta gives characteristic flavor without adding a lot of fat.

2   *tomatoes, cut into wedges*

1   *large cucumber, halved lengthwise and thinly sliced*

2   *green peppers, diced*

1   *small onion, sliced crosswise and separated into rings*

4   *slices Italian bread, toasted and cut into cubes*

⅓   *cup lemon juice*

1   *tablespoon olive oil*

2   *teaspoons minced fresh oregano*

1   *clove garlic, minced*

2   *tablespoons crumbled feta cheese*

In a large bowl, toss together the tomatoes, cucumbers, peppers, onions and bread.

In a cup, combine the lemon juice, oil, oregano and garlic. Pour over the tomato mixture and toss to mix well.

Divide among individual plates and sprinkle with the feta.

Preparation time: 15 minutes

Per serving: 174 calories, 5 g. fat (24% of calories), 3.3 g. dietary fiber, 4 mg. cholesterol, 208 mg. sodium.

BROCCOLI AND MUSHROOM SALAD

SERVES 4

*Y*ou can decide how crunchy you want your broccoli for this salad. You can parboil it for a few minutes to brighten the color and maintain the crisp texture, or you can steam the florets for a few minutes longer to soften them. Although the percent of calories from fat in this recipe is high, the actual grams of fat are not.

3   *cups broccoli florets, parboiled or steamed*
8   *small mushrooms, thinly sliced*
3   *scallions, thinly sliced*
2   *tablespoons crumbled feta cheese*
2   *tablespoons defatted chicken stock*
1   *tablespoon lemon juice*
1   *tablespoon olive oil*
1   *clove garlic, minced*
¼   *teaspoon ground black pepper*
¼   *teaspoon dried marjoram*

In a large bowl, toss together the broccoli, mushrooms, scallions and feta.

In a cup, mix the stock, lemon juice, oil, garlic, pepper and marjoram. Pour over the broccoli mixture and toss to mix well.

Preparation time: 15 minutes

Per serving: 78 calories, 4.6 g. fat (47% of calories), 3.3 g. dietary fiber, 3 mg. cholesterol, 98 mg. sodium.

FRUIT SALAD WITH LIME DRESSING

*F*resh fruit is abundant in the warm countries of the Mediterranean. In this recipe, it's served with a creamy sweet-tart dressing that's low in fat. You may substitute other fruit according to what's in season.

>   2   *cups halved fresh figs*
>   1   *cup watermelon balls*
>   1   *cup blueberries*
>   1   *cup orange sections*
>   *Grated rind from 1 lime*
>   3   *tablespoons lime juice*
>   ¼   *cup nonfat mayonnaise*
>   ¼   *cup nonfat sour cream*
>   2   *tablespoons honey*
>   2   *cups torn lettuce*
>   2   *tablespoons chopped pecans*

In a large bowl, toss together the figs, watermelon, blueberries, oranges, lime rind and 1 tablespoon lime juice. Let stand for 10 minutes.

In a cup, whisk together the mayonnaise, sour cream, honey and the remaining 2 tablespoons lime juice.

Divide the lettuce among individual plates. Top with the fruit and dollops of the dressing. Sprinkle with the pecans.

Preparation time: 20 minutes

Per serving: 218 calories, 3 g. fat (12% of calories), 8.8 g. dietary fiber, no cholesterol, 222 mg. sodium.

SIMPLY TOMATOES

SERVES 4

*M*atthew Hoffman, who attended the Mediterranean conference and wrote the first chapter in this book, serves this salad all summer long using the freshest, ripest tomatoes he can find.

> 2 *large tomatoes*
> 3 *tablespoons shredded fresh basil*
> 1–2 *cloves garlic, minced*
> *Cracked black pepper*
> 2 *teaspoons olive oil*

Core the tomatoes and cut them crosswise into thick slices. Divide among individual plates. Sprinkle with the basil, garlic and pepper. Drizzle with the oil.

Preparation time: 5 minutes

Per serving: 78 calories, 2.8 g. fat (32% of calories), 0.5 g. dietary fiber, no cholesterol, 6 mg. sodium.

DRESS UP YOUR SALADS

*Q*uestion: When is a crisp garden salad a dieter's demise? When all the wonderful greens and vegetables are drowned under the weight of regular salad dressing.

Leafy greens, succulent vegetables and fresh fruits are among the leanest, healthiest fare imaginable. But dousing them with fatty dressings can sabotage your diet and undo all the benefits these foods have to offer. Here are some dressings that are lower in fat than most homemade offerings.

RASPBERRY DRESSING

MAKES 1 CUP

- 1 cup fresh or thawed and drained frozen raspberries
- ¼ cup balsamic vinegar
- 4 teaspoons olive oil

Press the raspberries through a fine sieve to remove the seeds. To the resulting puree, add the vinegar and oil.

Preparation time: 5 minutes

Per tablespoon: 15 calories, 1.1 g. fat (66% of calories), trace dietary fiber, no cholesterol, no sodium.

CREAMY BUTTERMILK DRESSING

MAKES 1¼ CUPS

- ¾ cup buttermilk
- ¼ cup nonfat mayonnaise
- 2 tablespoons lemon juice

1   tablespoon olive oil
2   tablespoons minced scallion tops or snipped
     chives
1   tablespoon minced fresh tarragon
½   teaspoon ground black pepper

In a small bowl, whisk together the buttermilk, mayonnaise, lemon juice and oil. Stir in the scallions or chives, tarragon and pepper.

Preparation time: 5 minutes

Per tablespoon: 11 calories, 0.8 g. fat (65% of calories), trace dietary fiber, trace cholesterol, 35 mg. sodium.

POPPY SEED DRESSING

MAKES ¾ CUP

¼   cup defatted chicken stock
3   tablespoons orange juice
2   tablespoons lemon juice
1   tablespoon olive oil
2   teaspoons honey
2   teaspoons poppy seeds
1   teaspoon Dijon mustard
¼   teaspoon ground coriander

In a small bowl, whisk together the stock, orange juice, lemon juice, oil, honey, poppy seeds, mustard and coriander.

Preparation time: 5 minutes

Per tablespoon: 19 calories, 1.3 g. fat (62% of calories), trace dietary fiber, no cholesterol, 13 mg. sodium.

(continued)

STRAWBERRY VINAIGRETTE

MAKES 1 ¼ CUPS

1   cup sliced strawberries
½   cup orange juice
2   tablespoons white wine vinegar
1   tablespoon olive oil
1   tablespoon honey

In a blender, combine the strawberries, juice, vinegar, oil and honey. Process until smooth.

Preparation time: 5 minutes

Per tablespoon: 14 calories, 0.8 g. fat (51% of calories), trace dietary fiber, no cholesterol, trace sodium.

CREAMY PARMESAN-PEPPER DRESSING

MAKES 1 CUP

⅔   cup dry-curd cottage cheese
⅓   cup buttermilk
1   tablespoon white wine vinegar
2   tablespoons grated Parmesan cheese
1   teaspoon ground black pepper

Place the cottage cheese in a food processor. Process for 3 minutes, or until very smooth. With the machine running, pour in the buttermilk and vinegar. Process until smooth. Add the Parmesan and pepper. Blend briefly to distribute evenly.

Preparation time: 5 minutes

Per tablespoon: 14 calories, 0.4 g. fat (26% of calories), trace dietary fiber, 1 mg. cholesterol, 18 mg. sodium.

E N J O Y   T H E
B O U N T Y   O F
T H E   D E E P

$\mathscr{S}$EAFOOD DELIGHTS

$\mathscr{A}$s you can well imagine, countries in and around the Mediterranean have a wealth of seafood to choose from and feature on their menus. The recipes in this chapter reflect the diversity of that bounty. And although we've tried, for the sake of simplicity, to use fish commonly available in American markets, you should feel free to substitute other varieties according to your own taste. Consult with your fish seller for substitutions, or check the suggestions that appear with many of the recipes. Remember that most seafood contains omega-3 fatty acids, which can help lower cholesterol, so it's worth featuring fish and shellfish on your own menus on a regular basis.

BRAISED FILLET OF CATFISH

SERVES 4

*F*arm-raised catfish is becoming very popular and is increasingly easy to find in stores. This recipe, created by Houston Chef Raymond Potter for the American Cancer Society, prepares the fish very simply. Serve it with pasta or couscous. You may also use whiting, hake or pink salmon.

4   *catfish fillets (4 ounces each)*
2   *tablespoons lemon juice*
4   *medium tomatoes, seeded and diced*
1   *cup diced yellow peppers*
8   *scallions, chopped*
1   *clove garlic, minced*
1   *teaspoon oil*
2   *cups tomato juice*
4   *teaspoons cornstarch*
2   *tablespoons water*

Sprinkle the catfish with the lemon juice and set aside.

In a large no-stick frying pan over medium-high heat, sauté the tomatoes, peppers, scallions and garlic in the oil for 10 minutes, or until the vegetables are wilted and the juice released from the tomatoes has started to evaporate.

Reduce the heat to medium and add the tomato juice. Bring to a simmer.

In a cup, dissolve the cornstarch in the water. Stir into the pan; continue stirring until the mixture begins to thicken.

Add the catfish to the pan and spoon the sauce over the fillets. Cover the pan and simmer for 5 minutes, or until the fish is cooked through.

Preparation time: 10 minutes
Cooking time: 20 minutes

Per serving: 211 calories, 6.6 g. fat (27% of calories), 3.7 g. dietary fiber, 65 mg. cholesterol, 97 mg. sodium.

Dijon Cod

*A*topping of mayonnaise and mustard helps keep these cod fillets from drying out as they bake. Other fillets that would work nicely include haddock, halibut, tilefish, grouper, snapper and wolffish.

4	*cod fillets (6 ounces each)*
3	*tablespoons nonfat mayonnaise*
1	*tablespoon Dijon mustard*
½	*teaspoon prepared horseradish*
½	*teaspoon dried dill*
2	*tablespoons dry bread crumbs*
1	*teaspoon olive oil*

Choose a baking dish large enough to hold the cod in a single layer. Coat the dish with no-stick spray. Place the cod in the dish; turn under any thin ends so the fillets are an even thickness.

In a cup, mix the mayonnaise, mustard, horseradish and dill. Spread evenly over the cod. Sprinkle with the bread crumbs. Drizzle with the oil.

Bake at 350° for 20 minutes, or until the cod is cooked through.

Preparation time: 5 minutes
Cooking time: 20 minutes

Per serving: 164 calories, 2.6 g. fat (15% of calories), 0.1 g. dietary fiber, 67 mg. cholesterol, 319 mg. sodium.

SPICY HADDOCK WITH CORIANDER

SERVES 4

*H*ere's an especially quick way to prepare fish. Serve with couscous or rice and a cooked vegetable, such as carrots. Cod, halibut, tilefish and other medium-firm but mild fillets would also work in this recipe.

1	*papaya, diced*
¼	*cup chopped fresh coriander*
1	*small hot chili pepper, minced (wear plastic gloves when handling)*
	Juice of ½ lime
4	*haddock fillets (6 ounces each)*
2	*cloves garlic, minced*
½	*teaspoon paprika*

In a large bowl, combine the papaya, coriander, peppers and lime juice. Cover and let stand at room temperature for 20 minutes.

Pat the haddock dry with paper towels. Rub on all sides with the garlic. Sprinkle with the paprika. Broil or grill for about 4 minutes per side, or until cooked through. Serve topped with the papaya mixture.

Preparation time: 10 minutes plus standing time
Cooking time: 10 minutes

Per serving: 182 calories, 3.4 g. fat (17% of calories), 0.5 g. dietary fiber, 46 mg. cholesterol, 80 mg. sodium.

HALIBUT WITH ROASTED GARLIC AND MUSHROOMS

SERVES 4

*T*his recipe was created by Seattle Chef Caprial Pence. Serve the fish with a grain, such as bulgur, and additional roasted garlic, if desired.

5	*unpeeled cloves garlic*
1	*tablespoon sherry vinegar*
1	*tablespoon water*
2	*shallots, minced*
1	*tablespoon olive oil*
½	*cup sliced shiitake mushrooms*
3	*plum tomatoes, diced*
⅛	*teaspoon ground black pepper*
¾	*cup defatted chicken stock*
	Juice of 1 lemon
¼	*teaspoon dried thyme*
4	*halibut steaks (6 ounces each; ½" thick)*

Place 3 garlic cloves in a custard cup and roast at 400° for 15 minutes, or until soft. Peel, chop and place in a medium bowl. Add the vinegar, water and shallots. Whisk in the oil. Add the mushrooms, tomatoes and pepper. Set aside.

While the garlic is baking, peel and crush the remaining 2 cloves garlic. Place in a large pot. Add the stock, lemon juice and thyme. Bring to a boil.

Place the halibut on a steamer rack and set in the pan. Cover and steam for 7 to 10 minutes, or until cooked through. Remove from the pan and serve with the mushroom mixture.

Preparation time: 10 minutes
Cooking time: 10 minutes
Baking time: 15 minutes

Per serving: 209 calories, 6.8 g. fat (30% of calories), 0.4 g. dietary fiber, 45 mg. cholesterol, 99 mg. sodium.

HADDOCK WITH SPICY MUSTARD MARINADE

SERVES 4

*M*icrowaving is an ideal way to cook seafood. Delicate fillets always stay tender, steaks cook completely through without drying out, and shellfish remains appetizingly plump and moist. Better yet, the short cooking time leaves natural flavors intact so you never need heavy sauces to render your fish palatable. This recipe for haddock can easily be used with other types of fillets.

2   *tablespoons coarse mustard*
2   *tablespoons lime juice*
½   *teaspoon dried thyme*
     Dash of hot-pepper sauce
     Pinch of ground black pepper
1   *pound haddock fillets*

In a 9" glass pie plate, combine the mustard, lime juice, thyme, hot-pepper sauce and pepper. Add the haddock and turn the pieces to coat both sides. Let stand at room temperature for 20 minutes.

If the fillets have thin ends, tuck them under so the fish is evenly thick. Arrange the fillets around the outside edge of the pie plate and cover with vented plastic wrap.

Microwave on high power for a total of 4½ minutes, or until the fish is opaque; halfway through the cooking time, give the plate a quarter turn. Let stand for 4 minutes before serving.

Preparation time: 5 minutes plus marinating time
Cooking time: 5 minutes

Per serving: 100 calories, 0.6 g. fat (5% of calories), no dietary fiber, 55 mg. cholesterol, 173 mg. sodium.

French Duck Salad (page 106)

Spanish Pepper Shrimp (page 149)

Steamed Red Snapper with Pepper Relish (page 142)

Grilled Salmon with Cucumber Relish (page 139)

Halibut with Roasted Garlic and Mushrooms (page 127)

Grilled Chicken with Spinach (page 158)

Turkey Croquette (page 189)

Chicken Fricassee with Parsley Dumplings (page 164)

SAUTÉED MAHIMAHI

Mahimahi is a medium-firm fish with flavorful flesh. You can use this simple way of preparing fillets with other fish such as ocean perch, striped bass, pollock, pompano and perch.

1	*pound mahimahi fillets*
2	*tablespoons unbleached flour*
½	*teaspoon dried marjoram*
½	*teaspoon dried oregano*
¼	*teaspoon ground black pepper*
⅓	*cup fat-free egg substitute*
1	*teaspoon olive oil*

Cut the mahimahi into serving-size pieces.

In a small shallow bowl, mix the flour, marjoram, oregano and pepper. Place the eggs in another small shallow bowl.

In a large no-stick frying pan over medium heat, warm the oil for 2 minutes.

Dredge each piece of the mahimahi first in the flour mixture, then in the eggs. Place in the pan and sauté for 5 minutes per side, or until cooked through.

Preparation time: 5 minutes
Cooking time: 10 minutes

Chef's note: Before cooking any fish fillets, be sure to check the flesh carefully for any small bones. Pull them out with your fingers or with clean tweezers.

Per serving: 131 calories, 2 g. fat (14% of calories), 0.1 g. dietary fiber, 83 mg. cholesterol, 126 mg. sodium.

SALMON WITH DILL VEGETABLES

SERVES 4

*H*ere is a really easy way to prepare any type of fish steak. And because the fish bakes in foil packets, there's little cleanup involved. Serve the fish with microwave-baked potatoes, corn on the cob and one of the sauces on page 140. Don't be alarmed by the high percentage of calories from fat. They're an indication that salmon is a rich source of heart-smart omega-3s. And the percent of fat in your entire meal will be considerably reduced when you combine the salmon with low-fat side dishes.

¼	*cup cider vinegar*
¼	*teaspoon Dijon mustard*
¼	*teaspoon dried dill*
4	*salmon steaks (6 ounces each; ½″ thick)*
1	*green pepper, thinly sliced*
1	*large tomato, thinly sliced*
1	*onion, thinly sliced*

In a glass baking dish just large enough to hold the fish in a single layer, combine the vinegar, mustard and dill. Add the salmon and turn to coat both sides. Let marinate for 5 minutes. Flip the pieces and marinate for 5 more minutes.

Cut 4 squares of aluminum foil and coat the dull side of each with no-stick spray. Place a piece of salmon in the center of each square. Top with the peppers, tomatoes and onions. Drizzle with the marinade. Seal the packets and place on a baking sheet.

Bake at 375° for 20 minutes.

Preparation time: 5 minutes plus marinating time
Baking time: 20 minutes

Per serving: 249 calories, 10.1 g. fat (37% of calories), 1.3 g. dietary fiber, 86 mg. cholesterol, 77 mg. sodium.

GRILLED SALMON WITH CUCUMBER RELISH

*T*his salmon recipe with Mediterranean overtones was created by Seattle Chef Caprial Pence. Serve the fish with pasta or rice.

½	*cup diced red onions*
½	*cup white wine vinegar*
2	*shallots, minced*
2	*cloves garlic, minced*
1	*teaspoon minced fresh ginger*
1	*teaspoon grated orange rind*
¼	*teaspoon low-sodium soy sauce*
2	*cucumbers, thinly sliced*
⅛	*teaspoon ground black pepper*
4	*salmon fillets (6 ounces each)*
2	*teaspoons olive oil*

In a large no-stick frying pan over medium-high heat, combine the onions, vinegar, shallots, garlic, ginger, orange rind and soy sauce. Bring to a boil, stir and cook for 30 seconds. Remove from the heat.

Add the cucumbers and pepper. Set aside.

Rub the salmon with the oil and grill or broil for 4 to 5 minutes per side. Serve topped with the cucumber mixture.

Preparation time: 10 minutes
Cooking time: 10 minutes

Per serving: 294 calories, 13.3 g. fat (41% of calories), 2.1 g. dietary fiber, 94 mg. cholesterol, 95 mg. sodium.

CREAMY LOW-FAT SAUCES

Steamed, broiled or baked seafood is wonderfully low in fat and calories. Keep it that way with creamy sauces made from nonfat yogurt, mayonnaise, cottage cheese or sour cream. The following sauces are suitable for everything from abalone to wolffish. You can vary them by changing the herbs.

COTTAGE CHEESE AND DILL SAUCE

MAKES 1 CUP

- ½ cup dry-curd cottage cheese
- ¼ cup nonfat mayonnaise
- ¼ cup skim milk
- 1 tablespoon lemon juice
- 1 clove garlic, minced
- 1 tablespoon chopped fresh dill

Place the cottage cheese in a food processor and blend for 2 minutes, or until very smooth; stop and scrape down the sides of the container as necessary. Add the mayonnaise, milk, lemon juice, garlic and dill. Process with on/off turns until well mixed.

Preparation time: 5 minutes

Per tablespoon: 9 calories, trace fat (4% of calories), no dietary fiber, <1 mg. cholesterol, 34 mg. sodium.

TARTAR SAUCE

MAKES 1 CUP

- 1 cup nonfat mayonnaise
- 1 dill pickle spear, finely chopped
- 2 tablespoons minced fresh parsley
- 1 tablespoon lemon juice
- 2 teaspoons capers, rinsed and chopped

In a small bowl, mix the mayonnaise, pickles, parsley, lemon juice and capers.

Preparation time: 5 minutes

Per tablespoon: 9 calories, trace fat (3% of calories), no dietary fiber, no cholesterol, 153 mg. sodium.

YOGURT AND MUSTARD SAUCE

MAKES 1 CUP

1   cup nonfat yogurt
2   tablespoons snipped chives
1   tablespoon minced fresh tarragon
2   teaspoons Dijon mustard
½   teaspoon ground black pepper

In a small bowl, mix the yogurt, chives, tarragon, mustard and pepper.

Preparation time: 5 minutes

Per tablespoon: 8 calories, trace fat (8% of calories), no dietary fiber, no cholesterol, 30 mg. sodium.

HORSERADISH SAUCE

MAKES 1 CUP

1   cup nonfat sour cream
2   tablespoons minced fresh parsley
1   tablespoon prepared horseradish
1   tablespoon lemon juice
1   teaspoon Dijon mustard
    Dash of hot-pepper sauce

In a small bowl, mix the sour cream, parsley, horseradish, lemon juice, mustard and hot-pepper sauce.

Preparation time: 5 minutes

Per tablespoon: 15 calories, trace fat (6% of calories), no dietary fiber, no cholesterol, 30 mg. sodium.

STEAMED RED SNAPPER WITH PEPPER RELISH

SERVES 4

August Mrozowski of the Cafe L'Europe in Sarasota, Florida, created this recipe. Serve the fish with quick-cooking brown rice and steamed snap peas or another green vegetable. You may replace the snapper with cod, haddock, halibut or tilefish for variety.

1 *sweet red pepper*
1 *yellow pepper*
1 *green pepper*
2 *tablespoons balsamic vinegar*
1 *tablespoon chopped fresh coriander*
3 *scallions, minced*
2 *teaspoons olive oil*
½ *teaspoon hot-pepper sauce*
4 *red snapper fillets (6 ounces each)*

Place the red, yellow and green peppers on a baking sheet and broil about 3" from the heat for 15 minutes, or until charred on all sides. Set aside for 5 minutes to cool. Remove the blackened skin, cores and seeds; dice the flesh. Transfer to a medium bowl.

Add the vinegar, coriander, scallions, oil and hot-pepper sauce. Set aside.

Steam the fish over boiling water for 8 to 10 minutes, or until cooked through. Serve with the pepper mixture.

Preparation time: 10 minutes
Cooking time: 10 minutes
Broiling time: 15 minutes

Per serving: 202 calories, 5 g. fat (22% of calories), 0.6 g. dietary fiber, 62 mg. cholesterol, 110 mg. sodium.

GINGER SNAPPER

*T*his easy snapper recipe won a prize for Randolph Bush of Trumbull, Connecticut, in *Prevention*'s first annual Cooking for Health recipe contest. If you want to make the snapper a little fancier, add some flaked crab to the sauce.

Sauce

1	scallion, thinly sliced
2	tablespoons minced shallots
1	tablespoon powdered ginger
½	teaspoon olive oil
1	cup defatted chicken stock

Snapper

4	red snapper fillets (4 ounces each)
1	tablespoon powdered ginger
¼	cup cornstarch
1	tablespoon olive oil

To make the sauce: In a 1-quart saucepan over medium heat, sauté the scallions, shallots and ginger in the oil for 2 minutes. Add the stock. Raise the heat to high and boil for 5 minutes, or until the stock is reduced by half. Keep warm.

To make the snapper: Sprinkle the snapper with the ginger. Place the cornstarch in a small sieve and shake over the fish to coat on all sides.

In a large no-stick frying pan over medium-high heat, warm the oil. Add the snapper and sauté for 4 minutes per side, or until cooked through. Transfer to serving plates and top with the sauce.

Preparation time: 5 minutes
Cooking time: 15 minutes

Per serving: 187 calories, 4.8 g. fat (24% of calories), trace dietary fiber, 42 mg. cholesterol, 94 mg. sodium.

STOVETOP GRILLED FISH

Cast iron is the original no-stick cookware. It leaves foods naturally juicy without added fat. The new ridged stovetop grill pans have nifty grooves that allow any fat in food to drain harmlessly away. These pans are great for quickly cooking lean foods such as fish fillets and chicken breasts—and giving them the taste and appearance of grilled food. If you don't have a grill pan, use a well-seasoned regular cast-iron pan. This recipe couldn't be easier, and you can use the technique for any fish steak, such as tuna, salmon or shark. Serve the fish with cole slaw and steamed baby potatoes.

> 1   *pound fish steaks (½″ thick)*
> 1   *tablespoon nonfat mayonnaise*
> ½ *teaspoon dried dill*

Rub the fish all over with the mayonnaise and sprinkle with the dill.

Preheat a cast-iron grill pan on high for 5 minutes. Add the fish and reduce the heat to medium-high. Let the fish sizzle for about 45 seconds, then flip so grill marks appear on both sides. Sizzle the fish for 5 minutes, or until cooked through.

Preparation time: 5 minutes
Cooking time: 10 minutes

Per serving: 122 calories, 3.9 g. fat (29% of calories), no dietary fiber, 38 mg. cholesterol, 135 mg. sodium.

ITALIAN TUNA AND PASTA

SERVES 4

*T*his is a very simple dish to whip up after work. Canned salmon would also work very well in this recipe.

1 cup sliced mushrooms

1 cup sliced onions

1 tablespoon olive oil

1 cup diced tomatoes

1 can (12¼ ounces) water-packed albacore tuna, drained and flaked

¼ cup defatted chicken stock

Pinch of hot-pepper flakes

8 ounces fettuccine

2 tablespoons minced fresh basil

3 tablespoons grated Parmesan cheese

In a large no-stick frying pan over medium-high heat, sauté the mushrooms and onions in the oil for 5 minutes, or until tender. Add the tomatoes, tuna, stock and pepper flakes. Cover and simmer over low heat for 5 minutes.

Meanwhile, cook the fettuccine in a large pot of boiling water for 10 minutes, or until tender. Drain and place in a large bowl. Add the tuna mixture and basil; toss well to combine. Sprinkle with the Parmesan.

Preparation time: 15 minutes
Cooking time: 10 minutes

Per serving: 398 calories, 8.8 g. fat (20% of calories), 1.4 g. dietary fiber, 89 mg. cholesterol, 590 mg. sodium.

TUNA CURRY SANDWICH

When you want a really quick lunch sandwich that's a little out of the ordinary, try this offering from Elizabeth Goldstein of Yardley, Pennsylvania. This recipe won her a prize in *Prevention*'s first annual Cooking for Health recipe contest. If you want variety, substitute flaked cooked white fish or opt for chopped shrimp or flaked crab.

1   can (12¼ ounces) water-packed albacore
    tuna, drained and flaked
½   cup chopped onions
¼   cup low-fat mayonnaise
2   teaspoons Dijon mustard
1   teaspoon curry powder
2   small bananas, sliced
8   slices bread
8   cucumber slices

In a medium bowl, combine the tuna, onions, mayonnaise, mustard and curry powder. Fold in the bananas.

Spread the mixture on 4 slices of the bread. Top with the cucumbers and the remaining 4 slices bread.

Preparation time: 10 minutes

Per serving: 369 calories, 8.4 g. fat (20% of calories), 5 g. dietary fiber, 37 mg. cholesterol, 676 mg. sodium.

EASY SEAFOOD RISOTTO

*R*isotto is a classic Italian dish that can demand a lot of time and physical effort from the cook. Standard recipes require that you stand over the stove and constantly stir the rice for at least 30 minutes. Your microwave can immensely simplify the process. Traditional recipes call for Arborio rice, a special short-grain variety from Italy, but regular long-grain rice works just as well in this recipe. For variety, you may substitute other types of seafood or chopped cooked poultry for the scallops.

1	cup long-grain white rice
1	cup minced onions
½	cup minced green peppers
2	teaspoons olive oil
3½	cups defatted chicken stock, heated
12	ounces small bay scallops
2	tablespoons grated Parmesan cheese
1–2	tablespoons minced fresh dill or basil
½	teaspoon ground black pepper

In a 2-quart glass casserole, combine the rice, onions, green peppers and oil. Stir well. Microwave on high for 3 minutes. Stir.

Add the stock. Microwave on high for 10 minutes. Stir. Microwave on high for 10 minutes. Stir in the scallops. Microwave on high for 5 minutes, or until most of the liquid has been absorbed and the rice is tender. Stir in the Parmesan, dill or basil and black pepper. Cover and let stand for 5 minutes.

Preparation time: 5 minutes
Cooking time: 30 minutes

Per serving: 332 calories, 5.6 g. fat (15% of calories), 1.3 g. dietary fiber, 31 mg. cholesterol, 273 mg. sodium.

SHRIMP AND ORANGES

*Y*ou can make this dish mild or spicy, depending on how much of the pepper flakes you use. Serve the shrimp over rice or bulgur. Scallops would also be delicious prepared this way.

1	tablespoon olive oil
2	cloves garlic, minced
1	teaspoon dried thyme
¼	teaspoon ground black pepper
	Pinch of crushed red-pepper flakes
1	pound medium shrimp, peeled and deveined
1	sweet red pepper, julienned
4	scallions, thinly sliced
1	cup orange segments

In a large bowl, combine the oil, garlic, thyme, black pepper and pepper flakes. Add the shrimp and toss to coat. Cover and marinate at room temperature for 15 minutes.

Heat a large no-stick frying pan over medium-high heat until hot. Add the shrimp and sauté for 5 minutes, or until the shrimp are lightly browned. Remove the shrimp with a slotted spoon.

Add the red peppers and scallions. Sauté for 5 minutes, or until the peppers are tender. Stir in the oranges. Return the shrimp to the pan and reheat briefly.

Preparation time: 15 minutes
Cooking time: 10 minutes

Per serving: 162 calories, 5.9 g. fat (33% of calories), 0.9 g. dietary fiber, 151 mg. cholesterol, 447 mg. sodium.

SPANISH PEPPER SHRIMP

This simple recipe from Spain combines shrimp with a mixture of fresh herbs and a bit of olive oil. For authentic flavor, use extra virgin Spanish olive oil. Serve the shrimp over pasta or rice. This also makes a good appetizer and would work just as nicely with large scallops.

1   *pound large shrimp, peeled and deveined*
1   *tablespoon olive oil*
1   *tablespoon minced fresh rosemary*
1   *tablespoon minced fresh thyme*
2   *teaspoons minced garlic*
1   *teaspoon coarse black pepper*
    Pinch of ground red pepper
    Juice of 1 lime

In a medium bowl, combine the shrimp, oil, rosemary, thyme, garlic, black pepper and red pepper. Mix well to coat the shrimp. Let stand at room temperature for 20 minutes.

Heat a large no-stick frying pan over medium-high heat for 3 minutes. Add the shrimp in a single layer. Cook for 3 minutes per side, or until the shrimp are pink and just cooked through. Do not overcook. Remove from the heat and stir in the lime juice.

Preparation time: 10 minutes plus marinating time
Cooking time: 10 minutes

Per serving: 128 calories, 5 g. fat (35% of calories), no dietary fiber, 140 mg. cholesterol, 136 mg. sodium.

CRAB PATTIES

You ou could easily turn these into salmon, tuna or other fish patties by replacing the crab with flaked cooked fish.

1   pound crabmeat, flaked
1   cup dry bread crumbs
¼   cup nonfat mayonnaise
¼   cup fat-free egg substitute
2   teaspoons Dijon mustard
1   teaspoon dried thyme
1   tablespoon olive oil

In a large bowl, mix the crab and ½ cup bread crumbs.

In a small bowl, mix the mayonnaise, egg, mustard and thyme. Pour over the crab and mix well. Form into 8 patties.

Place the remaining ½ cup bread crumbs in a shallow bowl. Dredge the patties in the crumbs to coat well.

In a large no-stick frying pan over medium heat, warm the oil. Add the patties and sauté for 5 minutes per side, or until lightly browned.

Preparation time: 10 minutes
Cooking time: 10 minutes

Chef's note: Any type of crabmeat will work in this recipe. Lump backfin is the most expensive and makes the nicest patties, but you may use flaked body and claw meat or even the substitute "crab" made from fish. When using real crab, pick over the pieces carefully to remove any bits of shell or cartilage that may be mixed in with the meat.

Per serving: 259 calories, 6.7 g. fat (24% of calories), 0.9 g. dietary fiber, 108 mg. cholesterol, 729 mg. sodium.

ANGEL HAIR WITH CLAM SAUCE

*U*sing canned clams makes this sauce quick and easy. Adding olives and herbs to the sauce gives it a very Mediterranean feel. For variety, you could replace the clams with cooked small mussels and use bottled clam juice to prepare the sauce.

2	*cans (6½ ounces each) clams, with juice*
½	*cup skim milk*
3	*tablespoons unbleached flour*
⅓	*cup pitted and chopped black or green olives*
2	*tablespoons minced fresh parsley*
2	*tablespoons minced fresh sage*
8	*ounces angel hair pasta*

Drain the clams, reserving the juice. Set aside the clams. Measure the juice and add enough of the milk to equal 1½ cups.

Place the flour in a 2-quart saucepan. Gradually whisk in the juice mixture, being careful to avoid lumps. Cook over medium heat, stirring often, for 5 minutes, or until the mixture comes to a boil and thickens. Stir in the olives, parsley, sage and the reserved clams. Keep warm.

Cook the pasta in a large pot of boiling water for 5 minutes, or until just tender. Do not overcook. Drain and serve topped with the clam sauce.

Preparation time: 5 minutes
Cooking time: 10 minutes

Per serving: 373 calories, 4.5 g. fat (11% of calories), 0.4 g. dietary fiber, 111 mg. cholesterol, 155 mg. sodium.

LUNCH IN PROVENCE

*W*riter and cookbook author Judith Olney has spent much time in the south of France. Below she describes a typical lunch in that part of the Mediterranean and tells how you can enjoy a similar repast.

First course: radishes, olives, fresh bread and olive oil. The French can make a whole course of radishes and olives. Clean and trim some red radishes, but leave an inch of green leaves on top for a handle. Place the radishes in a small rustic bowl. Place small olives in another bowl and add a bay leaf and thyme sprigs for garnish. Give each person a small bowl of olive oil. Dip chunks of fresh bread into the oil. Alternate bites of radishes, olives and bread.

Second course: grilled whole fish with fennel. Walk up the nearest hillside and cut down branches of wild fennel weed. Failing that, buy a fennel bulb. Slice the tender white hearts into a salad; save the stalks and feathery tops for your fish.

Mince a tablespoon of the feathery greens and add it to a tablespoon or two of olive oil in a cup. Pour half of the mixture over a whole fish and rub it in well. Leave the fish to marinate, refrigerated, for one hour. Meanwhile, heat a grill.

Grill the fish. While it is cooking, dip a stalk of fennel into the leftover oil mixture and brush the fish frequently. Eat the fish with bread, taking the time to pick the fish from the bones.

Salad: mixed greens. Choose from an assortment of tender young leaves like arugula (also known as rocket or roquette) and mâche. Dress lightly with olive oil and a splash of wine vinegar.

Dessert: white cheese with fruit. Cheese and fruit is the typical dessert in Provence. Brousse cheese, made from fresh sheep's milk, is sold at local markets. Substitute a mild, soft white cheese. Serve it with bing cherries, fresh figs or other seasonal fruit. If you're lucky enough to have fresh figs, eat them as the French do: Cut off the stem, then make two slices at right angles halfway down the fruit. Hold the fruit from the bottom, squeeze it open and gently suck the pink-seeded pulp off the skin, which any true connoisseur will then discard.

CHAPTER 7

THE BEST
OF THE
BARNYARD

FIRST-CLASS POULTRY

oultry is an undisputed favorite worldwide, including in the various countries of the Mediterranean. Here in America we also love chicken and turkey. In fact, in the past few years, poultry consumption has taken flight, rising to an all-time yearly high of almost 70 pounds per person. That's not chicken feed! The reasons for poultry's popularity are no mystery. Turkey and chicken are lean and healthy food choices, and they're supremely versatile—you can dress them up, dress them down and serve them seven days a week without having the same dish twice! Best of all, boneless cuts cook very quickly. Give the following recipes a try and see for yourself why poultry is a superstar.

Honey-Basil Chicken

SERVES 4

*S*erve this chicken the way they do at the Doral Saturnia International Spa Resort in Miami—over rice or noodles. Or turn the cooked chicken into a summer salad by chilling it and serving it over mixed greens.

1	*cup raspberry vinegar*
3	*tablespoons Dijon mustard*
2	*tablespoons low-sodium soy sauce*
2	*tablespoons honey*
2	*tablespoons minced fresh basil*
½	*teaspoon dried thyme*
	Pinch of ground black pepper
4	*boneless, skinless chicken breast halves*

In a shallow glass baking dish, mix the vinegar, mustard, soy sauce, honey, basil, thyme and pepper. Add the chicken and turn to coat all sides. Allow to marinate at room temperature for 15 minutes.

Transfer the chicken to a grill or broiling rack; reserve the marinade and place in a 1-quart saucepan.

Grill or broil the chicken for 5 minutes per side, or until cooked through.

While the chicken is cooking, boil the marinade until reduced by half. To serve, pour the marinade over the chicken.

Preparation time: 5 minutes plus marinating time
Cooking time: 10 minutes

Per serving: 175 calories, 1.7 g. fat (8% of calories), 0.2 g. dietary fiber, 66 mg. cholesterol, 521 mg. sodium.

LEMON-MUSTARD CHICKEN BREASTS

SERVES 4

*T*his easy herb rub is suitable for any type of poultry, including whole chicken. If doing a whole bird, loosen the skin over the breast area and rub the mixture directly into the flesh.

> 2 *tablespoons minced fresh parsley*
> 1 *clove garlic, minced*
> 1 *teaspoon Dijon mustard*
> ¼ *teaspoon red-pepper flakes*
> ½ *teaspoon fennel seeds, crushed*
> *Juice of 1 lemon*
> 4 *boneless, skinless chicken breast halves*

In a cup, combine the parsley, garlic, mustard, pepper flakes and fennel seeds. Stir in the lemon juice. Rub the mixture all over the chicken breasts. Allow to marinate at room temperature for 15 minutes.

Grill or broil the chicken for 5 minutes per side, or until cooked through.

Preparation time: 5 minutes plus marinating time
Cooking time: 10 minutes

Per serving: 148 calories, 3.2 g. fat (20% of calories), 0.2 g. dietary fiber, 73 mg. cholesterol, 82 mg. sodium.

CINNAMON-SCENTED CHICKEN BREASTS

SERVES 4

*T*his marinade is also good on Cornish hens. If using them, cut them in half and marinate up to 24 hours. Bake at 375° for about 40 minutes.

- 3 tablespoons lemon juice
- 1 clove garlic, minced
- ½ teaspoon dried savory
- ½ teaspoon dried dill
- ¼ teaspoon ground cinnamon
- ¼ teaspoon curry powder
- 4 boneless, skinless chicken breast halves

In a large glass baking dish, combine the lemon juice, garlic, savory, dill, cinnamon and curry powder. Add the chicken and turn to coat all sides. Allow to marinate at room temperature for 15 minutes.

Grill or broil the chicken for 5 minutes per side, or until cooked through.

Preparation time: 5 minutes plus marinating time
Cooking time: 10 minutes

Per serving: 130 calories, 1.4 g. fat (10% of calories), trace dietary fiber, 66 mg. cholesterol, 75 mg. sodium.

CARDAMOM CHICKEN

SERVES 4

*H*ere is a very simple way to prepare chicken breasts. You can also use the cardamom marinade for turkey cutlets.

- 4 *boneless, skinless chicken breast halves*
- ½ *cup nonfat yogurt*
- ½ *cup minced onions*
- 1 *tablespoon minced fresh ginger*
- 1 *clove garlic, minced*
- 1 *teaspoon ground cardamom*
- 1 *teaspoon ground fennel seeds*
- ¼ *teaspoon crushed red-pepper flakes*

Place the chicken between sheets of plastic wrap or wax paper. Pound to an even thickness.

In a shallow baking dish, combine the yogurt, onions, ginger, garlic, cardamom, fennel seeds and pepper flakes. Add the chicken and turn to coat all sides. Allow to marinate at room temperature for 20 minutes.

Remove the chicken from the marinade and grill or broil for 5 minutes per side, or until cooked through.

Preparation time: 15 minutes plus marinating time
Cooking time: 10 minutes

Per serving: 146 calories, 1.8 g. fat (1% of calories), 0.3 g. dietary fiber, 67 mg. cholesterol, 89 mg. sodium.

GRILLED CHICKEN WITH SPINACH

SERVES 4

This marinated-chicken recipe won the Grand Prize for Nora Minor of Tampa, Florida, in *Prevention*'s second annual Cooking for Health recipe contest. This is a whole meal, consisting of the chicken, rice and a vegetable.

2 tablespoons minced garlic

2 tablespoons minced fresh ginger

4 teaspoons paprika

2 teaspoons ground cardamom

2 teaspoons ground coriander

2 teaspoons ground cumin

2 teaspoons turmeric

¼ cup lemon juice

1 cup nonfat yogurt

4 large boneless, skinless chicken thighs, trimmed of all visible fat

1¼ cups water

1½ cups quick-cooking brown rice

2 teaspoons olive oil

1 onion, diced

1 tomato, diced

1 teaspoon curry powder

8 cups coarsely chopped fresh spinach

½ cup crumbled feta cheese

In a large glass baking dish, mix the garlic, ginger, paprika, cardamom, coriander, cumin, turmeric and 2 tablespoons lemon juice. Whisk in the yogurt. Add the chicken, opening the pieces to expose the entire inner surface. Turn the pieces to coat all sides. Allow to marinate at room temperature for at least 20 minutes.

Remove the chicken from the marinade and grill or broil for 10 minutes per side, or until cooked through.

Meanwhile, bring the water to a boil in a 1-quart saucepan. Add the rice, cover and simmer over medium heat for 5 minutes. Remove from the heat and let stand for 5 minutes. Fluff with a fork and keep warm.

In a Dutch oven over medium heat, warm the oil. Add the onions; sauté for 5 minutes, or until tender. Stir in the tomatoes, curry powder and the remaining 2 tablespoons lemon juice. Add the spinach and stir for 5 minutes, or until the spinach is wilted. Stir in the feta.

Place the rice on a large serving platter. Add the spinach and chicken.

Preparation time: 20 minutes plus marinating time
Cooking time: 20 minutes

Per serving: 590 calories, 15.6 g. fat (24% of calories), 7.7 g. dietary fiber, 134 mg. cholesterol, 508 mg. sodium.

HERB MIXTURES FROM PROVENCE

*I*n the south of France, as in many other areas of the Mediterranean, herbs are used with abandon to flavor every dish imaginable. Many cooks make up their own dried-herb mixtures and keep a jarful handy so they can toss a generous amount into whatever they're preparing. Here are three typical mixtures. Certain herbs show up in all of them because they're regional favorites. Experiment with proportions until you find the blend that suits you best. For a particularly Provençal touch, add some dried lavender flowers.

- bay leaves (*pulverized* in a blender, spice grinder or mortar and pestle), oregano (include the flowers if you grow your own), rosemary, savory, thyme
- anise seeds, marjoram, rosemary, sage, savory, thyme
- basil, fennel seeds, marjoram, rosemary, sage, savory, thyme

CHICKEN BREASTS WITH SWEET PAPRIKA

SERVES 4

*A*lthough this recipe is based on a classic Hungarian dish, chicken paprikash, it features the tomatoes, peppers, garlic and onions so indicative of Mediterranean cuisine. Unlike the classic recipe—which contains lots of full-fat sour cream—this version is nicely low in fat and calories. This makeover is a specialty of Emrika Padus, the executive editor of *Prevention*. Serve the chicken over broad noodles.

2   *cups thinly sliced onions*
1   *tablespoon paprika*
½   *cup defatted chicken stock*
4   *boneless, skinless chicken breast halves*
1   *can (14 ounces) plum tomatoes, seeded, coarsely chopped and well drained*
1   *sweet red pepper, thinly sliced*
2   *tablespoons nonfat sour cream*
1   *tablespoon unbleached flour*
1   *tablespoon cold water*

Coat a large no-stick frying pan with no-stick spray. Add the onions and sauté over medium heat for 5 minutes, or until tender. Stir in ½ tablespoon paprika; mix well.

Add the stock, chicken, tomatoes and peppers. Bring to a boil over medium heat. Cover and simmer for 15 minutes, or until the chicken is cooked through. Use a slotted spoon to remove the chicken and vegetables from the pan. If there's more than 1 cup of liquid in the pan, boil it down to 1 cup.

In a cup, mix the sour cream, flour, water and the remaining ½ tablespoon paprika until smooth. Stir into the liquid remaining in the pan. Simmer, stirring constantly, for 5 minutes, or until the sauce is lightly thickened; do not let the sauce boil. Return the chicken and vegetables to the pan. Heat briefly.

Preparation time: 10 minutes
Cooking time: 25 minutes

Per serving: 185 calories, 2.1 g. fat (10% of calories), 0.8 g. dietary fiber, 66 mg. cholesterol, 94 mg. sodium.

PICCATA-STYLE CHICKEN WITH RICE

SERVES 4

*L*emon juice perks up the mild flavor of chicken breasts very nicely. This one-dish meal is reminiscent of chicken piccata, a dish of Italian origin.

4	*boneless, skinless chicken breast halves*
1	*tablespoon olive oil*
1½	*cups quick-cooking brown rice*
1¼	*cups defatted chicken stock*
¼	*cup minced fresh parsley*
¼	*cup lemon juice*
2	*tablespoons capers, rinsed and chopped*
2	*tablespoons chopped toasted almonds*

In a large no-stick frying pan over medium heat, cook the chicken in the oil for 5 minutes, or until lightly browned on both sides. Add the rice, stock, parsley, lemon juice and capers. Bring to a boil.

Cover and simmer over medium-low heat for 10 minutes, or until the chicken is cooked through. Remove from the heat. Let stand for 5 minutes. Sprinkle with the almonds.

Preparation time: 10 minutes
Cooking time: 15 minutes

Per serving: 460 calories, 10.6 g. fat (21% of calories), 4.6 g. dietary fiber, 73 mg. cholesterol, 342 mg. sodium.

ORANGE-SCENTED CHICKEN

SERVES 4

Oranges grow freely in Mediterranean countries and are often served with poultry and meats. Serve this dish over rice or bulgur.

  4   boneless, skinless chicken breast halves
  2   tablespoons unbleached flour
  ½   cup sliced scallions
  2   teaspoons olive oil
  ¾   cup defatted chicken stock
  ¼   cup thawed orange juice concentrate
  1   navel orange, peeled and sectioned

Dredge the chicken in the flour. Shake off the excess; reserve the remaining flour.

Coat a large no-stick frying pan with no-stick spray. Place over medium-high heat. Add the chicken and cook for 5 minutes, or until lightly browned on both sides. Remove from the pan and set aside.

Add the scallions and oil to the pan. Cook over medium heat for 5 minutes. Sprinkle with the reserved flour and stir to mix well. Add the stock and juice concentrate. Bring to a boil. Add the chicken. Cover and simmer over medium heat for 10 minutes, or until the chicken is cooked through. Add the oranges and heat briefly.

Preparation time: 15 minutes
Cooking time: 20 minutes

Chef's note: When sectioning the oranges for this dish, be sure to remove all the outer white pith and the transparent membranes surrounding each section. This takes a little extra time, but the oranges are more pleasing to eat this way.

Per serving: 218 calories, 5.4 g. fat (23% of calories), 0.5 g. dietary fiber, 73 mg. cholesterol, 227 mg. sodium.

Pepper Chicken with Rice

*T*his is a simplified version of jambalaya. For variety, you could replace some of the chicken with turkey sausage.

12	ounces boneless, skinless chicken breast, cut into 1½″ × 1″ strips
½	teaspoon ground black pepper
1	onion, chopped
1	green pepper, chopped
1	cup chopped celery
1	clove garlic, minced
1	teaspoon olive oil
1	cup long-grain white rice
¼	teaspoon ground red pepper
½	teaspoon dried thyme
1	bay leaf
1¼	cups defatted chicken stock
1	tomato, chopped

Coat a large no-stick frying pan with no-stick spray. Place over medium heat for 2 minutes. Add the chicken and cook, stirring often, for 5 minutes, or until the pieces are lightly browned. Remove from the pan and sprinkle with the black pepper.

Add the onions, green peppers, celery, garlic and oil to the pan. Sauté for 5 minutes, or until tender. Stir in the rice, red pepper, thyme and bay leaf. Add the stock and chicken. Bring to a boil. Cover and simmer for 20 minutes, or until all the liquid has been absorbed and the rice is tender. Stir in the tomatoes. Remove and discard the bay leaf.

Preparation time: 15 minutes
Cooking time: 30 minutes

Per serving: 315 calories, 3.1 g. fat (9% of calories), 2.5 g. dietary fiber, 49 mg. cholesterol, 124 mg. sodium.

Chicken Fricassee with Parsley Dumplings

Chicken fricassee is a popular dish that's often high in fat. This version tops well-trimmed chicken thighs with light but low-fat dumplings.

2	cups defatted chicken stock
1½	cups thinly sliced carrots
1½	cups thinly sliced celery
1	bay leaf
¼	teaspoon dried thyme
¼	teaspoon ground black pepper
4	large boneless, skinless chicken thighs, trimmed of all visible fat
¾	cup unbleached flour
1	teaspoon baking powder
1	tablespoon chilled margarine, cut into small pieces
⅓	cup buttermilk
1	tablespoon chopped fresh parsley

In a Dutch oven, combine the stock, carrots, celery, bay leaf, thyme and pepper. Bring to a boil over high heat.

Add the chicken and return to a boil. Cover, reduce the heat to low and simmer gently while you prepare the dumplings.

In a medium bowl, combine the flour and baking powder. Using a pastry blender or your fingers, work in the margarine until the mixture forms fine crumbs. Add the buttermilk and parsley. Stir until just mixed; the batter will be slightly lumpy.

Drop teaspoonfuls of batter on top of the simmering chicken mixture to form 12 dumplings. Cover and simmer for 25 minutes, or until the chicken is tender and the dumplings look dry on top and feel firm.

Preparation time: 15 minutes
Cooking time: 30 minutes

Per serving: 300 calories, 7.7 g. fat (23% of calories), 4.5 g. dietary fiber, 95 mg. cholesterol, 347 mg. sodium.

TAHINI CHICKEN

SERVES 4

A spicy tahini sauce helps dress up leftover cooked chicken. Serve the chicken over rice or couscous.

¾	*cup defatted chicken stock*
¼	*cup tahini*
2	*tablespoons low-sodium soy sauce*
1	*tablespoon honey*
1	*clove garlic, minced*
2	*teaspoons grated fresh ginger*
1	*teaspoon hot-pepper sauce*
2	*cups cubed cooked chicken*

In a 2-quart saucepan over medium heat, bring the stock to a boil. Reduce the heat to low. Whisk in the tahini, soy sauce, honey, garlic, ginger and pepper sauce until smooth. Stir in the chicken. Heat through.

Preparation time: 10 minutes
Cooking time: 5 minutes

Per serving: 205 calories, 10 g. fat (43% of calories), 1.3 g. dietary fiber, 48 mg. cholesterol, 512 mg. sodium.

CHICKEN WITH SPICY CHERRY SAUCE

*B*roiling is an ideal way to cook chicken breasts without adding a lot of fat. Here a spicy cherry chutney complements the flavor of curried chicken. The chutney also goes well with turkey, pork or lamb.

1	*tablespoon low-sodium soy sauce*
2	*teaspoons curry powder*
¼	*teaspoon ground black pepper*
¼	*teaspoon olive oil*
	Pinch of ground red pepper
4	*boneless, skinless chicken breast halves*
½	*cup chopped onions*
1	*clove garlic, minced*
½	*cup water*
2	*tablespoons cider vinegar*
1	*tablespoon cornstarch*
1	*tablespoon honey*
1	*tablespoon minced fresh ginger*
1½	*cups pitted dark sweet cherries, chopped*

In a large baking dish, mix the soy sauce, curry powder, black pepper, oil and red pepper. Add the chicken and turn to coat all sides. Allow to marinate at room temperature for 15 minutes.

Meanwhile, in a 1-quart glass bowl, combine the onions, garlic and 1 tablespoon water. Microwave on high for 2 minutes, or until the onions are soft.

Stir in the vinegar, cornstarch, honey, ginger and the remaining water. Mix well. Microwave on high for 2 minutes, or until the sauce is thickened and bubbly. Stir in the cherries. Microwave on high for 2 minutes. Stir well and microwave for 1 minute, or until the cherries are hot.

Broil the chicken for 5 minutes per side, or until cooked through. Serve with the cherry mixture.

Preparation time: 15 minutes plus marinating time
Cooking time: 20 minutes

Per serving: 252 calories, 2 g. fat (7% of calories), 4 g. dietary fiber, 66 mg. cholesterol, 227 mg. sodium.

CHICKEN IN PITA POCKETS

SERVES 4

*U*se this recipe when you've got leftover cooked chicken on hand. Naturally, the recipe would be just as good with cooked turkey.

2	cups diced cooked chicken breast
1	cup diced green peppers
2	plum tomatoes, diced
1	small onion, diced
¼	teaspoon dried tarragon
½	cup nonfat mayonnaise
4	pita breads, halved
1	cup shredded lettuce

In a large bowl, toss together the chicken, peppers, tomatoes, onions and tarragon. Add the mayonnaise and mix well.

Open the pita halves and divide the lettuce among them. Stuff with the chicken mixture.

Preparation time: 15 minutes

Per serving: 250 calories, 2.9 g. fat (11% of calories), 2.2 g. dietary fiber, 48 mg. cholesterol, 644 mg. sodium.

Moroccan Chicken Breasts

*T*he combination of spices and fruit makes this a very typical North African dish. Serve the chicken over couscous.

1	teaspoon ground cumin
½	teaspoon powdered ginger
½	teaspoon ground coriander
¼	teaspoon ground cinnamon
	Pinch of ground red pepper
4	boneless, skinless chicken breast halves
1	tablespoon olive oil
1	large onion, thinly sliced
1	cup defatted chicken stock
⅓	cup chopped pitted prunes

In a cup, mix the cumin, ginger, coriander, cinnamon and pepper. Rub into the chicken to coat all sides. Allow to marinate at room temperature for 15 minutes.

In a large no-stick frying pan over medium heat, warm the oil. Add the chicken and cook for 5 minutes per side, or until lightly browned. Remove from the pan. Add the onions and cook for 5 minutes, or until tender.

Return the chicken to the pan. Add the stock and prunes. Bring to a boil. Cover and simmer for 10 minutes, or until the chicken is cooked through.

Preparation time: 10 minutes plus marinating time
Cooking time: 20 minutes

Per serving: 224 calories, 6.7 g. fat (27% of calories), 1.6 g. dietary fiber, 73 mg. cholesterol, 283 mg. sodium.

Colorful Stuffed Peppers (page 206)

169

Arugula-Stuffed Calzones (page 207)

Chick-Pea Fritters with Pepper Sauce (page 208)

Asparagus and White Bean Frittata (page 194)

Lentils with Curried Vegetables (page 202)

Asparagus and Couscous (page 233)

Baby Lima Beans with Tomatoes and Sage (page 221)

175

Simple Spaghetti Squash (page 226)

POULET NIÇOISE

SERVES 4

*P*oulet Niçoise is a variation on a typical Provençal dish made with tomatoes, garlic and orange rind. If you'd like, you may add a pinch of saffron for an authentic touch. This recipe comes from Aliza Green, a Philadelphia chef and restaurant consultant.

4	*large boneless, skinless chicken thighs, trimmed of all visible fat*
2	*tablespoons unbleached flour*
¾	*cup defatted chicken stock*
1	*red onion, thinly sliced*
6	*cloves garlic, thinly sliced*
	Pinch of ground cloves
	Juice and grated rind of 1 orange
10	*small black olives, pitted and halved*
1	*pint cherry tomatoes, halved*
½	*cup fresh basil leaves, shredded*

Dredge the chicken in the flour to coat lightly.

In a large cast-iron frying pan over medium-high heat, warm ¼ cup stock. Add the chicken in a single layer. Cook for 5 minutes per side, or until browned. Remove and set aside.

Add the onions, garlic and cloves to the pan. Sauté for 2 minutes to soften the onions; do not let the garlic burn.

Add the orange juice, orange rind, olives and the remaining ½ cup stock. Mix well. Return the chicken to the pan. Bring the liquid to a boil. Reduce the heat to medium. Simmer for 10 minutes. Add the tomatoes and basil. Simmer for 5 minutes.

Preparation time: 15 minutes
Cooking time: 30 minutes

Per serving: 295 calories, 9.4 g. fat (29% of calories), 2.4 g. dietary fiber, 114 mg. cholesterol, 241 mg. sodium.

NEW TURKEY CUTS

*O*nce upon a time, a fresh turkey dinner required a cook to spend half a day toiling by a hot oven. But with the appearance of new skinless and boneless turkey thighs, cutlets and tenderloins, a hearty, healthy, family turkey dinner can appear in a few minutes.

Look in the refrigerated meat case for the following items. Some of these cuts are packaged by national manufacturers; others are prepared by the supermarket. Either way, be sure to check expiration dates to assure freshness.

- turkey cutlets, which are slices off the breast about ½" thick
- turkey tenderloins (also called fillets), which are thicker strips of breast meat that include the entire muscle from the inside center of the breast
- thigh steaks (dark meat from the turkey thigh) and drumstick steaks

SERVING IDEAS

- Here's an easy way to prepare turkey cutlets: Sprinkle the cutlets with your choice of seasonings; cook in a no-stick frying pan for 2 to 3 minutes on each side. During the last minute of cooking time, add ⅓ cup of liquid, such as broth or fruit juice.
- Cut turkey cutlets into strips. Cook and chill for salads.
- Slice turkey-breast tenderloins crosswise into round or oval-shaped medallions. Use as you would veal medallions.
- Thinly slice turkey for stir-fries. Cube it for kabobs and casseroles.
- Make a quick, substantial rice-and-bean turkey stew: In a large saucepan, sauté chopped onions in a small amount of olive oil. Add sliced turkey tenderloins and brown them. Stir in 2 cups of defatted chicken stock, 1 cup of quick-cooking brown rice and a 16-ounce can of pinto beans. Season with cumin and oregano. Bring to a boil. Cover and reduce the heat. Simmer for 10 minutes.

Turkey Meatballs with Tomato Sauce

SERVES 4

*M*eatballs needn't be full of fat if you use lean ground turkey breast. Serve these meatballs with pasta.

1½   *slices whole wheat bread, torn into small pieces*
8   *ounces ground turkey breast*
2   *tablespoons minced onions*
2   *teaspoons minced garlic*
½   *teaspoon dried basil*
½   *teaspoon dried oregano*
     Pinch of ground red pepper
1   *egg white, lightly beaten with a fork*
½   *cup defatted chicken stock*
1   *small onion, finely chopped*
2   *sweet red peppers, finely chopped*
4   *large tomatoes, seeded and diced*
¼   *cup tomato sauce*

Place the bread in a food processor. Process with on/off turns until fine crumbs form. Break up the turkey and add to the food processor. Sprinkle with the minced onions, garlic, basil, oregano and red pepper. Pour in the egg white. Process with on/off turns until well mixed. Shape into 1" balls.

Coat a Dutch oven or large frying pan with no-stick spray. Place over medium heat, add the meatballs and brown on all sides. Remove to a platter and set aside.

Add the stock to the pan and scrape up the cooked-on bits with a wooden spoon. Add the chopped onions and red peppers. Sauté, stirring frequently, for 5 minutes, or until tender. Add the tomatoes and tomato sauce. Cover and cook for 10 minutes, stirring frequently to prevent scorching. Add the meatballs and cook for 10 minutes.

Preparation time: 15 minutes
Cooking time: 30 minutes

Per serving: 178 calories, 3.4 g. fat (17% of calories), 1.9 g. dietary fiber, 33 mg. cholesterol, 149 mg. sodium.

TURKEY AND PEAR SAUTÉ

*T*his easy recipe combines quick-cooking turkey cutlets with fresh pears and couscous.

1¼	*cups defatted chicken stock*
1¼	*cups couscous*
1	*teaspoon cornstarch*
⅓	*cup apple juice*
⅓	*cup evaporated skim milk*
1	*tablespoon unbleached flour*
1	*pound turkey breast cutlets, about ¼″ thick*
1	*tablespoon olive oil*
1	*clove garlic, minced*
1	*teaspoon cracked black pepper*
¼	*teaspoon dried savory or thyme*
2	*ripe pears, halved, cored and thinly sliced*
1	*tablespoon snipped chives*

In a 1-quart saucepan over high heat, bring the stock to a boil. Stir in the couscous. Remove from the heat, cover and let stand for 15 minutes, until all the liquid has been absorbed.

Meanwhile, in a small bowl, dissolve the cornstarch in the apple juice. Stir in the milk. Set aside.

Place the flour on a sheet of wax paper. Dredge the turkey in it to lightly coat both sides.

In a large no-stick frying pan over medium-high heat, warm the oil for 1 minute. Add the turkey and brown for 2 minutes per side (do in batches if necessary). Remove the turkey to a plate.

Reduce the heat to medium. Add the milk mixture, garlic, pepper and savory or thyme to the pan. Stir well. Add the pears and top with the turkey. Cover and cook for 4 minutes, or until the pears have started to soften and the sauce has thickened slightly. Sprinkle with the chives.

Fluff the couscous with a fork. Spoon onto plates and top with the turkey and pears. Drizzle lightly with the sauce.

Preparation time: 10 minutes
Cooking time: 15 minutes

Per serving: 476 calories, 6.5 g. fat (12% of calories), 11.3 g. dietary fiber, 67 mg. cholesterol, 125 mg. sodium.

TURKEY MARINARA

SERVES 4

*B*oneless, skinless turkey breast cutlets are a real boon to time-pressed cooks.

1	*pound turkey breast cutlets, about ¼" thick*
1	*tablespoon unbleached flour*
1	*teaspoon olive oil*
½	*cup diced onions*
1	*clove garlic, minced*
½	*teaspoon ground black pepper*
½	*teaspoon dried thyme*
¼	*teaspoon dried basil*
2	*cups low-sodium tomato sauce*

Dredge the turkey in the flour to coat lightly on both sides.

Coat a large no-stick frying pan with no-stick spray. Place over medium-high heat. Add the turkey in a single layer and cook for 2 minutes per side, or until lightly browned. Remove from the pan and set aside.

Add the oil, onions, garlic, pepper, thyme and basil to the pan. Cook over medium heat, stirring constantly, for 5 minutes, or until the onions are tender. Add the tomato sauce and turkey. Cover and heat for 5 minutes.

Preparation time: 5 minutes
Cooking time: 15 minutes

Per serving: 184 calories, 3.5 g. fat (19% of calories), 2.1 g. dietary fiber, 49 mg. cholesterol, 79 mg. sodium.

TURKEY CACCIATORE

SERVES 4

*H*ere's a quicker variation of the ever-popular chicken cacciatore. Serve it over pasta.

8 *ounces turkey breast cutlets, cut into ½″ strips*

1 *tablespoon unbleached flour*

½ *cup defatted chicken stock*

1 *onion, thinly sliced*

1 *green pepper, thinly sliced*

3 *cloves garlic, minced*

3 *cups chopped tomatoes*

¾ *cup thinly sliced mushrooms*

½ *cup minced fresh parsley*

1 *teaspoon dried rosemary*

½ *teaspoon dried marjoram*

1 *bay leaf*

Sprinkle the turkey with the flour and toss to coat the pieces. Coat a large no-stick frying pan with no-stick spray. Place over medium-high heat. Add the turkey and sauté for 5 minutes, or until the turkey is lightly browned. Remove from the pan.

Add the stock to the pan. Boil rapidly, scraping the bottom of the pan with a wooden spoon, until the liquid has reduced by half. Reduce the heat to low and add the onions, peppers and garlic. Cook for 5 minutes, or until the vegetables are tender.

Add the tomatoes, mushrooms, parsley, rosemary, marjoram and bay leaf. Cover and simmer for 10 minutes. Add the turkey and heat through. Remove and discard the bay leaf.

Preparation time: 15 minutes
Cooking time: 20 minutes

Per serving: 125 calories, 1.6 g. fat (12% of calories), 2.7 g. dietary fiber, 34 mg. cholesterol, 59 mg. sodium.

BRAISED TURKEY WITH VEGETABLES

SERVES 4

You can substitute turkey breast for beef, veal and lamb in many stew and casserole recipes. This stewlike dish is best served over noodles or bulgur.

1	teaspoon olive oil
12	ounces turkey breast, cut into 1″ cubes
3	cups defatted chicken stock
1	cup thinly sliced carrots
1	cup thinly sliced celery
1	cup diced potatoes
1	cup chopped onions
1½	teaspoons dried thyme
½	teaspoon ground black pepper
1	bay leaf
2	tablespoons cornstarch
¼	cup cold water

Coat a Dutch oven with no-stick spray. Place over medium-high heat and add the oil. Let warm for 1 minute. Add the turkey and lightly brown on all sides.

Add the stock, carrots, celery, potatoes, onions, garlic, thyme, pepper and bay leaf to the pan. Bring to a boil. Reduce the heat to medium, cover the pan and simmer for 15 minutes, or until the vegetables are tender.

In a cup, dissolve the cornstarch in the water. Add to the pan. Simmer for a few minutes, until the sauce is slightly thickened. Discard the bay leaf.

Preparation time: 15 minutes
Cooking time: 25 minutes

Per serving: 179 calories, 3.1 g. fat (16% of calories), 2.5 g. dietary fiber, 37 mg. cholesterol, 726 mg. sodium.

TURKEY SANDWICH WITH FRUIT SAUCE

SERVES 4

*H*ere's an ideal way to use up leftover roast turkey at Thanksgiving or other special occasions. You can easily make the cranberry sauce ahead.

> 1 *bag (12 ounces) cranberries, sorted*
> 1 *cup apple juice*
> ½ *cup chopped red onions*
> ¼ *cup honey*
> 1 *tablespoon minced fresh ginger*
> 8 *thick slices whole-grain bread*
> 4 *teaspoons nonfat mayonnaise*
> 4 *teaspoons Dijon mustard*
> 4 *lettuce leaves*
> 12 *slices cooked turkey*

In a 2-quart saucepan, combine the cranberries, apple juice, onions, honey and ginger. Bring to a boil over medium heat. Reduce the heat to low and cook, stirring occasionally, for 10 minutes, or until the cranberries pop and the sauce has thickened. Cool to room temperature. Transfer to a container, cover and refrigerate until needed.

To assemble the sandwiches, spread 4 of the bread slices with 1 teaspoon each of the mayonnaise and mustard. Top with lettuce and turkey.

Take about ⅓ cup of the cranberry sauce and divide it among the remaining bread slices, spreading it on with a knife. (Save the remainder for other uses.) Top the sandwiches with the remaining 4 bread slices.

Preparation time: 15 minutes plus cooling time
Cooking time: 15 minutes

Per serving: 313 calories, 6 g. fat (17% of calories), 3 g. dietary fiber, 61 mg. cholesterol, 337 mg. sodium.

TURKEY WITH BLACK BEANS AND TOMATOES

SERVES 4

*U*se this recipe when you've got leftover cooked turkey that you don't know what to do with. This is pretty much a one-dish meal. All you need to round it out is a simple salad and some crusty bread.

2	*cups diced onions*
2	*cloves garlic, minced*
2	*cups diced cooked turkey breast*
1	*can (16 ounces) black beans, rinsed and drained*
1½	*cups nonfat sour cream*
1	*large tomato, seeded and diced*
2	*tablespoons vinegar*
1	*teaspoon ground cumin*
½	*teaspoon ground black pepper*
½	*cup fresh bread crumbs*
2	*tablespoons minced fresh parsley*
1	*tablespoon olive oil*

Coat a large no-stick frying pan with no-stick spray. Place over medium heat for 2 minutes. Add the onions and garlic. Sauté for 5 minutes, or until tender. Stir in the turkey, beans, sour cream, tomatoes, vinegar, cumin and pepper. Cover and cook over low heat for 5 minutes, or until heated through. Transfer to an oval baking dish.

In a small bowl, mix the bread crumbs, parsley and oil. Sprinkle over the turkey mixture. Broil for 5 minutes, or until the crumbs are lightly browned.

Preparation time: 15 minutes
Cooking time: 15 minutes
Broiling time: 5 minutes

Per serving: 443 calories, 7.4 g. fat (15% of calories), 2.4 g. dietary fiber, 49 mg. cholesterol, 105 mg. sodium.

TURKEY-SAUSAGE PAN PIZZA

SERVES 4

This pizza has a biscuitlike crust that is baked on top of the filling.

1 cup thinly sliced onions
1 yellow pepper, diced
2 tablespoons water
6 ounces spicy or mild turkey sausage
¾ cup tomato sauce
1 teaspoon dried savory
¼ teaspoon fennel seeds, crushed
½ cup shredded nonfat mozzarella cheese
¾ cup unbleached flour
½ cup whole-wheat flour
2 tablespoons grated Parmesan cheese
1 teaspoon baking powder
½ cup buttermilk
1 tablespoon olive oil

In an 8" cast-iron or ovenproof frying pan over medium-high heat, cook the onions and peppers in the water for 5 minutes, or until tender.

Remove any casings from the sausage. Crumble the meat into the pan. Brown, breaking up the pieces with a wooden spoon. Remove from the heat.

Line a large platter with several layers of paper towels. Spoon the filling onto the towels to soak up excess fat. Blot with more towels. Wipe out the frying pan. Return the filling to the pan. Stir in the tomato sauce, savory and fennel. Heat through. Remove from the heat and sprinkle with the mozzarella. Set aside.

In a large bowl, mix together the unbleached flour, whole-wheat flour, Parmesan and baking powder.

In a cup, stir together the buttermilk and oil. Pour over the flour mixture. Mix lightly with a fork until a soft dough forms. Turn out onto a lightly floured surface and roll into an 8" circle (to fit the diameter of the frying pan). Place the crust over the filling. Bake at 375° for 15 minutes, or until the crust is lightly browned.

Preparation time: 15 minutes
Cooking time: 15 minutes
Baking time: 15 minutes

Per serving: 313 calories, 8.4 g. fat (24% of calories), 4.1 g. dietary fiber, 31 mg. cholesterol, 546 mg. sodium.

TURKEY PARMESAN

SERVES 4

Old-fashioned recipes for Parmesan cutlets call for frying the pieces in lots of oil. Here we bake the cutlets instead.

> 2 *tablespoons unbleached flour*
> ¼ *teaspoon ground black pepper*
> ½ *cup fat-free egg substitute*
> ¾ *cup dry bread crumbs*
> ¼ *cup grated Parmesan cheese*
> 1 *pound turkey breast cutlets, about ¼″ thick*
> 1 *cup tomato sauce, heated*

Combine the flour and pepper on a sheet of wax paper. Place the eggs in a shallow bowl. Combine the bread crumbs and Parmesan in a flat dish.

Dredge the turkey in the flour mixture to lightly coat both sides. Dip each cutlet first into the eggs then into the Parmesan mixture to coat it well.

Coat a large no-stick baking sheet with no-stick spray. Place the cutlets on the sheet. Bake at 400° for 5 minutes. Flip the pieces and bake for another 5 minutes, or until the cutlets are golden and crisp. Serve topped with the tomato sauce.

Preparation time: 10 minutes
Cooking time: 10 minutes

Per serving: 297 calories, 5.7 g. fat (17% of calories), 1 g. dietary fiber, 71 mg. cholesterol, 550 mg. sodium.

Turkey and Mushroom Casserole

*T*his is similar to turkey tetrazzini, which traditionally contains a fatty cream sauce.

  ¾ *cup orzo*
  2 *tablespoons cornstarch*
  2 *cups defatted chicken stock*
  1¾ *cups buttermilk*
  ½ *teaspoon dried sage*
  ½ *teaspoon ground black pepper*
  2 *cups chopped cooked turkey breast*
  2 *cups frozen pearl onions*
  ½ *cup minced fresh parsley*
  2 *cups small mushrooms, quartered*
  2 *tablespoons water*
  ½ *cup fresh bread crumbs*
  1 *tablespoon olive oil*

Cook the orzo in boiling water for 10 minutes, or until tender. Drain and set aside.

Meanwhile, place the cornstarch in a 3-quart saucepan. Add a little stock and mix until the cornstarch is dissolved. Stir in the remaining stock. Add the buttermilk, sage and pepper. Place over medium-high heat and bring to a boil, whisking constantly. Reduce the heat and simmer, whisking occasionally, for 5 minutes, or until slightly thickened. Stir in the orzo, turkey, onions and parsley. Set aside.

In a large no-stick frying pan over medium-high heat, cook the mushrooms and water for 5 minutes, or until the mushrooms are tender and all the liquid has evaporated. Add to the turkey mixture. Transfer the mixture to an oval baking dish.

In a small bowl, mix the bread crumbs and oil. Sprinkle over the turkey mixture. Broil for 5 minutes, or until the crumbs are lightly browned.

Preparation time: 10 minutes
Cooking time: 15 minutes
Broiling time: 5 minutes

Chef's note: To make fresh bread crumbs, tear several slices of white, whole-wheat, oat or other bread into pieces. Place in a food processor and grind with on/off turns until fine.

Per serving: 371 calories, 8 g. fat (19% of calories), 1.6 g. dietary fiber, 53 mg. cholesterol, 202 mg. sodium.

TURKEY CROQUETTES

SERVES 4

*H*ere's another way to use up leftover cooked turkey.

4	cups diced cooked turkey
½	cup diced onions
¼	cup diced celery
¼	cup minced fresh parsley
2	hard-cooked egg whites, finely chopped
⅓	cup nonfat mayonnaise
2	teaspoons Worcestershire sauce
½	teaspoon paprika
¼	teaspoon dry mustard
¼	teaspoon ground black pepper
1	egg white, lightly beaten
1½	cups fresh bread crumbs
1	teaspoon olive oil
1½	cups nonfat yogurt
2	tablespoons snipped chives
1	teaspoon lemon juice

In a large bowl, combine the turkey, onions, celery, parsley and cooked egg whites.

(continued)

In a small bowl, whisk together the mayonnaise, Worcestershire sauce, paprika, mustard and pepper. Stir into the turkey mixture and blend well. Form into 4 thick patties. Cover and refrigerate for at least 15 minutes to set the mixture.

Place the lightly beaten egg white in a shallow bowl. Place the bread crumbs in a flat dish. Dip each patty first into the egg white, then into the bread crumbs to coat them well.

In a large no-stick frying pan over medium-high heat, warm the oil. Add the patties and sauté for 5 minutes per side, or until golden.

In a small bowl, whisk together the yogurt, chives and lemon juice. Serve as a sauce with the patties.

Preparation time: 15 minutes plus chilling time
Cooking time: 10 minutes

Per serving: 335 calories, 7.7 g. fat (21% of calories), 1.2 g. dietary fiber, 88 mg. cholesterol, 410 mg. sodium.

TURKEY TENDERLOIN AU POIVRE

SERVES 4

*T*urkey tenderloins are readily available in supermarkets. They're very convenient to use and cook quickly. And they're just what's called for when you don't want to roast a whole turkey breast.

2	turkey tenderloins (8 ounces each)
¼	cup balsamic vinegar
2	tablespoons low-sodium soy sauce
2	tablespoons ground coriander
2	tablespoons ground black pepper
4	cloves garlic, minced
1	teaspoon dried thyme
4	teaspoons olive oil
4	tart apples, cored and thinly sliced
1	cup cider

Butterfly the turkey tenderloins by splitting them down the center lengthwise with a sharp knife to cut almost in half. Flatten the pieces with your hand. Rinse and pat dry.

In a large glass baking dish, combine the vinegar, soy sauce, coriander, pepper, garlic and thyme. Add the turkey and turn to coat all sides. Allow to marinate at room temperature for 20 minutes.

Brush a large cast-iron pan with 2 teaspoons oil and place over high heat for a few minutes until it just begins to smoke. Reduce the heat to medium-high. Add the turkey. Press the meat down with the back of a metal spatula so it makes good contact with the pan. Grill for 5 minutes, or until well browned. Baste with some of the leftover marinade (then discard the rest). Flip the turkey and grill the other side for about 5 minutes, or until cooked through.

Meanwhile, heat the remaining 2 teaspoons oil in a large no-stick frying pan over medium-high heat. Add the apples and cook for about 5 minutes, or until golden. Add the cider. Cook for about 5 minutes, or until the apples are soft.

To serve, cut the turkey tenderloins in half, then slice each piece on the diagonal into thin slices. Serve topped with the apples.

Preparation time: 10 minutes plus marinating time
Cooking time: 20 minutes

Per serving: 319 calories, 7.4 g. fat (20% of calories), 3.8 g. dietary fiber, 68 mg. cholesterol, 379 mg. sodium.

CHAPTER 8

MAIN
DISHES
WITHOUT
MEAT

VEGETARIAN ENTRÉES

In many parts of the world, meat rarely shows up on the table. And when it does, it's more in the form of a condiment than the meal's centerpiece. Vegetarian main courses are the norm in those areas. People have discovered that dishes like the ones in this chapter are quite filling and satisfying. Frittatas, omelets and other egg dishes provide plenty of protein, and they are so easy to vary simply by changing the vegetables or herbs that flavor the eggs. In the same vein, the almost infinite variety of pasta shapes and beans makes it easy to feast on these foods and still not tire of them. Try the following recipes and judge for yourself.

GARDEN-FRESH FRITTATA

*Y*ou can vary this Italian-style omelet according to what's in season.

1   *large baking potato*
1   *tablespoon olive oil*
1   *cup thinly sliced fresh spinach*
⅓   *cup thinly sliced scallions*
⅓   *cup diced sweet red peppers*
1   *tablespoon minced fresh dill*
    Pinch of grated nutmeg
1½ *cups fat-free egg substitute*

Pierce the potato all over with a fork. Place a paper towel directly on the floor of a microwave. Center the potato on the towel. Microwave on high for 2½ minutes. Flip the potato. Microwave on high for 2½ minutes, or until the potato is easily pierced with a fork. Let stand for 5 minutes to cool. Peel and cut into ½" cubes.

Place the oil in a large no-stick frying pan and warm over medium heat. Add the potatoes and sauté for 5 minutes, or until lightly browned. Add the spinach, scallions and peppers. Sauté for 4 minutes, or until the spinach is wilted. Stir in the dill and nutmeg.

Add the eggs. Cook, lifting the edges of the egg mixture so uncooked portions can flow underneath, until almost set. Cover and cook for 1 minute, or until the top is dry.

Preparation time: 10 minutes
Cooking time: 15 minutes

Chef's note: If you don't have a microwave, bake the potato at 375° for 1 hour, or until easily pierced with a fork.

Per serving: 118 calories, 3.7 g. fat (28% of calories), 1.2 g. dietary fiber, 8 mg. cholesterol, 135 mg. sodium.

ASPARAGUS AND WHITE BEAN FRITTATA

SERVES 4

$\mathcal{T}$his is perfect for a brunch or light lunch.

1	teaspoon olive oil
½	cup thinly sliced scallions
1	clove garlic, minced
2	tablespoons chopped fresh tarragon
1	cup fat-free egg substitute
1	can (16 ounces) cannellini beans, rinsed and drained
¼	cup skim milk
⅛	teaspoon ground mace
¼	cup shredded reduced-fat Cheddar cheese
8	asparagus spears, blanched

In a large ovenproof frying pan over medium-high heat, warm the oil. Add the scallions and sauté for 1 minute. Add the garlic and tarragon; cook for 1 minute. Remove from the heat.

In a medium bowl, combine the eggs, beans, milk and mace. Add the onion mixture.

Pour the mixture into the frying pan. Sprinkle with the Cheddar and top with the asparagus in a pinwheel design.

Place over medium-high heat and cook for 2 minutes. Reduce the heat to medium and cook for 5 minutes, or until the edges are set and the top is just slightly moist.

Place under the broiler, about 3" from the heat, and broil for 3 minutes, or until the frittata is puffed and lightly browned.

Preparation time: 10 minutes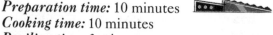
Cooking time: 10 minutes
Broiling time: 3 minutes

Per serving: 192 calories, 3 g. fat (14% of calories), 7.2 g. dietary fiber, 5 mg. cholesterol, 541 mg. sodium.

ONION OMELET

SERVES 4

*T*his is a savory way to get plenty of cholesterol-lowering onions into your diet.

2	*cups thinly sliced onions*
1	*teaspoon olive oil*
½	*cup dry bread crumbs*
2	*tablespoons grated Romano cheese*
1	*teaspoon dried basil*
1	*teaspoon Dijon mustard*
¼	*teaspoon ground black pepper*
2	*cups fat-free egg substitute*
2	*tablespoons water*
2	*teaspoons margarine*

Place the onions and oil in a 2-quart casserole. Cover with a lid or vented plastic wrap and microwave on high for 4 minutes, or until tender. Transfer to a large no-stick frying pan. Sauté over medium heat for 5 minutes. Stir in the bread crumbs, Romano, basil, mustard and pepper. Transfer to a medium bowl and set aside.

In another medium bowl, whisk together the eggs and water.

Wipe out the frying pan with paper towels. Place it over medium-high heat. Add 1 teaspoon margarine and swirl the pan. Add half of the eggs. Lift and rotate the pan so the eggs are evenly distributed. As the eggs set around the edges, lift them to allow uncooked portions to flow underneath. When the eggs are mostly set, spread half of the onion mixture over them. Use a spatula to fold the omelet in half. Transfer to a serving platter.

Repeat with the remaining margarine, eggs and filling.

Preparation time: 5 minutes
Cooking time: 20 minutes

Per serving: 173 calories, 4.8 g. fat (25% of calories), 1.8 g. dietary fiber, 2 mg. cholesterol, 345 mg. sodium.

BROCCOLI AND EGGS

SERVES 4

When you crave scrambled eggs on a low-cholesterol diet, turn to egg substitute, which is made largely from egg whites and is therefore cholesterol-free. These breakfast or brunch burritos are easy to make and infinitely variable. If you don't have broccoli on hand, substitute asparagus, zucchini, green beans or tomatoes.

1	*cup fat-free egg substitute*
¼	*cup skim milk*
¼	*cup minced fresh coriander*
¼	*teaspoon ground black pepper*
1	*cup chopped cooked broccoli*
2	*teaspoons margarine*
4	*flour tortillas*
1	*cup mild or medium salsa*
½	*cup nonfat yogurt*

In a small bowl, whisk together the eggs, milk, coriander and pepper. Stir in the broccoli.

Heat a large no-stick frying pan over medium heat for 3 minutes. Add the margarine and swirl the pan to distribute it well. Add the egg mixture and cook, stirring frequently, until set. Remove from the heat.

Wrap the tortillas in a damp paper towel. Microwave on high for 30 seconds, or until hot and pliable.

Divide the eggs among the tortillas and roll to enclose the filling. Serve with the salsa and yogurt.

Preparation time: 5 minutes
Cooking time: 5 minutes

Per serving: 190 calories, 5.3 g. fat (23% of calories), 1.9 g. dietary fiber, <1 mg. cholesterol, 359 mg. sodium.

BROCCOLI QUICHE

SERVES 4

*H*ere's a good way to use up leftover cooked broccoli. Other vegetables, such as carrots, cauliflower, green beans and asparagus, would also work nicely. The beauty of this quiche is that it doesn't have a crust, which would add lots of fat to the dish and take extra time to prepare.

1	*cup skim milk*
¾	*cup fat-free egg substitute*
2	*cups chopped cooked broccoli*
½	*cup diced green peppers*
½	*cup shredded reduced-fat Monterey Jack cheese*
3	*scallions, thinly sliced*
2	*tablespoons minced fresh dill*
2	*tablespoons grated Parmesan cheese*

In a large bowl, mix the milk and eggs. Stir in the broccoli, peppers, Monterey Jack, scallions and dill.

Coat a 9" pie plate with no-stick spray. Add the broccoli mixture. Sprinkle with the Parmesan.

Bake at 375° for 30 minutes, or until a knife inserted in the center comes out clean and the quiche is lightly puffed and golden on top.

Preparation time: 10 minutes
Cooking time: 30 minutes

Chef's note: If you don't have any ready-cooked broccoli, simply steam some florets for 5 minutes. Let cool a few minutes, then chop as desired.

Per serving: 136 calories, 4.3 g. fat (28% of calories), 2.1 g. dietary fiber, 19 mg. cholesterol, 221 mg. sodium.

SHELLS WITH VEGETABLES AND CHEESE

SERVES 4

Stuffed shells are an Italian staple. These are superlow in fat because the filling starts with dry-curd cottage cheese instead of full-fat ricotta.

12	large pasta shells
⅔	cup dry-curd cottage cheese
¼	cup snipped chives
4	scallions, minced
1	carrot, shredded
1	teaspoon Dijon mustard
½	teaspoon dried tarragon
1	egg white
⅛	teaspoon ground black pepper
1	cup tomato sauce
1	tablespoon grated Parmesan cheese

Cook the shells in a large pot of boiling water for 10 minutes, or until tender. Drain.

While the shells are cooking, in a medium bowl mix the cottage cheese, chives, scallions, carrots, mustard, tarragon, egg white and pepper. Use a spoon to stuff the filling into the shells.

Spread ½ cup tomato sauce in the bottom of a 9" × 9" baking dish. Add the shells in a single layer. Drizzle with the remaining ½ cup sauce. Sprinkle with the Parmesan.

Cover the dish with a lid or foil. Bake at 375° for 20 minutes, or until the filling has set.

Preparation time: 15 minutes
Cooking time: 10 minutes
Baking time: 20 minutes

Per serving: 187 calories, 2.6 g. fat (12% of calories), 1 g. dietary fiber, 3 mg. cholesterol, 317 mg. sodium.

CAVATELLI WITH SPINACH-BASIL PESTO

SERVES 4

*P*esto is a very fragrant herb sauce that's a perfect topping for noodles of all sorts. The drawback of many pesto recipes is their large quantity of oil, cheese and nuts. This version gets super flavor from just a little olive oil and Parmesan blended with defatted chicken stock.

1½	cups packed fresh spinach leaves
⅔	cup packed fresh basil
¼	cup packed fresh parsley
1½	ounces Parmesan cheese, cut into small chunks
6	tablespoons defatted chicken stock
5	teaspoons olive oil
1	clove garlic, chopped
¼	teaspoon ground black pepper
⅛	teaspoon red-pepper flakes
12	ounces cavatelli

In a food processor, combine the spinach, basil, parsley, Parmesan, stock, oil, garlic, black pepper and pepper flakes. Process for 3 to 5 minutes, stopping occasionally to scrape down the sides of the bowl, until the mixture is pureed.

Cook the cavatelli in a large pot of boiling water for 10 minutes, or until just tender. Drain and place in a large bowl. Add the pesto and toss to coat well.

Preparation time: 10 minutes
Cooking time: 10 minutes

Per serving: 431 calories, 10.6 g. fat (22% of calories), 2 g. dietary fiber, 8 mg. cholesterol, 222 mg. sodium.

EGGPLANT AND BOW-TIE NOODLES

SERVES 4

*T*his dish is reminiscent of eggplant Parmesan, but with an important difference. The eggplant is cooked in the microwave, so you don't need to sauté it in a large amount of oil. Serve the noodles with warm crusty bread and a simple antipasto salad made with artichoke hearts, low-fat cheese, tomato wedges, lettuce and fat-free Italian dressing. If you're on a low-sodium diet, make sure to use reduced-sodium tomato sauce. Most of the sodium in this dish comes from the sauce.

8 *ounces bow-tie noodles*
8 *cups peeled and cubed eggplant*
2 *cups diced onions*
3 *cups low-sodium tomato sauce*
   Pinch of ground red pepper
½ *cup grated Parmesan cheese*

Cook the noodles in a large pot of boiling water for 15 minutes, or until just tender. Drain and keep warm.

Meanwhile, place the eggplant and onions in a 3-quart casserole. Cover with a lid or vented plastic wrap. Microwave on high for a total of 8 minutes, or until soft; stop and stir halfway through the cooking period. Stir in the tomato sauce and pepper. Cover again and microwave on high for 4 minutes, or until bubbly. Serve over the noodles. Sprinkle with the Parmesan.

Preparation time: 10 minutes
Cooking time: 15 minutes

Chef's note: If you don't have a microwave, steam the eggplant and onions for about 10 minutes. Transfer to a large saucepan, and add the tomato sauce and pepper; warm through.

Per serving: 475 calories, 11.7 g. fat (22% of calories), 5 g. dietary fiber, 10 mg. cholesterol, 300 mg. sodium.

LASAGNA SWIRLS

*W*hen you don't want to make a traditional layered version, whip up these individual rolls.

12 lasagna noodles

1 box (10 ounces) frozen chopped spinach, thawed

1½ cups nonfat ricotta cheese

¼ cup grated Parmesan cheese

¼ cup fat-free egg substitute

2 tablespoons minced fresh basil

2 tablespoons minced fresh parsley

½ teaspoon ground black pepper

2 cups tomato sauce

4 ounces nonfat mozzarella cheese, shredded

Cook the noodles in a large pot of boiling water for 10 minutes, or until tender. Drain, rinse with cold water, lay the noodles flat on a tray and set aside.

Meanwhile, squeeze the spinach with your hands to extract all excess moisture. Place the spinach in a large bowl and use a fork to break it up. Stir in the ricotta, Parmesan, egg, basil, parsley and pepper.

Spoon about 1 cup of the tomato sauce into the bottom of a 9" × 13" glass baking dish.

Spread about 3 tablespoons of the filling along the entire length of each noodle. Roll up the noodles and stand them on end in the baking dish. Spoon the remaining 1 cup of tomato sauce over the noodles. Sprinkle with the mozzarella. Bake at 350° for 20 minutes.

Preparation time: 10 minutes
Cooking time: 10 minutes
Baking time: 20 minutes

Per serving: 246 calories, 5.8 g. fat (19% of calories), 0.8 g. dietary fiber, 6 mg. cholesterol, 782 mg. sodium.

LENTILS WITH CURRIED VEGETABLES

*L*entils make a very hearty main dish.

1	*onion, thinly sliced*
½	*cup thinly sliced carrots*
½	*cup thinly sliced celery*
1	*tablespoon olive oil*
1	*clove garlic, minced*
1	*tablespoon curry powder*
1	*teaspoon ground cumin*
¼	*teaspoon turmeric*
¼	*teaspoon ground cardamom*
1	*thin slice fresh ginger, minced*
2	*cups defatted chicken stock*
1	*cup dry brown lentils, sorted and rinsed*
1	*sweet potato, peeled and diced*
1	*bay leaf*
1	*cup chopped (½" pieces) green beans*
½	*cup peas*
1	*cup nonfat yogurt*

In a large no-stick frying pan over medium heat, sauté the onions, carrots and celery in the oil for 4 minutes. Add the garlic, curry powder, cumin, turmeric, cardamom and ginger. Stir for 1 minute.

Add the stock, lentils, sweet potatoes and bay leaf. Bring to a boil. Cover and cook, stirring occasionally, for 20 minutes, or until the lentils are tender. (If the mixture becomes too dry, add a little additional stock or some water.) Remove and discard the bay leaf.

Add the beans and peas. Cover and cook for 5 minutes. Remove from the heat and stir in the yogurt.

Preparation time: 15 minutes
Cooking time: 30 minutes

PASTA WITH RED LENTILS IN SPICY TOMATO SAUCE

SERVES 4

*R*ed lentils are among the quickest-cooking legumes. And they don't require soaking before being cooked.

2	*cups water*
½	*cup dry red lentils, sorted and rinsed*
1	*bay leaf*
1	*can (28 ounces) plum tomatoes, drained*
1	*teaspoon olive oil*
1	*clove garlic, minced*
½	*teaspoon red-pepper flakes*
2	*cups macaroni or ditalini*
2	*tablespoons shredded reduced-fat Cheddar cheese*

In a 2-quart saucepan over high heat, bring the water to a boil. Add the lentils and bay leaf. Reduce the heat to medium and cook, stirring occasionally, for 15 minutes, or until the lentils are tender but not mushy. Drain. Remove and discard the bay leaf.

While the lentils are cooking, place the tomatoes in a large no-stick frying pan and coarsely break them up with a spoon. Add the oil, garlic and pepper flakes. Cook over medium heat, stirring frequently, for 5 minutes, or until most of the moisture from the tomatoes has evaporated. Stir in the lentils.

Also while the lentils are cooking, cook the pasta in a large pot of boiling water for 8 minutes, or until just tender. Drain and add to the frying pan with the lentils. Sprinkle with the Cheddar.

Preparation time: 5 minutes
Cooking time: 15 minutes

Per serving: 345 calories, 3.7 g. fat (10% of calories), 4.2 g. dietary fiber, 2 mg. cholesterol, 392 mg. sodium.

GREEK ORZO

SERVES 4

*F*eta cheese and capers give this simple dish a very Greek accent. Orzo is small pasta that resembles grains of rice.

1   *small onion, diced*
1   *clove garlic, minced*
1   *teaspoon olive oil*
1   *can (28 ounces) plum tomatoes, drained*
1   *tablespoon capers, rinsed and drained*
1   *teaspoon dried oregano*
½   *teaspoon dried sage*
½   *teaspoon ground black pepper*
¼   *teaspoon red-pepper flakes*
1   *cup orzo*
⅓   *cup crumbled feta cheese*

In a large no-stick frying pan over medium heat, sauté the onions and garlic in the oil for 5 minutes, or until tender. Add the tomatoes and break them up with a spoon. Stir in the capers, oregano, sage, black pepper and pepper flakes. Simmer, stirring occasionally, for 15 minutes, or until most of the liquid given off by the tomatoes has evaporated.

Meanwhile, cook the orzo in a pot of boiling water for 10 minutes, or until tender. Drain and add to the pan. Stir in the feta and cook for 1 minute, or until the feta starts to melt.

Preparation time: 5 minutes
Cooking time: 15 minutes

Per serving: 183 calories, 4.1 g. fat (20% of calories), 2 g. dietary fiber, 8 mg. cholesterol, 433 mg. sodium.

RISOTTO WITH KALE

SERVES 4

*T*his recipe uses the traditional way of preparing risotto, a creamy Italian rice dish.

4	cups defatted chicken stock
1	small onion, diced
3	cloves garlic, minced
1½	tablespoons olive oil
1	cup Arborio rice
2	cups packed kale leaves, thinly sliced
1	teaspoon chopped fresh thyme
3	tablespoons grated Parmesan cheese
½	teaspoon ground black pepper
1	teaspoon white wine vinegar

In a 2-quart saucepan over medium-high heat, bring the stock to a boil. Reduce the heat to low and keep the stock warm.

In a large frying pan or 3-quart saucepan over medium heat, sauté the onions and garlic in the oil for 5 minutes, or until tender. Stir in the rice.

Add a ladleful of stock (just enough to cover the rice). Cook, stirring constantly, until the stock has been absorbed, about 3 to 5 minutes. Repeat this procedure several more times, until about 20 minutes has elapsed.

Stir in the kale and thyme. Continue adding stock by the ladleful until all the stock has been used (this will take another 10 minutes). The rice should be tender and creamy.

Stir in the Parmesan, pepper and vinegar.

Preparation time: 5 minutes
Cooking time: 35 minutes

Per serving: 311 calories, 8.5 g. fat (25% of calories), 2.1 g. dietary fiber, 4 mg. cholesterol, 185 mg. sodium.

COLORFUL STUFFED PEPPERS

SERVES 4

*S*tuffed peppers are very easy to prepare, and they freeze well, so you can make them ahead.

1½	*cups defatted chicken stock*
½	*cup diced onions*
½	*cup corn*
½	*cup diced carrots*
½	*teaspoon dried savory*
1	*clove garlic, minced*
1¼	*cups quick-cooking brown rice*
4	*large green, red or yellow peppers*
1	*cup shredded nonfat mozzarella cheese*
½	*cup partially thawed frozen peas*

In a 2-quart saucepan, combine the stock, onions, corn, carrots, savory and garlic. Bring to a boil over medium-high heat. Stir in the rice. Reduce the heat to low, cover the pan and simmer for 10 minutes, or until the rice has absorbed all the liquid. Remove from the heat and fluff with a fork.

Meanwhile, cut each pepper in half lengthwise. Carefully remove the stem end and scoop out the seeds. Bring a large pot of water to a boil. Add the peppers and blanch for 5 minutes. Drain and set aside to cool.

Lightly stir the mozzarella and peas into the rice. Divide the mixture among the pepper halves, mounding the tops slightly.

Coat a 9" × 13" baking dish with no-stick spray. Add the peppers in a single layer. Cover with foil and bake at 400° for 15 minutes.

Preparation time: 10 minutes
Cooking time: 10 minutes
Baking time: 15 minutes

Per serving: 187 calories, 1 g. fat (4% of calories), 5 g. dietary fiber, 9 mg. cholesterol, 485 mg. sodium.

Arugula-Stuffed Calzones

*C*alzones are small stuffed pizzas that resemble turnovers. This version is so simple that you'll never again have to settle for the fatty pizzeria variety.

1	tablespoon olive oil
1	green pepper, diced
2	cloves garlic, minced
1	small bunch arugula, chopped
1	cup nonfat ricotta cheese
½	cup shredded nonfat mozzarella cheese
¼	cup chopped fresh basil
	Pinch of ground red pepper
1	tube (10 ounces) refrigerated pizza dough
1	tablespoon cornmeal

In a large no-stick frying pan over medium heat, warm the oil for 1 minute. Add the green peppers and garlic. Cook, stirring frequently, for 2 minutes. Add the arugula. Cook for 2 minutes, or until wilted. Remove from the heat. Stir in the ricotta, mozzarella, basil and red pepper.

Divide the dough into 4 pieces. Working on a lightly floured surface, roll or press each piece into a 6" circle or a 4" × 6" rectangle. Divide the filling among the pieces, mounding it on half of the dough and leaving a ½" margin. Fold the dough over the filling and crimp the edges well to seal.

Sprinkle a large baking sheet with the cornmeal. Place the calzones on the sheet. Bake at 500° for 8 to 10 minutes, or until golden.

Preparation time: 15 minutes
Cooking time: 5 minutes
Baking time: 10 minutes

Per serving: 248 calories, 8.8 g. fat (29% of calories), 1.6 g. dietary fiber, 2 mg. cholesterol, 737 mg. sodium.

CHICK-PEA FRITTERS WITH PEPPER SAUCE

SERVES 4

*S*erve these fritters for dinner or even for brunch.

1   *cup diced roasted sweet red peppers*
1   *tomato, diced*
1   *clove garlic, minced*
2   *teaspoons balsamic vinegar*
¼   *teaspoon honey*
1¾   *cups rinsed and drained canned chick-peas*
1   *small sweet potato, peeled and shredded*
¼   *cup finely chopped scallions*
1   *tablespoon unbleached flour*
2   *teaspoons lemon juice*
    Pinch of ground black pepper
½   *cup fat-free egg substitute*
2   *tablespoons olive oil*

In a small bowl, combine the red peppers, tomatoes, garlic, vinegar and honey. Set aside.

In a medium bowl, coarsely mash the chick-peas.

In a large bowl, mix the sweet potatoes, scallions, flour, lemon juice and black pepper. Stir in the chick-peas and eggs.

In a large no-stick frying pan over medium heat, warm 1 tablespoon oil. Drop rounded tablespoonfuls of the chick-pea mixture into the pan, allowing room for them to spread. Cook for 3 minutes per side, or until lightly browned and cooked through. Transfer to a platter and keep warm. Continue making fritters, adding more oil as needed. Serve the fritters with the pepper sauce.

Preparation time: 15 minutes
Cooking time: 20 minutes

Per serving: 270 calories, 9 g. fat (30% of calories), 6.6 g. dietary fiber, no cholesterol, 66 mg. sodium.

Herbed Tofu with Noodles

*T*ofu makes a great substitute for meat because it's high in protein.

8 *ounces firm tofu, well drained and squeezed dry between paper towels*

1 *teaspoon dried basil*

1 *teaspoon dried rosemary, crumbled*

⅛ *teaspoon ground black pepper*

1 *tablespoon olive oil*

1 *can (19 ounces) red kidney beans, undrained*

2 *cans (14½ ounces each) low-sodium stewed tomatoes*

1 *teaspoon dried oregano*

Pinch of red-pepper flakes

12 *ounces no-yolk broad egg noodles*

½ *cup shredded nonfat mozzarella cheese*

Dice the tofu and place in a small bowl. Sprinkle with the basil, rosemary and black pepper; toss to coat the cubes.

In a large no-stick frying pan over medium heat, warm the oil for 1 minute. Add the tofu; cook, stirring frequently, for 5 minutes, or until the tofu is browned.

Stir in the beans (with their liquid), tomatoes, oregano and pepper flakes; bring to a boil. Reduce the heat to low and simmer for 15 minutes, or until the sauce thickens.

Meanwhile, in a large pot of boiling water, cook the noodles for 10 minutes, or until tender. Drain. Place in a large serving bowl. Add the tofu mixture; toss to mix well. Sprinkle with the mozzarella.

Preparation time: 15 minutes
Cooking time: 20 minutes

Per serving: 426 calories, 8.9 g. fat (18% of calories), 6.8 g. dietary fiber, no cholesterol, 402 mg. sodium.

GETTING THE MOST FROM FRESH HERBS

Nothing adds sparkle to low-fat food like fresh herbs. They have a taste and texture that their dried counterparts just can't match. Here are some quick tips for preserving their natural goodness.

- The less you handle fresh herbs, the better you'll protect their essential oils. So if they're not dirty, don't wash them. If the herbs do need a rinse, make it a quick one under cool water, and then gently pat them dry. Chop just before using.

- If your herbs come from the supermarket rather than your own garden, where you can pick them at will, store them properly. Wrap them in a barely damp paper towel, enclose in plastic and refrigerate. Check every day and remove any wilting or browning leaves.

- A mini food processor makes chopping a quantity of herbs easy. Process with on/off turns to avoid turning them to paste.

- When adding fresh herbs to cooked dishes, do so late in the cooking process so they retain their freshness. Overexposure to heat dissipates the essential oils that give herbs their unique flavor.

- Put lots of herbs in marinades for fish, poultry, meat and vegetables. Then, when broiling or grilling those foods, use a rosemary sprig as your basting brush. You'll get an extra dash of flavor.

- Similarly, strip the leaves from sturdy long rosemary, thyme or sage branches and press the twigs into service as skewers for vegetable, poultry or seafood kabobs. (They're not strong enough to use for red meat.) Grilling will release flavor from the stems and impart it to the food.

- When making salads, think of herbs as "greens." They'll add so much extra flavor, you'll need only a very light dressing. Throw in whole leaves of basil, coriander, marjoram, chervil, parsley, whatever. Add the herb flowers, too. Chive blossoms, for instance, have an intriguing onion flavor; break apart the blooms and scatter them over your salad.

- Use large leaves of basil, mint, lovage, sorrel or other herbs as wrappers. Put a dab of chicken salad, shrimp salad, bean spread, yogurt cheese or any other filling in the middle of a leaf and roll it up. You'll have delicious little tidbits for appetizers.

- Bruise mint leaves and add them to summer drinks.

- If you grow your own herbs, you can preserve some of their summertime freshness for winter enjoyment. Pack clean dry leaves in freezer bags and seal airtight. Although freezing safeguards flavor, it will change the herbs' texture, so use them in cooked foods, such as sauces, stews and soups. (And remember to add them at the end of the cooking period.)

- When using rosemary, which has pinelike needles, pull the leaves off the stems and crush them lightly. You can give olive oil wonderful flavor by pouring a little over the rosemary and letting it steep for 15 minutes.

- Stuff sage leaves under the skin of chicken to add flavor during roasting.

- When picking marjoram, harvest it after the "knots" have formed and before they begin to flower. It's at its flavor peak then.

- Harvest oregano when the flowers are bright purple and fully open.

TOFU CUTLETS

---

*Y*ou may serve these cutlets in any number of ways. First, they're fine just plain. Accompany them with noodles, a steamed vegetable and low-fat gravy from the supermarket. But you may also turn them into a Parmesan version by topping the cutlets with a little spaghetti sauce, mozzarella and Parmesan before baking. You may notice that the percent of calories from fat is a little high, but almost all the fat comes from the tofu and is unsaturated.

12	*ounces firm tofu, drained and squeezed dry between paper towels*
½	*cup fat-free egg substitute*
2	*tablespoons skim milk*
	Pinch of ground black pepper
½	*cup seasoned dry bread crumbs*
2	*tablespoons chopped fresh coriander*
1	*tablespoon finely shredded Provolone cheese*
2	*teaspoons low-sodium soy sauce*

Cut the tofu into ¼" thick slices.

In a shallow bowl, whisk together the eggs, milk and pepper.

On a large piece of wax paper, combine the bread crumbs, coriander and Provolone.

Dip the tofu slices into the egg mixture, then into the crumb mixture, coating both sides.

Coat a large baking sheet with no-stick spray. Place the tofu on the sheet. Sprinkle the pieces with the soy sauce.

Bake at 350° for 20 minutes. Flip the slices and bake for 15 minutes, or until golden.

Preparation time: 10 minutes
Cooking time: 35 minutes

Per serving: 390 calories, 17.4 g. fat (40% of calories), 2.8 g. dietary fiber, 3 mg. cholesterol, 326 mg. sodium.

HEARTY EGGPLANT AND BARLEY

SERVES 4

*E*ggplant is popular in Mediterranean dishes. Here Margaret Donohue of Bellevue, Nebraska, combines it with barley to make a tasty entrée.

1	*cup peeled and cubed eggplant*
½	*cup chopped onions*
½	*cup chopped mushrooms*
¼	*cup chopped green peppers*
1	*tablespoon minced garlic*
1	*teaspoon olive oil*
1	*can (16 ounces) tomatoes, with juice*
1½	*cups water*
¾	*cup quick-cooking barley*
½	*cup chili sauce*
¼	*cup chopped fresh parsley*
1	*teaspoon honey*
1	*teaspoon Worcestershire sauce*
½	*teaspoon dried marjoram*
¼	*teaspoon ground black pepper*

In a large no-stick frying pan over medium heat, sauté the eggplant, onions, mushrooms, green peppers and garlic in the oil for 5 minutes, or until softened.

Add the tomatoes (with juice) to the pan; use a spoon to break them up. Stir in the water, barley, chili sauce, parsley, honey, Worcestershire sauce, marjoram and black pepper. Bring to a boil, then reduce the heat and simmer for 20 minutes.

Preparation time: 10 minutes
Cooking time: 30 minutes

Per serving: 224 calories, 2 g. fat (8% of calories), 7.3 g. dietary fiber, no cholesterol, 439 mg. sodium.

SPINACH ENCHILADAS

SERVES 4

*T*his easy recipe won a prize for Carol Patten of Grand Junction, Colorado, in the second *Prevention* Cooking for Health recipe contest.

2   *cups defatted chicken stock*
1   *cup diced mild canned green chili peppers*
2   *tomatoes, peeled and diced*
2   *tablespoons finely chopped onions*
2   *cloves garlic, minced*
2   *tablespoons cornstarch*
2   *tablespoons water*
1¼ *pounds fresh spinach, coarsely chopped*
8   *corn tortillas*

In a 2-quart saucepan, combine the stock, peppers, tomatoes, onions and garlic. Bring to a boil. Simmer over medium heat for 15 minutes.

In a cup, combine the cornstarch and water. Add to the pan. Cook, stirring, until the mixture thickens. Remove from the heat.

While the sauce is cooking, steam the spinach for 5 minutes, or until wilted. Divide the spinach among the tortillas and roll to enclose it.

Coat a 9" × 13" baking dish with no-stick spray. Add the tortillas in a single layer. Top with the tomato mixture. Bake at 400° for 10 minutes.

Preparation time: 10 minutes
Cooking time: 15 minutes
Baking time: 10 minutes

Per serving: 204 calories, 3 g. fat (12% of calories), 6.6 g. dietary fiber, no cholesterol, 190 mg. sodium.

Eggplant Parmesan

*E*ggplant Parmesan is usually high in fat because traditional recipes call for sautéing the eggplant in lots of oil. Here we bake the eggplant.

2	*medium eggplants (about 1½ pounds total)*
4	*egg whites, beaten until frothy*
½	*cup dry bread crumbs*
½	*teaspoon dried basil*
½	*teaspoon dried oregano*
½	*teaspoon garlic powder*
¼	*teaspoon ground black pepper*
3	*cups tomato sauce*
8	*ounces nonfat mozzarella cheese, shredded*
¼	*cup grated sapsago cheese*
2	*tablespoons chopped fresh parsley*

Cut the eggplants crosswise into ½" slices.

Place the egg whites in a shallow bowl. In another shallow bowl, mix the bread crumbs, basil, oregano, garlic powder and pepper.

Dip each eggplant slice first into the egg whites, then into the crumb mixture. Place on a no-stick baking sheet and broil about 4" from the heat for 5 minutes per side, or until lightly browned.

Spread about ½ cup tomato sauce in the bottom of a 9" × 13" baking dish. Arrange a layer of eggplant slices on top of it. Sprinkle with a little mozzarella and sapsago. Repeat the layers of sauce, eggplant and cheese—ending with tomato sauce—until all the ingredients have been used up. Sprinkle with the parsley.

Cover with foil and bake at 350° for 30 minutes.

Preparation time: 10 minutes
Broiling time: 10 minutes
Baking time: 30 minutes

Per serving: 233 calories, 1.4 g. fat (5% of calories), 6.8 g. dietary fiber, 12 mg. cholesterol, 822 mg. sodium.

Beans and Rice

SERVES 4

Beans and rice is a combo that appears in many cuisines worldwide. The two just naturally go together and make a filling meal that doesn't need meat to be satisfying. You can make this version spicy by adding some minced hot peppers to the beans before simmering them.

1¼	cups water
1½	cups quick-cooking brown rice
2	cups diced onions
4	cloves garlic, minced
1	tablespoon ground cumin
2	tablespoons olive oil
1	can (16 ounces) red kidney beans, rinsed and drained
½	cup tomato juice
2	tablespoons minced parsley
1	teaspoon dried marjoram
1	teaspoon dried oregano
1	cup nonfat yogurt

Bring the water to boil in a 1-quart saucepan. Add the rice, cover and simmer over medium heat for 5 minutes. Remove from the heat and let stand for 5 minutes.

While the rice is cooking, in a large no-stick frying pan over medium heat, sauté the onions, garlic and cumin in the oil for 5 minutes, or until the onions are tender. Add the beans, tomato juice, parsley, marjoram and oregano. Cover and simmer until the rice is ready.

Fluff the rice and stir into the pan. Serve with the yogurt.

Preparation time: 5 minutes
Cooking time: 10 minutes

Per serving: 499 calories, 10 g. fat (18% of calories), 11.3 g. dietary fiber, 1 mg. cholesterol, 535 mg. sodium.

POLENTA, BEAN AND PASTA CASSEROLE

SERVES 4

*T*his won a prize for Martha Jane Parasida of Baden, Pennsylvania, in *Prevention*'s Cooking for Health contest.

½   *cup cornmeal*

½   *cup cold water*

1½ *cups boiling water*

½   *cup corn*

¼   *cup wheat germ*

1   *green pepper, chopped*

4   *scallions, chopped*

1   *teaspoon olive oil*

2   *ounces brick cheese, shredded*

4   *ounces penne or mostaccioli pasta*

1   *can (16 ounces) black-eyed peas or kidney beans, rinsed and drained*

1½ *cups tomato sauce*

In a 2-quart saucepan, whisk together the cornmeal and cold water. Slowly whisk in the boiling water. Bring to a boil over medium heat and cook, stirring constantly, for 10 minutes, or until thick. Stir in the corn and wheat germ. Set aside.

Coat a 10" × 10" casserole with no-stick spray. Spread the cornmeal mixture in the pan. Refrigerate while you prepare the topping.

In a large no-stick frying pan, sauté the peppers and scallions in the oil for 5 minutes, or until crisp-tender. Spread over the cornmeal. Sprinkle with the cheese.

While the vegetables are cooking, cook the pasta in a large pot of boiling water for 7 minutes, or until just tender. Drain and place in a large bowl. Add the beans and tomato sauce. Mix well and pour over the vegetables.

Cover with a lid. Microwave on high (100% power) for a total of 10 minutes; give the dish a quarter turn 3 times during this period.

(continued)

Preparation time: 5 minutes
Cooking time: 25 minutes

Chef's note: If you don't have a microwave, bake the casserole at 350° for 20 minutes.

Per serving: 382 calories, 9.5 g. fat (21% of calories), 9.5 g. dietary fiber, 13 mg. cholesterol, 427 mg. sodium.

MATTHEW'S LAST-MINUTE PASTA

SERVES 4

*W*hen you think there's nothing in the house to eat, you'll probably still be able to throw together an easy pasta entrée like this. If you don't have fresh tomatoes, use some drained canned ones. And virtually any type of pasta will do.

2	*anchovies, mashed (optional)*
¼	*teaspoon capers, rinsed and drained*
4	*teaspoons olive oil*
3	*large tomatoes, seeded and diced*
¼	*cup minced fresh parsley*
2	*tablespoons balsamic vinegar*
1	*clove garlic, minced*
1	*green pepper, thinly sliced*
1	*sweet red or yellow pepper, thinly sliced*
1	*onion, thinly sliced*
½	*teaspoon cracked black pepper*
⅛	*teaspoon fennel seeds*
12	*ounces perciatelli or other thick pasta*

In a 2-quart saucepan over medium heat, combine the anchovies (if used), capers and 1 teaspoon oil. Cook, stirring, for 1 minute. Add the tomatoes, parsley, vinegar and garlic. Cook, stirring occasionally, for 15 minutes, or until most of the liquid from the tomatoes has evaporated.

While the sauce is cooking, in a large no-stick frying pan over medium heat, sauté the green peppers, red or yellow peppers and onions in the remaining 3 teaspoons oil for 5 minutes, or until tender. Stir in the black pepper and fennel seeds. Cook for 1 minute. Keep warm.

Also while the sauce is cooking, cook the pasta in a large pot of boiling water for 12 minutes, or until just tender. Drain and divide among individual dinner plates. Top with the sauce and the peppers mixture.

Preparation time: 10 minutes
Cooking time: 15 minutes

Chef's note: The easiest way to remove seeds from fresh tomatoes is to cut them in half crosswise and then gently squeeze the halves. Most of the seeds and some excess liquid will come right out. If you have a few extra minutes, you might want to peel the tomatoes before removing the seeds. Drop the tomatoes into boiling water (you can use the water you'll be cooking the pasta in) and let stand for 30 seconds. Remove with a slotted spoon, rinse with cold water and use a paring knife to slit the skin. It should peel off easily.

Per serving: 395 calories, 8.3 g. fat (19% of calories), 2.7 g. dietary fiber, 2 mg. cholesterol, 30 mg. sodium.

CHAPTER 9

VEGETABLES,
GRAINS AND
OTHER SIDE
DISHES

EASY ACCOMPANIMENTS

he bounty of the garden sustains many people in Mediterranean countries. Even if you don't have a little backyard plot of your own, you can enjoy some of the same dishes they do. Supermarkets and farmers' markets are offering ever-wider choices when it comes to fresh produce. It's not unusual to find broccoli rabe, a green Italian vegetable that has a pleasant bitter flavor, among the regular broccoli, carrots and zucchini. And in the grains section, you'll come across couscous, different types of rice and even quinoa, a high-protein grain favored by the ancient Incas. You can use all of them—and more—to toss together quick, delicious side dishes your family will love.

BABY LIMA BEANS WITH TOMATOES AND SAGE

SERVES 4

aby lima beans are a super source of dietary fiber. In this recipe from Philadelphia chef and restaurant consultant Aliza Green, they're cooked with lots of garlic. Aliza says that when you buy garlic, you should look for fresh young cloves that have not begun to sprout. She's especially partial to the pink-skinned Italian variety, which has large cloves and a parchmentlike skin that's easy to peel.

½   head garlic
1   tablespoon olive oil
1   tablespoon minced fresh sage
1   box (10 ounces) partially thawed frozen baby lima beans
¾   cup diced tomatoes
¼   cup water
¼   teaspoon ground black pepper

Separate the garlic into individual cloves. Peel and slice them.

In a large heavy-bottomed frying pan, combine the garlic, oil and sage. Cook over low heat, stirring frequently, for 5 minutes, or until the garlic begins to turn golden. Don't let it burn or turn brown.

Add the beans, tomatoes and water. Bring to a boil over medium heat. Simmer for 20 minutes, or until thick. Season with the pepper.

Preparation time: 5 minutes
Cooking time: 25 minutes

Chef's note: To partially thaw the lima beans, remove them from their box and place in a glass pie plate. Microwave on high for 1 minute, or until you can break the pieces apart.

Per serving: 140 calories, 4.2 g. fat (27% of calories), 5.8 g. dietary fiber, no cholesterol, 13 mg. sodium.

BUTTER-FLAVORED BROCCOLI

*T*his is a simply wonderful way to serve tender young broccoli—or any garden-fresh vegetable, such as snow peas, green beans, asparagus or beets.

1   *pound thin broccoli spears*
1   *tablespoon hot tap water*
2   *teaspoons butter-flavored sprinkles*
1   *tablespoon lemon juice*
1   *teaspoon grated lemon rind*

Steam the broccoli for 4 minutes, or until just crisp-tender.

In a cup, combine the water and butter-flavored sprinkles; stir until dissolved. Stir in the lemon juice and lemon rind.

Heat a large no-stick frying pan over medium-high heat. Add the broccoli. Pour the lemon mixture over it. Cook for 1 minute.

Preparation time: 5 minutes
Cooking time: 5 minutes

Per serving: 36 calories, 0.4 g. fat (8% of calories), 3.2 g. dietary fiber, no cholesterol, 64 mg. sodium.

CURRIED CAULIFLOWER

SERVES 4

*C*urry dishes may be either hot or mild. Tailor this recipe to your taste by adjusting the amount of ground pepper.

1	*head cauliflower, separated into florets*
1	*large onion, thinly sliced*
1	*sweet red pepper, thinly sliced*
1	*teaspoon olive oil*
1	*tablespoon minced fresh ginger*
2	*teaspoons ground coriander*
¾	*teaspoon ground cumin*
¾	*teaspoon turmeric*
¼	*teaspoon ground red pepper*
½	*cup nonfat yogurt*
½	*cup nonfat sour cream*
2	*tablespoons lemon juice*
¼	*cup minced fresh coriander*

Steam the cauliflower for 5 minutes, or until tender.

Meanwhile, in a large no-stick frying pan over medium heat, sauté the onions and red peppers in the oil for 5 minutes, or until tender. Add the ginger, ground coriander, cumin, turmeric and ground red pepper. Stir for 1 minute. Add the cauliflower and stir for 2 minutes.

In a small bowl, whisk together the yogurt, sour cream and lemon juice.

Reduce the heat to low. Stir the yogurt mixture into the frying pan and allow to warm for 2 minutes, stirring constantly. Sprinkle with the fresh coriander.

Preparation time: 10 minutes
Cooking time: 10 minutes

Per serving: 103 calories, 1.9 g. fat (15% of calories), 3.7 g. dietary fiber, <1 mg. cholesterol, 62 mg. sodium.

SWEET-AND-SOUR CAULIFLOWER

SERVES 4

Despite its Chinese-sounding name, this is an Italian dish. The recipe comes from cookbook author Judith Olney, who has spent much time in several of the Mediterranean countries. Although the percent of calories from fat is high, the actual grams of fat are not. And almost all the fat comes from the olive oil, so it's the healthy monounsaturated type.

1	clove garlic, minced
1	tablespoon olive oil
1	head cauliflower, separated into florets
1	large tomato, seeded and diced
2½	tablespoons red wine vinegar
3	tablespoons toasted pine nuts
3	tablespoons golden raisins

In a large no-stick frying pan over medium heat, sauté the garlic in the oil for 1 minute. Add the cauliflower, tomatoes and vinegar. Cover and cook for 7 minutes.

Stir in the pine nuts and raisins. Cover and cook for 2 minutes, or until the cauliflower is tender.

Preparation time: 5 minutes
Cooking time: 10 minutes

Per serving: 112 calories, 5.3 g. fat (43% of calories), 5.4 g. dietary fiber, no cholesterol, 26 mg. sodium.

GREEN BEANS WITH ROSEMARY

*R*osemary is an herb that's very popular in France and Italy but often forgotten about here. This recipe pairs it with fresh green beans. When buying green beans, look for young, tender ones that show no signs of seeds developing inside.

1	*pound green beans, cut into 1" pieces*
2	*teaspoons butter-flavored sprinkles*
2	*teaspoons minced fresh rosemary*
1	*teaspoon grated lemon rind*
½	*teaspoon olive oil*

Steam the beans for 5 minutes, or until tender. Place in a large bowl. Sprinkle with the butter-flavored sprinkles, rosemary, lemon rind and oil. Toss to coat well.

Preparation time: 5 minutes
Cooking time: 5 minutes

Per serving: 47 calories, 0.9 g. fat (5% of calories), 2 g. dietary fiber, no cholesterol, 4 mg. sodium.

SIMPLE SPAGHETTI SQUASH

Spaghetti squash is an unusual vegetable that's available in most large markets. When cooked, the flesh separates into spaghetti-like strands that you can use as a base for sauces, just as you would pasta. With a hearty sauce, it can be a main course. Here it's a light side dish.

1   spaghetti squash (about 3½ pounds), halved
    and seeded
1   thin zucchini, julienned
1   sweet red pepper, julienned
1   teaspoon olive oil
2   cloves garlic, minced
1   cup cherry tomatoes, halved
1   tablespoon white wine vinegar
1   tablespoon minced fresh basil
2   teaspoons minced fresh oregano
¼   teaspoon ground black pepper
2   tablespoons grated Parmesan cheese

Place 1 squash half, cut side down, in a glass pie plate. Microwave on high for 4 minutes, or until the strands become loose and tender. Let stand for 5 minutes. Microwave the other half; let stand.

While the squash is cooking, in a large no-stick frying pan over medium-high heat, sauté the zucchini and peppers in the oil for 3 minutes. Stir in the garlic and cook for 1 minute. Add the tomatoes, vinegar, basil, oregano and black pepper; sauté for 2 minutes.

Using 2 forks, fluff the flesh of the squash into strands. Add to the frying pan; sauté for 3 minutes. Sprinkle with the Parmesan.

Preparation time: 10 minutes plus standing time
Cooking time: 15 minutes

Chef's note: If you don't have a microwave, quarter the squash and place it in a Dutch oven or other large pot. Add about 1 cup of water. Cover and bring to a boil. Reduce the heat and simmer for 20 minutes, or until the squash fibers pull apart easily with a fork. Transfer to a large plate. Scoop out and discard the seeds.

Per serving: 100 calories, 2.8 g. fat (25% of calories), 10.1 g. dietary fiber, 2 mg. cholesterol, 92 mg. sodium.

BALSAMIC BROCCOLI RABE

SERVES 4

Broccoli rabe is a green vegetable that has long stalks and scattered clusters of buds that resemble broccoli flowers. It's got a pungent flavor that's made it a favorite in Italy for many years. Groceries in America are starting to carry broccoli rabe (also known as rapini and broccoli raab), and people here are beginning to appreciate its distinctive flavor.

1   pound broccoli rabe
1   tablespoon balsamic vinegar
1   tablespoon grated Parmesan cheese
2   teaspoons butter-flavored sprinkles
1   teaspoon minced fresh thyme

Wash the broccoli rabe in cold water. Shake off the stalks, but don't dry them completely. Cut the thick stems into 1" pieces; cut the leafy tops into 3" pieces. Place in a Dutch oven or other large pot with just the water left clinging to the pieces.

Cover and cook over medium heat for 5 minutes, or until tender. Remove from the heat. Sprinkle with the vinegar, Parmesan, butter-flavored sprinkles and thyme. Toss to mix.

Preparation time: 5 minutes
Cooking time: 5 minutes

Per serving: 45 calories, 0.9 g. fat (15% of calories), 3.1 g. dietary fiber, 1 mg. cholesterol, 59 mg. sodium.

MIXED GREENS AND VIDALIA ONIONS

SERVES 4

*V*idalia onions are a particularly mild variety. If you can't find them (they're usually available in early summer), substitute sweet Spanish onions or regular yellow ones. Although 2 pounds of fresh spinach might seem like a lot, it cooks down considerably.

1   *pound Vidalia onions, thinly sliced*
2   *teaspoons olive oil*
3   *cloves garlic, thinly sliced*
2   *pounds fresh spinach leaves*
1   *tablespoon cider vinegar*
½   *teaspoon red-pepper flakes*

In a Dutch oven or other large pot over medium heat, sauté the onions in the oil for 10 minutes, or until lightly browned. Add the garlic and stir for 2 minutes.

Meanwhile, wash the spinach in plenty of cold water. Shake off the excess. Remove tough stems and coarsely shred the leaves. Add to the pot and stir to mix with the onions. Cover and cook over low heat for 10 minutes, or until the spinach is wilted. Stir in the vinegar and pepper flakes.

Preparation time: 10 minutes
Cooking time: 20 minutes

Per serving: 118 calories, 3.1 g. fat (24% of calories), 7.5 g. dietary fiber, no cholesterol, 186 mg. sodium.

Yellow Squash Casserole

SERVES 4

This ultra-easy casserole, developed by the staff at Duke University for their weight-loss patients, makes a great side dish for poached fish or chicken. Since it's also a good protein source in its own right, you could serve it as a light main course for brunch or lunch.

½	cup nonfat yogurt
½	cup low-fat cottage cheese
½	cup fat-free egg substitute
¼	cup grated Parmesan cheese
¼	teaspoon dried marjoram
1	cup thinly sliced onions
3	cups thinly sliced yellow squash
¼	cup fresh bread crumbs

In a small bowl, whisk together the yogurt, cottage cheese, eggs, Parmesan and marjoram. Set aside.

Coat a large no-stick frying pan with no-stick spray. Add the onions and cook over medium heat for 5 minutes, or until tender.

Coat a 2-quart casserole with no-stick spray. Spread one-third of the squash slices in the dish. Top with one-third of the onions and one-third of the yogurt mixture. Repeat twice. Sprinkle with the bread crumbs.

Cover and bake at 375° for 20 minutes. Uncover and bake for 5 minutes, or until the top is brown.

Preparation time: 10 minutes
Cooking time: 5 minutes
Baking time: 25 minutes

Chef's note: To make fresh bread crumbs, tear several slices of white, whole-wheat, oat or other bread into pieces. Place in a food processor and grind with on/off turns until fine.

Per serving: 117 calories, 3 g. fat (23% of calories), 2.4 g. dietary fiber, 7 mg. cholesterol, 314 mg. sodium.

Baked Sweet Potatoes with Ginger and Honey

*S*weet potatoes are delicious almost any way they're prepared. Here they're paired with an interesting blend of spices for a really easy—and nutritious—side dish. This is particularly good at Thanksgiving and other holidays as an alternative to high-fat candied sweet potatoes or yams.

1	*can (16 ounces) vacuum-packed small whole sweet potatoes, cut into ½" cubes*
¼	*cup honey*
1½	*tablespoons grated fresh ginger*
1	*tablespoon olive oil*
½	*teaspoon ground cardamom*
¼	*teaspoon ground black pepper*

In a large bowl, combine the sweet potatoes, honey, ginger, oil, cardamom and pepper.

Coat an 8" × 8" baking dish with no-stick spray. Add the sweet-potato mixture. Bake at 400° for 20 minutes.

Preparation time: 5 minutes
Baking time: 20 minutes

Per serving: 218 calories, 3.5 g. fat (14% of calories), 3.4 g. dietary fiber, no cholesterol, 16 mg. sodium.

Golden Mashed Potatoes with Horseradish

SERVES 4

Classic recipes for mashed potatoes call for lots of butter. But you can get a rich flavor by replacing the butter with cottage cheese, as Chef Aliza Green has done here. For potatoes that *look* as though they've got butter whipped in, use yellow-fleshed spuds such as Yellow Finnish, Yukon Golds or Yellow Golds.

1½	*pounds yellow-fleshed potatoes, peeled and cubed*
1½	*cups low-fat small-curd cottage cheese*
1	*cup 1% low-fat milk, scalded*
4	*scallions, minced*
1	*tablespoon prepared horseradish*
½	*teaspoon ground black pepper*
	Pinch of grated nutmeg

Place the potatoes in a 3-quart saucepan. Add cold water to cover. Bring to a boil over high heat. Reduce the heat to medium and cook for 20 minutes, or until the potatoes are quite soft. Drain well and return to the pan or place in a large bowl. Mash the potatoes thoroughly.

While the potatoes are cooking, place the cottage cheese in a food processor and process for 2 minutes, or until smooth.

Using a heavy whisk or a potato masher, gradually incorporate the milk into the potatoes. Add the cottage cheese, scallions, horseradish, pepper and nutmeg.

Preparation time: 10 minutes
Cooking time: 20 minutes

Per serving: 244 calories, 1.8 g. fat (7% of calories), 2.2 g. dietary fiber, 8 mg. cholesterol, 426 mg. sodium.

ORZO FLAVORED WITH FETA CHEESE

SERVES 4

Orzo is small pasta that's shaped like rice grains. It cooks quickly and makes a nice alternative to rice. Here it gets a Greek accent with the addition of feta cheese and olives.

8   ounces orzo
3   tablespoons crumbled feta cheese
3   large pitted black olives, chopped
3   tablespoons minced fresh parsley
2   tablespoons snipped chives
2   teaspoons olive oil

Cook the orzo in a pot of boiling water for 10 minutes, or until tender. Drain and place in a large bowl. Add the feta, olives, parsley, chives and oil. Toss to mix well.

Preparation time: 5 minutes
Cooking time: 10 minutes

Per serving: 249 calories, 4.8 g. fat (17% of calories), 1.7 g. dietary fiber, 5 mg. cholesterol, 79 mg. sodium.

ASPARAGUS AND COUSCOUS

SERVES 4

*T*his is an excellent side dish to have when fresh asparagus is in season. But it's hearty enough to double as a light entrée; serve it with nonfat sour cream.

1	*onion, thinly sliced*
1	*teaspoon olive oil*
8	*ounces trimmed asparagus, cut into 1" pieces*
1½	*cups defatted chicken stock*
½	*teaspoon ground black pepper*
¼	*teaspoon hot-pepper sauce*
1	*cup couscous*
¼	*cup chopped fresh basil*
2	*tablespoons chopped toasted almonds*

In a large no-stick frying pan over medium-high heat, sauté the onions in the oil for 5 minutes, or until light brown. Add the asparagus, stock, black pepper and hot-pepper sauce. Cover and bring to a boil. Reduce the heat to medium and cook for 5 minutes. Remove from the heat.

Stir in the couscous, basil and almonds. Cover and let stand for 5 minutes, or until all the liquid has been absorbed. Fluff with a fork.

Preparation time: 10 minutes
Cooking time: 10 minutes

Per serving: 244 calories, 3.8 g. fat (14% of calories), 8.9 g. dietary fiber, no cholesterol, 337 mg. sodium.

PINEAPPLE PILAF

SERVES 4

*T*his easy dish can bake while you prepare the rest of the meal.

> 1 onion, diced
> ½ cup diced green peppers
> 2 tablespoons currants
> 1 clove garlic, minced
> 2 teaspoons olive oil
> 1 cup long-grain white rice
> ½ cup drained crushed pineapple
> ¼ cup toasted pine nuts
> 1 tablespoon minced fresh sage
> ½ teaspoon ground black pepper
> 2 cups defatted chicken stock
> ¼ cup chopped fresh coriander

In a 3-quart casserole suitable for stovetop cooking, combine the onions, green peppers, currants, garlic and oil. Sauté over medium heat for 5 minutes, or until the onions are tender.

Stir in the rice, pineapple, pine nuts, sage and black pepper. Add the stock and bring to a boil.

Bake at 375° for 25 minutes, or until the rice is tender and most of the liquid has been absorbed. Stir in the coriander. Let stand for 5 minutes before serving. Fluff with a fork.

Preparation time: 10 minutes plus standing time
Cooking time: 5 minutes
Baking time: 25 minutes

Per serving: 274 calories, 7.3 g. fat (24% of calories), 1.9 g. dietary fiber, no cholesterol, 446 mg. sodium.

QUINOA PILAF

SERVES 4

*Q*uinoa is a grain that's one of the best vegetable sources of protein. It's delicious cooked into a pilaf such as this one from Dieter Dopplefeld, a talented chef and instructor at the Culinary Institute of America.

2   *cups defatted chicken stock*
1   *cup quinoa*
¼   *cup minced sweet red peppers*
¼   *cup minced onions*
1   *clove garlic, minced*
1   *bay leaf*
¼   *teaspoon dried thyme*
¼   *teaspoon ground black pepper*

In a 1-quart saucepan over high heat, bring the stock to a boil. Keep warm.

In a large no-stick frying pan over medium heat, toast the quinoa, stirring frequently, for 5 minutes, or until lightly browned. Set aside.

While the quinoa is toasting, in an ovenproof 2-quart saucepan over medium heat, cook the red peppers, onions and garlic in about 2 tablespoons of the stock for 5 minutes, or until tender. Add the quinoa, bay leaf, thyme, black pepper and the remaining stock. Bring to a boil.

Cover and bake at 350° for 20 minutes, or until all the liquid has been absorbed and the quinoa is just tender. Fluff with a fork. Discard the bay leaf.

Preparation time: 5 minutes
Cooking time: 5 minutes
Baking time: 20 minutes

Per serving: 184 calories, 3.2 g. fat (15% of calories), 2.5 g. dietary fiber, no cholesterol, 50 mg. sodium.

CELEBRATION RICE

*A*ny occasion will be cause for celebration if you serve this festive dish. It was special enough to win a prize for Marjorie Kingston of Stockbridge, Massachusetts, in *Prevention*'s annual healthy-recipe contest.

1¼	*cups quick-cooking brown rice*
1	*cup water*
⅓	*cup orange juice*
1	*tablespoon low-sodium soy sauce*
1½	*teaspoons olive oil*
1	*teaspoon grated orange rind*
1	*teaspoon curry powder*
1	*tablespoon toasted sesame seeds*
2	*tablespoons snipped chives*
2	*tablespoons diced sweet red peppers*

In a 2-quart saucepan, mix the rice, water, orange juice, soy sauce, oil, orange rind and curry powder. Bring to a boil over high heat. Cover, reduce the heat to medium-low and simmer for 10 minutes, or until all the liquid has been absorbed.

Fluff the rice with a fork. Stir in the sesame seeds, chives and peppers.

Preparation time: 5 minutes
Cooking time: 10 minutes

Chef's note: Marjorie's original recipe included wild rice, which takes about 40 minutes to cook. If you have any cooked wild rice on hand, reduce the brown rice to 1 cup and stir in about ½ cup wild rice.

Per serving: 119 calories, 3.4 g. fat (25% of calories), 0.8 g. dietary fiber, no cholesterol, 156 mg. sodium.

CORN AND PARMESAN SPOON BREAD

*S*poon bread is a close relative of cornbread, but it's much softer in texture and needs to be eaten with a spoon or fork.

½	cup cornmeal
1	teaspoon baking powder
½	teaspoon dried thyme
½	teaspoon ground black pepper
¼	teaspoon baking soda
½	cup buttermilk
½	cup skim milk
2	tablespoons honey
1	tablespoon olive oil
½	cup corn
¼	cup fat-free egg substitute
3	tablespoons grated Parmesan cheese

In a small bowl, mix the cornmeal, baking powder, thyme, pepper and baking soda.

In a 3-quart saucepan, combine the buttermilk, skim milk, honey and oil. Place over medium heat and bring just to a simmer; the mixture may separate.

Remove from the heat. Whisk until smooth. Then whisk in the cornmeal mixture in a steady stream until well incorporated (the mixture will foam up). Whisk in the corn, egg and Parmesan.

Coat a 9" pie plate with no-stick spray. Pour in the cornmeal mixture. Bake at 375° for 35 minutes, or until the top is set and light gold but the center of the mixture is still slightly creamy.

Preparation time: 10 minutes
Cooking time: 35 minutes

Per serving: 187 calories, 5.7 g. fat (26% of calories), 2.9 g. dietary fiber, 5 mg. cholesterol, 296 mg. sodium.

SHALLOT AND MUSTARD SAUCE

*H*ere's an easy sauce that's great served over most any type of steamed vegetable or cooked rice. This is an adaptation of a recipe created by Chef Jean-Marc Fullsack, who creates wonderfully low-fat dishes for patients at the Preventive Medicine Research Institute in Sausalito, California. This recipe uses a fennel bulb to add body to the sauce.

1¼	cups defatted chicken stock
½	cup finely chopped fennel
4	shallots, minced
2	teaspoons Dijon mustard
1	teaspoon nonfat milk powder
1	teaspoon chopped fresh tarragon
¼	teaspoon ground black pepper

In a 2-quart saucepan, mix the stock, fennel, shallots, mustard and milk powder. Bring to a boil over medium-high heat. Cook for 10 minutes, or until the sauce is reduced to about 1 cup and the fennel is very tender. Stir in the tarragon and pepper.

Preparation time: 10 minutes
Cooking time: 10 minutes

Chef's note: For a deeper, richer flavor, roast the shallots before adding them to the sauce. Place whole, unpeeled shallots in a custard cup and bake at 350° for 35 minutes, or until soft and tender. Peel and chop finely.

Per ¼ cup: 21 calories, 0.2 g. fat (9% of calories), 0.6 g. dietary fiber, no cholesterol, 114 mg. sodium.

PEAR CHUTNEY

*T*his sweet and savory chutney goes especially well with chicken or pork. You can easily make it ahead. Serve warm, cold or at room temperature.

½	cup maple syrup
¼	cup cider vinegar
⅓	cup golden raisins
¼	cup thinly sliced crystallized ginger
¼	cup thinly sliced onions
1	clove garlic, thinly sliced
1	teaspoon mustard seeds
½	teaspoon ground red pepper
3	firm Bosc pears, peeled, cored and chopped
½	cup cranberries

In a 3-quart saucepan over medium-high heat, bring the maple syrup and vinegar to a boil. Reduce the heat to medium. Add the raisins, ginger, onions, garlic, mustard seeds and pepper. Mix well.

Stir in the pears and cook for about 15 minutes, or until the pears are soft and just beginning to lose their shape. Add the cranberries and cook an additional 5 minutes.

Preparation time: 10 minutes
Cooking time: 20 minutes

Per ½ cup: 95 calories, 0.3 g. fat (3% of calories), 1.1 g. dietary fiber, no cholesterol, 4 mg. sodium.

PINEAPPLE SALSA

MAKES ABOUT 5 CUPS

his mildly spicy salsa is an excellent accompaniment to fish of all sorts, including very simply roasted or grilled salmon. The recipe is particularly easy since it requires no cooking.

- ½   *tablespoon honey*
- 2   *tablespoons cider vinegar*
- 2½   *cups diced fresh pineapple*
- 1   *cup diced mango*
- 1   *small jalapeño pepper, finely chopped (wear plastic gloves when handling)*
- ½   *cup diced red onions*
- ½   *cup minced fresh coriander*
- 2   *tablespoons lime juice*
- 1   *tablespoon grated lime rind*

Place the honey in a large glass bowl. Add the vinegar and stir until the honey has dissolved. Add the pineapple, mangoes, peppers, onions, coriander, lime juice and lime rind. Cover and refrigerate until needed.

Preparation time: 15 minutes

Chef's note: You'll find it easier to grate the rind from the lime if you do so before cutting and juicing the fruit.

Per ½ cup: 35 calories, 0.2 g. fat (5% of calories), 0.9 g. dietary fiber, no cholesterol, 1 mg. sodium.

CLASSIC GARLIC MAYONNAISE SAUCE

In Provence, this sauce is called aïoli (ay-OH-lee), and it's served with all sorts of cooked vegetables as well as fish, meats and even crusty bread. In France, it's not unusual for cooks to incorporate a whole bulb of garlic into the sauce. You, of course, may opt for less, according to your own taste.

Because this sauce is made up almost entirely of oil, the percent of calories from fat is extremely high. So you'll want to use just a small amount and counterbalance it with lots of vegetables, bread and other foods. For a lower-fat version of aïoli, mash garlic and stir it into commercial nonfat mayonnaise.

AÏOLI

MAKES ABOUT 1 CUP

5 *cloves garlic, mashed into a paste*
3 *tablespoons fat-free egg substitute*
2 *tablespoons lemon juice*
¼ *teaspoon dry mustard*
¼ *teaspoon ground black pepper*
½ *cup olive oil*

In a blender or food processor, combine the garlic, egg, lemon juice, mustard and pepper. Process for about 15 seconds. With the motor running, very slowly add the oil in a thin stream.

Preparation time: 5 minutes

Per tablespoon: 63 calories, 6.8 g. fat (95% of calories), trace dietary fiber, no cholesterol, 4 mg. sodium.

CHAPTER 10

MUFFINS,
BREADS,
SCONES
AND MORE

YOUR OWN BAKERY

Breads and other grain-based products are an indispensable staple of the Mediterranean diet. Even the smallest town has a bakery that produces hearty, crusty loaves daily. Because bread is a complex carbohydrate and is very often low in fat, you should consider it an essential part of your own diet. You might not have access to a top-notch bakery, but you can prepare many breads and other baked goods at home—in less time than you might imagine. Muffins are particularly easy, and if you make them yourself, you can keep close tabs on their fat content. And by using quick-rise yeast and a microwave, you can have homemade rolls and other breads whenever you want.

FIG AND OAT MUFFINS

MAKES 12

*O*at bran is a good source of soluble fiber, which can help lower cholesterol. These easy muffins can help you increase your consumption of oat bran.

3	*cups oat-bran-flakes cereal, such as Common Sense*
1½	*cups orange juice*
½	*cup fat-free egg substitute*
¼	*cup honey*
2	*tablespoons canola oil*
1	*cup unbleached flour*
½	*cup whole-wheat flour*
4	*teaspoons baking powder*
1	*cup finely chopped dried figs*

Coat 12 muffin cups with no-stick spray.

In a medium bowl, combine the cereal and orange juice. Let stand for 10 minutes, or until the cereal is softened.

In a small bowl, whisk together the eggs, honey and oil. Stir into the cereal.

In a large bowl, whisk together the unbleached flour, whole-wheat flour and baking powder. Stir in the figs and make sure they're well distributed.

Pour the liquid ingredients into the flour mixture. Stir with a rubber spatula until all the flour is moistened; do not overmix.

Spoon the batter into the prepared muffin cups, just about filling them. Bake at 400° for 20 to 25 minutes, or until golden brown.

Preparation time: 10 minutes
Baking time: 25 minutes

Per muffin: 183 calories, 3 g. fat (14% of calories), 3.2 g. dietary fiber, no cholesterol, 163 mg. sodium.

FETA CORN MUFFINS

*Y*ou'll love these easy Greek muffins that make terrific accompaniments to salads and soups.

1 small onion, minced
1 cup buttermilk
¼ cup fat-free egg substitute
3 tablespoons honey
2 tablespoons olive oil
1 cup unbleached flour
1 cup cornmeal
2 teaspoons baking soda
1½ teaspoons ground cumin
1 teaspoon ground black pepper
½ teaspoon ground coriander
½ teaspoon dried oregano
½ teaspoon baking powder
4 ounces feta cheese, crumbled

Coat 12 muffin cups with no-stick spray.

Place the onions in a small bowl. Microwave on high for 1 minute.

In a medium bowl, mix the buttermilk, egg, honey and oil.

In a large bowl, mix the flour, cornmeal, baking soda, cumin, pepper, coriander, oregano and baking powder. Stir in the feta and onions.

Pour the buttermilk mixture over the flour mixture. Mix with a rubber spatula until the dry ingredients are moistened.

Spoon the batter into the prepared muffin cups, filling them about three-quarters full. Bake at 450° for 15 minutes.

Preparation time: 15 minutes
Baking time: 15 minutes

Per muffin: 151 calories, 5 g. fat (29% of calories), 2 g. dietary fiber, 9 mg. cholesterol, 289 mg. sodium.

SWEET POTATO WAFFLES

*T*hese waffles are often requested by the guests at Canyon Ranch in Tucson, Arizona, where they're a staple on the breakfast menu. For variety, serve the waffles with sliced fresh fruit or with one of the sauces on page 248.

2¼	*cups peeled and diced sweet potatoes*
1½	*cups 1% low-fat milk*
3	*egg whites*
1	*tablespoon canola oil*
1	*cup unbleached flour*
½	*cup whole-wheat flour*
1	*tablespoon baking powder*
½	*cup maple syrup*

Steam the sweet potatoes for 10 minutes, or until very soft. Transfer to a large bowl and mash well. Beat in the milk, egg whites and oil until smooth.

In a small bowl, whisk together the unbleached flour, whole-wheat flour and baking powder. Pour over the liquid ingredients and stir until smooth.

Heat a waffle iron and lightly brush the grids with oil. For each waffle, pour in about ½ cup of batter and spread it over the grids. Bake according to the manufacturer's directions.

Serve the waffles with the syrup.

Preparation time: 5 minutes
Cooking time: 10 minutes
Baking time: 25 minutes

Per serving: 201 calories, 2.5 g. fat (11% of calories), 2.7 g. dietary fiber, 3 mg. cholesterol, 207 mg. sodium.

TOMATO ORANGE MUFFINS

*Y*ou might never have considered using tomatoes in muffins, but they complement the flavor of the orange juice and rind. You'll need approximately 1 medium tomato. For best results, seed it before finely chopping it: Cut the tomato in half crosswise and gently squeeze the halves to remove the seeds and some of the excess juice.

1	*cup unbleached flour*
½	*cup whole-wheat flour*
1	*tablespoon baking powder*
1	*cup nonfat yogurt*
⅓	*cup honey*
⅓	*cup fat-free egg substitute*
¼	*cup orange juice*
2	*tablespoons canola oil*
2	*tablespoons grated orange rind*
½	*cup diced tomatoes*
½	*cup oat bran*

Coat 12 muffin cups with no-stick spray.

In a large bowl, mix the unbleached flour, whole-wheat flour and baking powder.

In a medium bowl, whisk together the yogurt, honey, eggs, orange juice, oil and orange rind. Stir in the tomatoes and oat bran. Pour over the flour mixture and stir until just combined; do not overmix (some lumps are acceptable).

Spoon the batter into the prepared muffin cups, filling them about two-thirds. Bake at 375° for 22 to 25 minutes, or until golden brown.

Preparation time: 10 minutes
Baking time: 25 minutes

Per muffin: 126 calories, 2.8 g. fat (18% of calories), 1.5 g. dietary fiber, no cholesterol, 107 mg. sodium.

DATE AND GINGER PANCAKES

SERVES 4

These pancakes are perfect for busy mornings because you can whip them up quickly.

1	cup unbleached flour
¾	cup whole-wheat flour
1	tablespoon baking powder
1½	cups buttermilk
⅓	cup chopped dates
1	teaspoon minced fresh ginger
¾	cup fat-free egg substitute
¼	cup honey
2	tablespoons canola oil
	About 1 cup skim milk

In a large bowl, mix the unbleached flour, whole-wheat flour and baking powder.

Place the buttermilk, dates and ginger in a blender. Process for 20 seconds to finely chop the dates. Add the eggs, honey and oil. Mix briefly to blend.

Pour the buttermilk mixture over the flour mixture. Mix. Add enough of the skim milk to make a pourable batter that's a little thicker than heavy cream.

Coat a griddle or large no-stick frying pan with no-stick spray. Heat over medium heat. Ladle in the batter, using about 2 tablespoons per pancake. Cook until lightly browned on both sides.

Preparation time: 5 minutes
Cooking time: 20 minutes

Chef's note: For variety, you may turn these pancakes into waffles. Omit the skim milk. Preheat a waffle iron and prepare the waffles according to the manufacturer's directions.

Per serving: 388 calories, 8.1 g. fat (18% of calories), 4.8 g. dietary fiber, 2 mg. cholesterol, 374 mg. sodium.

FAST FRUIT SAUCES

*P*ancakes, French toast and waffles don't *need* butter to make them delicious. Syrup or plain chopped fruit makes a wonderful fat-free topping that enhances the flavor of your breakfast treat. For something just a little more elaborate, try one of these easy sauces.

STRAWBERRY SAUCE

MAKES ABOUT 3 CUPS

3	*cups chopped strawberries*
½	*cup water*
2	*tablespoons maple syrup*
2	*teaspoons lemon juice*

Place 2 cups strawberries in a blender. Add the water, maple syrup and lemon juice. Blend until pureed. Transfer to a bowl and stir in the remaining 1 cup strawberries.

Preparation time: 5 minutes

Per ½ cup: 39 calories, 0.3 g. fat (7% of calories), 1.9 g. dietary fiber, no cholesterol, 2 mg. sodium.

PINEAPPLE SAUCE

MAKES ABOUT 2½ CUPS

1	*can (15¼ ounces) pineapple tidbits packed in juice*
¼	*cup honey*
2	*tablespoons orange juice*
1	*teaspoon grated orange rind*
½	*cup water*
1	*tablespoon cornstarch*

Drain the pineapple and place the juice in a 2-quart saucepan. Set the pineapple aside.

Add the honey, orange juice and orange rind to the pan. Bring to a boil over medium heat.

In a cup, mix the water and cornstarch. Pour into the pan. Cook, stirring, for 2 minutes, or until the sauce thickens. Stir in the pineapple.

Preparation time: 5 minutes
Cooking time: 5 minutes

Per ½ cup: 113 calories, <0.1 g. fat (1% of calories), 0.8 g. dietary fiber, no cholesterol, 2 mg. sodium.

MIXED BERRY SAUCE

MAKES ABOUT 2 ½ CUPS

3	tablespoons maple syrup
1	tablespoon lime juice
1	teaspoon grated lime rind
1	cup blueberries
1	cup red raspberries
½	cup black raspberries

In a large bowl, mix the maple syrup, lime juice and lime rind. Stir in the blueberries, red raspberries and black raspberries.

Preparation time: 5 minutes

Per ½ cup: 65 calories, 0.3 g. fat (4% of calories), 2.3 g. dietary fiber, no cholesterol, 3 mg. sodium.

(continued)

CINNAMON PEACH SAUCE

¼ cup honey
¼ teaspoon ground cinnamon
1 teaspoon lemon juice
¼ teaspoon almond extract
2 cups peeled and chopped peaches

In a large bowl, mix the honey and cinnamon. Microwave on high for 1 minute, or until the honey has liquefied and the aroma of the cinnamon has intensified. Stir in the lemon juice and almond extract. Add the peaches and stir to coat.

Preparation time: 10 minutes
Cooking time: 1 minute

Per ½ cup: 103 calories, <0.1 g. fat (1% of calories), 1.4 g. dietary fiber, no cholesterol, 1 mg. sodium.

ORANGE AND BLUEBERRY SAUCE

MAKES ABOUT 2½ CUPS

1 cup orange juice
3 tablespoons maple syrup
1 tablespoon cornstarch
1 teaspoon grated fresh ginger
2 cups chopped orange segments
¼ cup blueberries

In a 2-quart saucepan, combine the orange juice, maple syrup, cornstarch and ginger. Bring to a boil over medium heat, stirring constantly. Cook, stirring, for 2 minutes, or until the sauce thickens. Stir in the oranges and blueberries.

Preparation time: 10 minutes
Cooking time: 5 minutes

Per ½ cup: 98 calories, 0.2 g. fat (2% of calories), 2 g. dietary fiber, no cholesterol, 2 mg. sodium.

CINNAMON-SCENTED FRENCH TOAST

SERVES 4

*F*rench toast is always popular. Some recipes call for soaking the bread overnight, but it's not necessary in this version. The use of egg substitute cuts out all the cholesterol you'd get from using whole eggs.

¾	*cup skim milk*
¾	*cup fat-free egg substitute*
1	*teaspoon canola oil*
½	*teaspoon vanilla*
¼	*teaspoon ground cinnamon*
8	*slices oat-bran bread*

In a 9" × 13" baking dish, mix the milk, eggs, oil, vanilla and cinnamon. Add the bread in a single layer. Turn the pieces to expose both sides to the mixture.

Coat a griddle or large no-stick frying pan with no-stick spray. Place over medium heat until hot. Transfer the bread slices to the pan, working in batches if necessary. Brown on both sides.

Preparation time: 5 minutes
Cooking time: 10 minutes

Per serving: 218 calories, 3.2 g. fat (13% of calories), 5.1 g. dietary fiber, 1 mg. cholesterol, 280 mg. sodium.

GOLDEN RAISIN AND APRICOT SKILLET CAKE

Skillet cakes are easy to prepare and are good for breakfast, brunch or a coffee break.

½	cup skim milk
½	cup nonfat yogurt
½	cup fat-free egg substitute
¼	cup honey
1	cup unbleached flour
½	cup oat bran
2	teaspoons baking powder
½	teaspoon baking soda
⅓	cup golden raisins
⅓	cup chopped dried apricots
2	tablespoons chopped walnuts

In a small bowl, mix the milk, yogurt, eggs and honey.

In a large bowl, mix the flour, oat bran, baking powder and baking soda. Stir in the raisins and apricots.

Place a 9" cast-iron frying pan over low heat and warm for 3 minutes. Lightly coat the pan with no-stick spray.

While the pan is heating, pour the milk mixture over the flour mixture. Stir gently until just blended. Pour into the prepared pan. Scatter the walnuts on the top.

Bake at 375° for 20 to 25 minutes, or until a cake tester inserted in the middle comes out clean.

Preparation time: 10 minutes
Baking time: 25 minutes

Per wedge: 213 calories, 2.4 g. fat (10% of calories), 2.1 g. dietary fiber, 1 mg. cholesterol, 233 mg. sodium.

TURKEY SAUSAGE AND SAGE SKILLET CAKE

MAKES 6 WEDGES

*S*age gives an especially nice flavor to this breadlike breakfast entrée.

1	cup buttermilk
1/2	cup fat-free egg substitute
1/4	cup maple syrup
6	ounces cooked turkey sausage, diced
3–4	tablespoons chopped fresh sage
1	cup unbleached flour
1/4	cup bran
2	teaspoons baking powder
1/2	teaspoon baking soda
6	large fresh sage leaves
1/4	teaspoon ground black pepper

In a medium bowl, mix the buttermilk, eggs and maple syrup. Stir in the turkey and chopped sage.

In a large bowl, mix the flour, bran, baking powder and baking soda.

Place a 9" cast-iron frying pan over low heat and warm for 3 minutes. Lightly coat the pan with no-stick spray.

While the pan is heating, pour the buttermilk mixture over the flour mixture. Mix gently to moisten all the flour. Pour the batter into the prepared pan. Arrange the sage leaves in a decorative pattern on top and press them into place. Sprinkle with the pepper.

Bake at 375° for 20 to 25 minutes, or until a cake tester inserted in the middle comes out clean.

Preparation time: 10 minutes
Baking time: 25 minutes

Per serving: 179 calories, 3.7 g. fat (19% of calories), 1.3 g. dietary fiber, 21 mg. cholesterol, 533 mg. sodium.

LEMON POPPY SCONES

*T*hese light and fluffy pastries make a guilt-free, elegant treat that you can serve anytime. They won a prize for Roxanne Chan of Albany, California, in *Prevention*'s second healthy-recipe contest. Cake flour, which contains little gluten, helps make these scones tender.

½ cup currants

2 tablespoons boiling water

1¼ cups unbleached flour

1¼ cups cake flour

2 tablespoons poppy seeds

2 teaspoons baking powder

1 teaspoon baking soda

1 teaspoon grated lemon rind

½ teaspoon ground cinnamon

¼ cup margarine

1 cup low-fat lemon yogurt

2 egg whites, lightly beaten

In a small bowl, combine the currants and water. Let stand while you prepare the other ingredients.

In a large bowl, mix the unbleached flour, cake flour, poppy seeds, baking powder, baking soda, lemon rind and cinnamon.

Using a pastry blender, cut the margarine into the flour until the mixture resembles coarse crumbs.

Stir in the yogurt, egg whites and the currants and water. Mix well; the dough will be sticky and soft.

On a floured surface, roll the dough out to ½" thickness. Cut into rounds using a 2½" cutter. Gather up the scraps and reroll; cut more scones to use all the dough.

Coat a baking sheet with no-stick spray. Place the scones on the sheet, leaving about ½" between them. Bake at 425° for 10 minutes, or until lightly browned.

Per scone: 100 calories, 2.3 g. fat (21% of calories), 0.5 g. dietary fiber, <1 mg. cholesterol, 111 mg. sodium.

FIG BREAKFAST PUDDING

SERVES 4

*F*resh figs are plentiful in Mediterranean countries and figure prominently in this custardlike breakfast dish. If they're unavailable, substitute cherries, apricots, strawberries, peaches, pineapple or other soft fruit.

½	*cup toasted wheat germ*
1	*cup nonfat vanilla yogurt*
1	*cup fat-free egg substitute*
¼	*cup honey*
¼	*cup unbleached flour*
¼	*teaspoon grated nutmeg*
2	*cups quartered figs*

Lightly coat a 1½-quart straight-sided casserole or baking dish with no-stick spray. Dust with ¼ cup of the wheat germ to coat the interior evenly.

In a medium bowl, whisk the yogurt briefly until smooth. Add the eggs, honey, flour, nutmeg and the remaining ¼ cup wheat germ. Mix well.

Place the figs in the bottom of the dish. Add the batter. Place on the top shelf of the oven. Bake at 400° for 30 to 35 minutes, or until the top is golden brown and a cake tester inserted in the middle comes out clean. Serve warm or cold.

Preparation time: 5 minutes
Baking time: 35 minutes

Per serving: 320 calories, 2.2 g. fat (5% of calories), 7.3 g. dietary fiber, 1 mg. cholesterol, 130 mg. sodium.

MINI RAISIN SODA BREADS

MAKES 8

*I*ndividual small soda breads take much less time to bake than a large bread.

1¼	cups unbleached flour
1	cup whole-wheat flour
1½	teaspoons baking powder
¼	teaspoon baking soda
½	cup currants
½	cup buttermilk
½	cup thawed orange juice concentrate
2	tablespoons canola oil

In a large bowl, mix the unbleached flour, whole-wheat flour, baking powder and baking soda. Stir in the currants.

In a small bowl, mix the buttermilk, juice concentrate and oil. Pour over the flour mixture and mix to get a stiff dough.

Turn the dough out onto a lightly floured surface. With floured hands, knead for about 30 seconds to combine the ingredients well. If necessary, add a bit more flour to keep the dough from sticking to your hands.

Divide the dough into 8 equal pieces. Form the pieces into slightly flattened balls about 2" in diameter. Using a sharp knife, cut an × about ¼" deep in the top of each.

Coat a baking sheet with no-stick spray. Transfer the wedges to the sheet, leaving at least 1" between them. Bake at 375° for 15 to 20 minutes, or until golden brown.

Preparation time: 20 minutes
Baking time: 20 minutes

Chef's note: For variety, cut the dough into wedges. Pat the dough into an 8" circle. With a sharp knife, cut it into 8 wedges. Bake for the same amount of time as the round breads.

Per bread: 184 calories, 4.1 g. fat (20% of calories), 2.5 g. dietary fiber, 1 mg. cholesterol, 105 mg. sodium.

HERBED RICE BREAD

MAKES 9 SQUARES

*L*ow in fat and flavored with mixed herbs and a dusting of Parmesan, this unique bread is a real delight. It garnered a prize for its creator, Virginia Moon of Harvest, Alabama, in *Prevention*'s Cooking for Health recipe contest. The bread goes particularly well with chili and other spicy entrées.

1	cup cold cooked white rice
1	tablespoon olive oil
1	cup cornmeal
1	tablespoon grated Parmesan cheese
1	teaspoon baking powder
1	teaspoon onion powder
½	teaspoon garlic powder
½	teaspoon dried mixed herbs
1	cup skim milk
¼	cup fat-free egg substitute
¼	cup nonfat sour cream

Coat an 8" × 8" baking dish with no-stick spray.

In a small bowl, mix the rice and oil. Use a fork or potato masher to lightly mash the rice.

In another small bowl, mix the cornmeal, Parmesan, baking powder, onion powder, garlic powder and herbs.

In a large bowl, whisk together the milk, egg and sour cream. Add the cornmeal mixture and stir to combine. Fold in the rice.

Transfer the batter to the prepared baking dish. Bake at 400° for 30 minutes, or until a cake tester inserted in the center comes out clean.

Preparation time: 10 minutes
Baking time: 30 minutes

Per square: 113 calories, 1.2 g. fat (10% of calories), 1 g. dietary fiber, 1 mg. cholesterol, 92 mg. sodium.

Herb Dinner Rolls

nder ordinary circumstances, yeast rolls and breads take quite a while to prepare. You can cut that time considerably by using quick-rising yeast along with your food processor and microwave. This recipe calls for white-wheat flour. It's a whole-grain product made from a strain of wheat known as white wheat. It's particularly nice to bake with because it has the light color and texture of unbleached flour but the nutritional benefits—including fiber—of whole-wheat. Look for it in supermarkets or contact the manufacturer, King Arthur Flour (P.O. Box 876, Norwich, VT 05055). You can use white-wheat flour in most any baked goods.

½   *cup water*
½   *cup plus 1 tablespoon skim milk*
1   *package quick-rising active dry yeast*
1   *tablespoon olive oil*
1   *teaspoon honey*
1   *cup white-wheat or whole-wheat flour*
½   *teaspoon dried thyme*
½   *teaspoon salt*
¼   *teaspoon dried marjoram*
¼   *teaspoon dried oregano*
¼   *teaspoon ground black pepper*
    About 1¼ cups unbleached flour

In a small glass bowl, combine the water and ½ cup of the milk. Microwave on high for 30 seconds, or until lukewarm. Mix in the yeast, oil and honey. Let stand for 5 minutes, or until the yeast has started to foam.

In a food processor, combine the white-wheat or whole-wheat flour, thyme, salt, marjoram, oregano, pepper and 1¼ cups unbleached flour. Process briefly to mix well. With the machine running, pour in the yeast mixture through the feed tube. Process for about 1 minute, or until the mixture forms itself into a ball of dough that sits on top of the blade.

Turn the dough out onto a lightly floured surface. Knead for 5 minutes (adding a little more flour if necessary to keep the dough from sticking) until the dough is smooth.

Coat a large glass bowl with no-stick spray. Add the ball of dough. Lightly mist the top of the dough with no-stick spray. Cover with vented plastic wrap or a damp tea towel. Microwave on *low power (10%)* for 5 minutes. (Do not use a higher power; the heat might kill the yeast.)

Give the bowl a quarter turn. Microwave on low for another 5 minutes. If the dough has not doubled in bulk, microwave on low for another 5 minutes.

Punch it down, place on a lightly floured surface and knead for 1 minute. Form into a rope about 18" long; cut into 12 equal pieces. Form each piece into a ball.

Coat a large baking sheet with no-stick spray. Place the balls on the sheet, leaving about 2" between them. Cover with a sheet of plastic wrap and set in a warm, draft-free place for 15 minutes, or until the balls have doubled in bulk. Remove the plastic and lightly brush the balls with the remaining 1 tablespoon milk.

Bake at 400° for 15 to 20 minutes, or until the rolls are lightly browned and sound hollow when tapped.

Preparation time: 20 minutes plus rising time
Baking time: 20 minutes

Chef's note: For variety, you may form the dough into different shapes. To make *coils*, form each ball into a 12" rope; wind into a coil shape. To make *knots*, form each ball into an 8" rope; loosely tie it into a knot. To make *braids*, divide each ball into thirds and form each third into a 6" rope; braid the pieces together. To make *clover rolls*, divide each ball into thirds and form each piece into a small ball; group the balls together to form a clover. To make *Vienna loaves*, form each ball into a small elongated loaf about 3" long; use a sharp knife to make 3 diagonal slashes ¼" deep in the top. To make *cottage loaves*, divide each ball into 2 pieces, with 1 twice the size of the other, and stack the small piece on top of the larger one; flour your finger and press it straight down through both pieces to form a small hole in the center.

Per roll: 99 calories, 1.5 g. fat (13% of calories), 1.8 g. dietary fiber, no cholesterol, 96 mg. sodium.

Basic Cornbread

MAKES 9 SQUARES

When you need a very quick cornbread to accompany your meal, this version is the one you should turn to. Although most types of cornbread *are* easy to prepare, this one requires no chopping or precooking of any ingredients.

1	cup unbleached flour
1	cup cornmeal
1	tablespoon baking powder
½	teaspoon dried thyme
½	teaspoon onion flakes
½	teaspoon ground black pepper
1	cup skim milk
¼	cup fat-free egg substitute
2	tablespoons olive oil

Coat an 8" × 8" baking pan with no-stick spray.

In a large bowl, mix the flour, cornmeal, baking powder, thyme, onion flakes and pepper.

In a small bowl, mix the milk, egg and oil. Pour over the flour mixture. Mix with a rubber spatula until the dry ingredients are moistened; do not overmix.

Spread in the prepared pan. Bake at 400° for 20 minutes, or until a cake tester inserted in the middle comes out clean.

Preparation time: 5 minutes
Cooking time: 20 minutes

Per square: 137 calories, 3.7 g. fat (24% of calories), 2.5 g. dietary fiber, <1 mg. cholesterol, 135 mg. sodium.

SPICY CORNBREAD

This version of cornbread incorporates flavors from the American Southwest, but it complements all sorts of Mediterranean entrées, including grilled fish and poultry dishes. For extra spiciness, mix some minced jalapeño peppers into the batter.

1	cup unbleached flour
¾	cup cornmeal
2	teaspoons baking powder
1	teaspoon chili powder
½	teaspoon dried oregano
1	cup corn
2	scallions, minced
1	cup 1% low-fat milk
½	cup fat-free egg substitute
2	tablespoons honey
1	tablespoon olive oil

Coat an 8" × 8" baking pan with no-stick spray.

In a large bowl, mix the flour, cornmeal, baking powder, chili powder and oregano. Stir in the corn and scallions.

In a medium bowl, whisk together the milk, eggs, honey and oil. Pour over the flour mixture. Mix with a rubber spatula until the dry ingredients are moistened; do not overmix.

Spread in the prepared pan. Bake at 350° for 25 minutes, or until a cake tester inserted in the middle comes out clean.

Preparation time: 10 minutes
Baking time: 25 minutes

Per serving: 145 calories, 2.5 g. fat (15% of calories), 2.1 g. dietary fiber, 1 mg. cholesterol, 129 mg. sodium.

OLIVE FOCACCIA

MAKES 8 WEDGES

*ocaccia is a type of Italian flatbread. Unlike pizza, the flavoring ingredients are mixed right in with the dough. This version is quick to make because the microwave cuts down on the amount of time needed for the dough to rise.

¾	*cup water*
1	*package quick-rising active dry yeast*
1	*teaspoon honey*
2	*tablespoons olive oil*
10	*large black olives, pitted and halved lengthwise*
1	*cup white-wheat or whole-wheat flour*
2–3	*tablespoons minced fresh rosemary*
½	*teaspoon ground black pepper*
½	*teaspoon salt*
1¼–1½	*cups unbleached flour*

Place the water in a small glass bowl. Microwave on high for 30 seconds, or until lukewarm. Mix in the yeast, honey and 1½ tablespoons oil. Let stand for 5 minutes, or until the yeast has started to foam.

Pat the olives dry with paper towels. Coarsely chop.

Place the white-wheat or whole-wheat flour, rosemary, pepper, salt and 1¼ cups unbleached flour in a food processor. Process briefly to mix well. Sprinkle with the olives and process briefly to mix them in.

With the machine running, pour in the yeast mixture through the feed tube. Process until the mixture forms itself into a ball of dough that sits on top of the blade. (If necessary, sprinkle the dough with a little of the remaining unbleached flour to make it form a ball.)

Turn the dough out onto a lightly floured surface. Knead for a minute or so, or until the dough is smooth and not sticky; as you knead, incorporate as much of the remaining unbleached flour as needed to keep the dough from sticking.

Coat a large glass bowl with no-stick spray. Add the ball of dough. Lightly mist the top of the dough with no-stick spray. Cover with vented plastic wrap or a damp tea towel. Microwave on *low power (10%)* for 5 minutes. (Do not use a higher power; the heat might kill the yeast.)

Give the bowl a quarter turn. Microwave on low for another 5 minutes. If the dough has not doubled in bulk, microwave on low for another 5 minutes.

Punch down the dough, place it on a lightly floured surface and knead briefly.

Coat a large baking sheet with no-stick spray. Pat the dough into a 10" circle on the sheet. Make random indentations in the surface with your finger. Drizzle with the remaining ½ tablespoon olive oil.

Bake at 425° for 15 to 20 minutes, or until lightly browned and puffed. Remove from the oven and check the underside of the focaccia. If it is still fairly soft, slide it from the baking sheet directly onto the oven rack and let bake for an additional 1 or 2 minutes to crisp it.

Preparation time: 20 minutes plus rising time
Baking time: 20 minutes

Per wedge: 152 calories, 4.8 g. fat (27% of calories), 2.7 g. dietary fiber, no cholesterol, 159 mg. sodium.

CHAPTER 11

FRESH
IDEAS FOR
GRAND
FINALES

JOYFUL DESSERTS

f dessert is your favorite part of the meal, rejoice. You need not forgo it—even if you're committed to the low-fat lifestyle. Do as they do in the Mediterranean: Make succulent, vine-ripe fruit your first choice. You'll be amazed by how satisfying fresh seasonal fruit can be. But if you simply must have a more traditional sweet, incorporate the fruit into your dessert and have the best of both worlds. Fruit-based crisps, mousses, parfaits and pies taste terrific, and they have lots of health-building fiber. Best of all, they can still appease your sweet tooth even though they're low in fat.

CREAMY APRICOT MOUSSE

*N*onfat yogurt cheese is a godsend for the health-minded cook. It has the creamy texture of regular cream cheese and sour cream but none of their fat. And it's so easy to make using a yogurt cheese funnel or a strainer lined with cheesecloth. Be sure to use yogurt that doesn't contain gelatin or other binders that would deter drainage. If you don't have a special yogurt funnel, improvise by lining a colander or sieve with cheesecloth or a paper coffee filter.

1   *cup nonfat plain yogurt*
1   *cup nonfat vanilla yogurt*
1   *can (16 ounces) apricots packed in juice*
1   *envelope unflavored gelatin*
¼   *teaspoon almond extract*

Spoon the plain yogurt and vanilla yogurt into a yogurt cheese funnel. Set over a mug or tall drinking glass. Cover with a piece of plastic, refrigerate and allow to drain for 30 minutes.

Drain the apricots, reserving the juice. Set aside the apricots.

Measure the juice and, if needed, add enough water to equal 1 cup. Transfer to a 1-quart saucepan and sprinkle the gelatin over top. Let soften for 5 minutes.

Bring to a boil over medium-high heat, stirring well to dissolve the gelatin. Remove from the heat. Let cool for 5 minutes.

In a blender, puree the apricots, almond extract and gelatin mixture.

Place the yogurt cheese in a large bowl. Gradually whisk in the puree. Pour into individual dessert dishes. Refrigerate until firm, about 1 hour.

Preparation time: 35 minutes plus chilling time
Cooking time: 2 minutes

Per serving: 139 calories, 0.1 g. fat (1% of calories), 1.3 g. dietary fiber, 2 mg. cholesterol, 85 mg. sodium.

Poached Pears with Raspberry Yogurt Sauce

*P*ears are particularly good when poached. Serve them chilled or at room temperature, accompanied by the refreshing mint and raspberry sauce that follows. This recipe was created by Dallas chef Victor Gielisse for a program the American Cancer Society calls its Great American Food Fight against Cancer.

> 3   *cups nonalcoholic white wine or white grape juice*
>
> 1   *cup water*
>
> 1   *cup orange juice*
>
> 1   *tablespoon grated lemon rind*
>
> 1   *tablespoon grated orange rind*
>
> 1   *cinnamon stick*
>
> 3   *whole cloves*
>
> 2   *teaspoons vanilla*
>
> 6   *Comice or Bosc pears, peeled and cored from the bottom*
>
> 1   *pint raspberries*
>
> 3   *tablespoons nonfat yogurt*
>
> 1   *teaspoon chopped fresh mint*

In a large frying pan, combine the wine or grape juice, water, orange juice, lemon rind, orange rind, cinnamon, cloves and vanilla. Bring to a boil over high heat. Reduce the heat to medium and add the pears, submerging them as much as possible.

Cover and simmer for 20 minutes, or until the pears are tender when tested with a sharp knife. Do not overcook. Remove from the liquid and set aside to cool. If desired, chill the pears.

Bring the cooking liquid to a boil over high heat and cook for 10 minutes, or until reduced to ½ cup. Strain into a small bowl. Set in the freezer for 10 minutes to cool.

In a blender or food processor, puree the raspberries with the poaching liquid. Add the yogurt and mint. Process until well blended. Serve with the pears.

Preparation time: 20 minutes plus chilling time
Cooking time: 25 minutes

Per serving: 234 calories, 1 g. fat (4% of calories), 5.8 g. dietary fiber, <1 mg. cholesterol, 13 mg. sodium.

APRICOT, FIG AND YOGURT SWIRL

SERVES 6

*H*ere's an easy dessert for midwinter, when fresh fruit is often scarce.

2   cups nonfat vanilla yogurt
12 ounces dried apricots
4   ounces dried figs, halved
2   cups water
1   teaspoon vanilla extract
1   star anise pod
1   cinnamon stick

Spoon the yogurt into a yogurt cheese funnel. Set over a mug or tall drinking glass. Cover with a piece of plastic, refrigerate and allow to drain for 30 minutes.

Meanwhile, in a 2-quart saucepan, combine the apricots, figs, water, vanilla, star anise and cinnamon. Bring to a simmer over medium heat and cook for 30 minutes, or until the fruit is very soft.

Remove and discard the spices. Spoon the fruit (with a little of its poaching liquid) and yogurt into individual dessert dishes or parfait glasses.

Preparation time: 5 minutes
Cooking time: 30 minutes

Per serving: 235 calories, 0.7 g. fat (3% of calories), 6.1 g. dietary fiber, 1 mg. cholesterol, 68 mg. sodium.

Slim Pickin's

*W*hen it comes to quick and healthy low-fat desserts, nothing fits the bill as conveniently as fresh fruit. It's naturally sweet, full of fiber and free of fat. All you have to do is peel (maybe) and eat.

Fruit harvested in season and eaten at the peak of its flavor is the most satisfying. It doesn't require any embellishments to gratify your sweet tooth. Here are some tips for choosing the freshest, most succulent fruits.

Apples. Look for smooth, unblemished skins with no signs of bruises.

Apricots. A ripe apricot is gold all over and free of wrinkles. Some varieties have a red blush. If still firm, let soften at room temperature for a day.

Bananas. Don't let green skins deter you; bananas continue to ripen after being picked. Let stand at room temperature until the skin has turned yellow, with perhaps a few brown spots.

Blackberries. Make sure the berries have a deep purplish-black to black color and no signs of being bruised.

Blueberries. Look for dry berries with a dusty, frosty coating.

Cantaloupes. Choose those with a golden glow and sweet fragrance.

Cherries. Pick clean, dry cherries with a green (not dark) stem. Sticky fruit is overripe and probably brown inside.

Figs. Look for good color for the variety, whether it's black, greenish-yellow or yellow. The delicate flesh should be just firm to the touch and the fruit should look plump, not wrinkled.

Grapes. Make sure the grapes are plump, with no mold, soft spots or bruises. A frosty white coating is an indication of freshness.

Honeydew melons. The skin should be ivory gold and slightly sticky to the touch. Look for a sweet fragrance. The skin should give slightly when pressed.

Kiwifruit. Pick fruit that's firm but yields to gentle

pressure and has no signs of bruises. Let ripen further at room temperature.

Mangoes. The skin may vary in color from green to yellow and be tinged with red. There should be a fruity smell, and the flesh should feel firm when pressed gently. Allow to ripen at room temperature for several days.

Nectarines. Fragrance is essential. Look for those with tight, moist skin.

Papayas. Select fruit that is at least half yellow, with smooth skin and no blemishes. The flesh should feel a little soft when gently pressed.

Peaches. The fruit should be firm with an even yellow or creamy background color. (A red blush doesn't necessarily indicate sweetness.) Let soften at home for a day or two.

Pears. Look for fruit that has no bruises or cuts. It's okay to buy fruit that's quite firm; it will soften if allowed to ripen further at room temperature.

Persimmons. Choose fruit with a brilliant orange color, smooth skin and a green cap. The larger, acorn-shaped fruit (Hachiya) should be soft or it will be inedible. The smaller, rounded variety (fuyu) can be firm and will have a crisp, applelike texture.

Pineapple. The fruit should have a plump shape. The stem end should smell sweet but not heavy or fermented. A golden color is preferable to green. Avoid pineapples with dried-out, brownish leaves.

Plums. Look for those with a dull, matte skin. Unripe plums are shiny.

Raspberries. Look for uniform color, whether it's red, black or yellow. Avoid stained containers, which indicate some of the fruit has been crushed.

Strawberries. Look for all-over red color; avoid those with white shoulders. Fresh, green caps and a sweet fragrance are good signs.

Watermelons. You cannot really tell a ripe watermelon without cutting into it. No amount of thumping can guarantee sweetness. Ask if the seller will cut a plug out so you can see that the flesh is bright red.

STRAWBERRY FLUFF DESSERTS

SERVES 6

*U*sing frozen strawberries helps the gelatin in this dessert set quickly. This is similar to a dessert created by Jean Holmes of Emmaus, Pennsylvania, and served at her Lavender 'n' Lace Tea Room.

¼ cup cold water

1 teaspoon unflavored gelatin

1 package (0.3 ounce) sugar-free strawberry gelatin

1 cup boiling water

3 cups frozen strawberries, thawed for 5 minutes

½ cup nonfat vanilla yogurt

½ cup nonfat sour cream

1 cup blueberries

Place the cold water in a cup. Sprinkle with the unflavored gelatin and set aside for 5 minutes to soften.

Place the strawberry gelatin in a medium heatproof bowl. Stir in the boiling water and mix well to dissolve the gelatin. Stir in the softened unflavored gelatin.

Place the strawberries in a blender. Pour in the gelatin mixture. Blend until the berries are coarsely chopped. Pour the mixture into a large bowl. Whisk in the yogurt and sour cream. Fold in the blueberries.

Divide among individual serving dishes or parfait glasses. Chill for 20 minutes, or until set.

Preparation time: 15 minutes plus chilling time

Per serving: 177 calories, 0.3 g. fat (1% of calories), 10.5 g. dietary fiber, no cholesterol, 85 mg. sodium.

PUMPKIN PIE

This version of pumpkin pie is much lower in fat and cholesterol than standard versions.

½	*cup gingersnap crumbs*
½	*cup graham cracker crumbs*
2	*tablespoons extra-light margarine, melted*
1	*cup canned mashed pumpkin*
1	*cup fat-free egg substitute*
1	*cup evaporated skim milk*
⅓	*cup honey*
½	*teaspoon ground cinnamon*
½	*teaspoon powdered ginger*
⅛	*teaspoon grated nutmeg*
⅛	*teaspoon ground allspice*

In a medium bowl, mix the gingersnap crumbs and graham cracker crumbs. Add the margarine and mix well.

Coat a 9" pie plate with no-stick spray. Add the crumb mixture and press it evenly into the pan. Bake at 350° for 7 minutes.

While the crust is baking, in a large bowl, whisk together the pumpkin, eggs, milk, honey, cinnamon, ginger, nutmeg and allspice. Pour into the crust.

Bake for 40 minutes, or until the center of the filling doesn't jiggle when you gently shake the pan. Allow to cool before cutting.

Preparation time: 15 minutes plus cooling time
Baking time: 50 minutes

Per serving: 194 calories, 2.9 g. fat (13% of calories), 0.9 g. dietary fiber, 1 mg. cholesterol, 191 mg. sodium.

ORANGES SUPREME

When you want a light but festive-looking dessert, serve these oranges. The pomegranate seeds make them especially beautiful for a holiday table.

4	*navel oranges*
2	*cups water*
3	*tablespoons honey*
1	*teaspoon vanilla*
¼	*teaspoon ground coriander*
3	*whole cloves*
1	*cup pomegranate seeds*

Using a vegetable peeler, remove the colored part of each orange rind (do not include any underlying white pith). Cut the rind into very thin slivers and set aside.

Using a very sharp knife, remove all the white pith from the oranges and discard it. Transfer the oranges to a large bowl, cover with plastic wrap and refrigerate until needed.

In a 1-quart saucepan, combine the water and honey. Bring to a boil over medium-high heat. Stir in the vanilla, coriander, cloves and reserved orange rind. Cook for 10 minutes, or until the mixture has reduced by half. Remove and discard the cloves.

Pour the syrup over the oranges and stir them gently to coat them well. Refrigerate for at least 30 minutes. Serve sprinkled with the pomegranate seeds.

Preparation time: 20 minutes plus chilling time
Cooking time: 10 minutes

Per serving: 86 calories, 0.2 g. fat (2% of calories), 5.2 g. dietary fiber, no cholesterol, 2 mg. sodium.

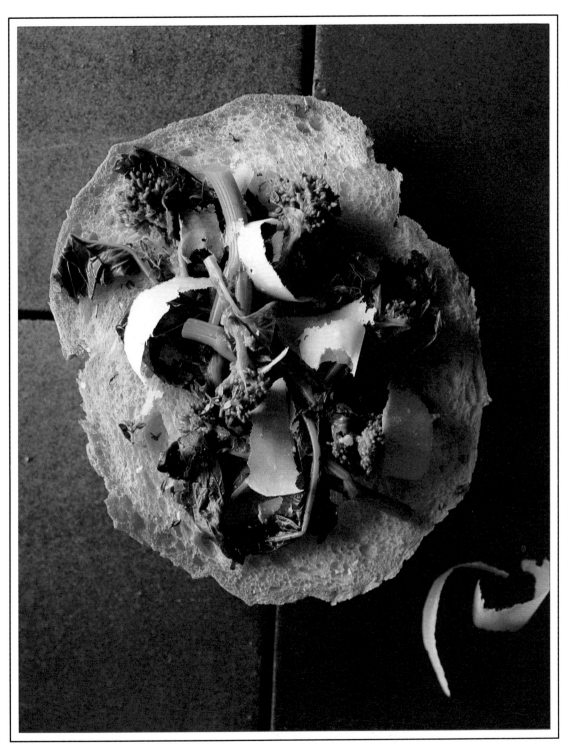

Balsamic Broccoli Rabe (page 227)

273

Mini Raisin Soda Breads (page 256)

Sweet Potato Waffles (page 245)

Turkey Sausage and Sage Skillet Cake (page 253)

Oranges Supreme (page 272)

Apricot, Fig and Yogurt Swirl (page 267)

278

Christmas Fruitcake (page 286)

Poached Pears with Raspberry Yogurt Sauce (page 266)

PATRIOTIC PARFAITS

SERVES 6

Y ou needn't wait for a national holiday to enjoy these easy parfaits. Although the fruits called for here are in season around the Fourth of July, you can substitute others at different times of the year. You can even use thawed unsweetened fruit in the dead of winter.

½ cup honey
3 tablespoons cornstarch
2 cups 1% low-fat milk
½ cup fat-free egg substitute
1 teaspoon vanilla
1½ cups blueberries
1½ cups red raspberries

In a 2-quart saucepan, whisk together the honey and cornstarch. Whisk in the milk. Bring the mixture to a boil over medium heat, stirring constantly. Cook, stirring, until thickened. Remove from the heat.

Place the eggs in a small bowl. Mix in a small amount of the milk mixture to warm the eggs. Whisk this mixture into the pan. Cook, stirring constantly, for 2 minutes. Stir in the vanilla. Allow to cool.

Spoon a layer of the milk mixture into each of 6 parfait glasses. Top with a layer of blueberries. Add another layer of the milk mixture. Top with a layer of raspberries. Repeat the layering to use all the ingredients. Serve immediately or chill.

Preparation time: 10 minutes plus cooling
and chilling time
Cooking time: 5 minutes

Per serving: 212 calories, 0.6 g. fat (2% of calories), 2.7 g. dietary fiber, 3 mg. cholesterol, 127 mg. sodium.

ORIENTAL RICE PUDDING

SERVES 6

*A*dding Chinese spices and dried fruit to rice pudding earned Ellen Burr of Truro, Massachusetts, a prize in *Prevention*'s first annual Cooking for Health recipe contest.

2	*cups water*
1	*cup long-grain white rice*
1	*tablespoon canola oil*
1	*tablespoon grated tangerine or orange rind*
1	*teaspoon five-spice powder*
1	*can (15 ounces) evaporated skim milk*
½	*cup chopped dates*
¼	*cup chopped dried figs*
2	*tablespoons minced crystallized ginger*
2	*tablespoons toasted pine nuts*
	Ground cinnamon

In a 3-quart saucepan, combine the water, rice, oil, tangerine or orange rind and five-spice powder. Bring to a boil over high heat. Cover, reduce the heat to medium and simmer for 20 minutes.

Stir in the milk, dates and figs. Cook, uncovered, over medium-low heat for 15 minutes, or until the mixture is thick and creamy; stir often during this period.

Serve sprinkled with the ginger, pine nuts and cinnamon.

Preparation time: 10 minutes
Cooking time: 35 minutes

Per serving: 113 calories, 4.5 g. fat (14% of calories), 2.4 g. dietary fiber, 3 mg. cholesterol, 87 mg. sodium.

282   JOYFUL DESSERTS

BLACKBERRY CRISP

SERVES 4

hanks to all the tiny seeds they contain, blackberries are loaded with fiber, something many conventional desserts lack. Although they make great out-of-hand eating, blackberries are also delicious in pies and crisps, such as this one.

> 4   cups blackberries
> ½   cup maple syrup
> 2   tablespoons water
> 2   tablespoons cornstarch
> 1   tablespoon lemon juice
> 1   teaspoon vanilla
> ⅔   cup rolled oats
> ½   cup wheat germ

Place the blackberries in a large bowl. Drizzle with ¼ cup maple syrup and toss lightly.

In a cup, mix the water, cornstarch, lemon juice and vanilla. Pour over the blackberries and mix well, being careful not to crush the berries.

Coat a 1½-quart casserole with no-stick spray. Add the berry mixture.

In a small bowl, mix the oats and wheat germ. Drizzle with the remaining ¼ cup maple syrup and toss well to moisten the dry ingredients. Sprinkle over the berries.

Bake at 350° for about 25 minutes, or until the filling is bubbly and thickened.

Preparation time: 10 minutes
Baking time: 25 minutes

Per serving: 298 calories, 2.8 g. fat (8% of calories), 11.1 g. dietary fiber, no cholesterol, 9 mg. sodium.

CHEESECAKE TART

SERVES 8

heesecake needn't be a forbidden pleasure—even when you're on a low-fat diet. This dessert was created by Erin Bause-Landry, a chef and caterer in Pottstown, Pennsylvania. Because the cheesecake needs to chill, you'll want to make it ahead of time.

4	*tablespoons apricot jelly*
2½	*cups graham cracker crumbs*
1	*container (15 ounces) nonfat or low-fat ricotta cheese*
2	*cups nonfat yogurt*
⅓	*cup honey*
3	*tablespoons cornstarch*
2	*tablespoons lime juice*
1	*tablespoon vanilla*
3	*cups sliced fruit*

In a 2-quart saucepan, melt 2 tablespoons jelly. Remove from the heat, add the crumbs and mix well. Lightly oil an 8" pie plate. Press the crumbs into the pan to make a crust.

In a food processor or blender, puree the ricotta until very smooth. Add the yogurt, honey, cornstarch, lime juice and vanilla. Process for about 30 seconds, or until well mixed. Pour the mixture into the prepared pan.

Bake at 350° for 30 to 40 minutes, or until a knife inserted in the center comes out clean. Cool at room temperature for 30 minutes. Refrigerate for at least 3 hours.

Just before serving, melt the remaining 2 tablespoons jelly in a 2-quart saucepan. Remove from the heat. Stir in the fruit and mix well. Top the cheesecake with the fruit.

Preparation time: 15 minutes plus chilling time
Baking time: 40 minutes

Per serving: 287 calories, 2 g. fat (7% of calories), 2.6 g. dietary fiber, 1 mg. cholesterol, 225 mg. sodium.

PEAR AND RASPBERRY CLAFOUTI

SERVES 6

Gloria Bradley of Naperville, Illinois, won a prize for this low-fat, high-fiber dessert in *Prevention*'s healthy-cooking contest. She often serves the clafouti topped with nonfat frozen raspberry yogurt.

1	can (29 ounces) pear halves packed in juice, drained and chopped
¾	cup rolled oats
1	cup skim milk
½	cup fat-free egg substitute
2	tablespoons vanilla
1	tablespoon honey
1	teaspoon grated lemon rind
½	cup raspberries
¼	teaspoon ground cinnamon

Coat a deep-dish 9" pie plate with no-stick spray. Spread the pears in the dish in an even layer.

Place the oats in a blender. Cover and process on high for 1 minute, or until finely chopped. Add the milk, eggs, vanilla, honey and lemon rind. Process until well blended, stopping occasionally to scrape down the sides of the container.

Gently pour the batter over the pears. Sprinkle with the raspberries and cinnamon. Bake at 350° for 35 minutes, or until puffed and cooked through. Cool slightly.

Preparation time: 10 minutes
Baking time: 35 minutes

Per serving: 113 calories, 0.8 g. fat (7% of calories), 2.3 g. dietary fiber, no cholesterol, 50 mg. sodium.

CHRISTMAS FRUITCAKE

f you don't care for standard fruitcakes, you'll probably still like this one.

2	*cups very thinly sliced carrots*
3	*cups unbleached flour*
2	*teaspoons baking soda*
1	*teaspoon baking powder*
½	*teaspoon powdered ginger*
½	*teaspoon grated nutmeg*
1	*cup buttermilk*
½	*cup applesauce*
½	*cup fat-free egg substitute*
⅓	*cup maple syrup*
2	*tablespoons canola oil*
½	*teaspoon almond extract*
⅔	*cup chopped dried apricots*
⅓	*cup chopped dates*
⅓	*cup raisins*

Steam the carrots for 10 minutes, or until very soft.

Meanwhile, in a large bowl, mix the flour, baking soda, baking powder, ginger and nutmeg. Set aside.

Transfer the carrots to a blender. Add the buttermilk and process until the carrots are pureed. Add the applesauce, eggs, maple syrup, oil and almond extract.

Pour the liquid ingredients into the bowl with the flour. Mix well. Fold in the apricots, dates and raisins.

Coat a 6-cup Bundt pan with no-stick spray. Add the batter and smooth the top. Bake at 350° for 35 minutes, or until a cake tester inserted in the center comes out clean. Invert onto a wire rack.

Preparation time: 20 minutes
Cooking time: 10 minutes
Baking time: 35 minutes

Per slice: 139 calories, 1.8 g. fat (12% of calories), 2.5 g. dietary fiber, <1 mg. cholesterol, 119 mg. sodium.

LEMON ICEBOX PIE

SERVES 8

*G*ood old-fashioned flavor prevails in this updated version of a traditional pie. The use of a graham cracker crust in place of a standard pie shell helps cut calories and fat. This recipe was special enough to earn a prize for Virginia Moon of Harvest, Alabama, in *Prevention*'s healthy-cooking contest. Although preparing the pie is easy, you'll want to allow plenty of time for the yogurt in the filling to drain and let the finished pie chill.

1	*cup nonfat plain yogurt*
6	*whole graham crackers*
1	*tablespoon canola oil*
¼	*cup cornstarch*
½	*cup plus 1 tablespoon honey*
2	*cups low-fat vanilla yogurt*
½	*cup fat-free egg substitute*
½	*cup lemon juice*
½	*teaspoon lemon extract*
¼	*teaspoon almond extract*
3	*egg whites*
½	*teaspoon cream of tartar*
1	*teaspoon vanilla*

(continued)

Spoon the plain yogurt into a yogurt cheese funnel. Set over a mug or tall drinking glass. Cover with a piece of plastic, refrigerate and allow to drain for 8 hours or until very thick.

While the yogurt is draining, prepare the crust. Crumble the graham crackers into a food processor. Process with on/off turns to make crumbs. Add the oil and process to combine. Coat a 10" pie plate with no-stick spray. Press the crumbs into the pan to make a crust. Chill until needed.

After the yogurt has drained, in a 2-quart saucepan, whisk together the cornstarch and ½ cup honey. Whisk in the vanilla yogurt and the drained yogurt. Place over medium heat. Cook, stirring constantly, for 5 minutes, or until the mixture comes to a boil and thickens.

Remove from the heat. Very slowly whisk in the eggs. Reduce the heat to low. Cook, stirring constantly, for 2 minutes. Remove from the heat and whisk in the lemon juice, lemon extract and almond extract. Spoon into the prepared crust.

In a medium bowl, beat the egg whites and cream of tartar with an electric mixer at medium speed until foamy. Add the vanilla and the remaining 1 tablespoon honey. Beat at high speed until stiff peaks form. Spread over the pie filling, making sure to leave no gaps where the meringue topping meets the crust.

Bake at 325° for 10 minutes, or until the meringue is golden brown. Chill for several hours before cutting.

Preparation time: 15 minutes plus draining
                    and chilling time
Cooking time: 10 minutes
Baking time: 10 minutes

Per serving: 221 calories, 3.3 g. fat (13% of calories), 0.4 g. dietary fiber, 3 mg. cholesterol, 145 mg. sodium.

APPLE CAKE WITH ORANGE SYRUP

SERVES 10

*F*resh fruits and honey-spiced syrup make this a deliciously moist cake that you'll be proud to serve to company. The cake was special enough to win a prize for Angela Bond of Wilkesboro, North Carolina, in the *Prevention* Cooking for Health recipe contest.

Cake

⅔	cup whole-wheat flour
⅔	cup unbleached flour
½	cup quick-cooking rolled oats
1½	teaspoons baking soda
1	teaspoon ground cinnamon
4	egg whites
⅓	cup honey
¼	cup canola oil
1	teaspoon vanilla
⅓	cup orange juice
¾	cup shredded apples
½	cup cranberries
¼	cup raisins
¼	cup chopped dates

Orange Syrup

½	cup orange juice
⅓	cup honey
½	teaspoon ground cinnamon

To make the cake: In a large bowl, combine the whole-wheat flour, unbleached flour, oats, baking soda and cinnamon.

(continued)

In a medium bowl, whisk together the egg whites and honey. Whisk in the oil and vanilla, then the orange juice. Stir in the apples, cranberries, raisins and dates.

Pour the fruit mixture over the dry ingredients. Fold until the dry ingredients are just moistened; do not overmix.

Coat a 9" × 13" baking dish with no-stick spray. Add the batter and spread evenly. Bake at 350° for 25 minutes, or until browned and firm to the touch. Remove from the oven and place on a wire rack.

To make the syrup: While the cake is baking, in a 1-quart saucepan, combine the orange juice, honey and cinnamon. Bring to a boil over medium heat. Reduce the heat to medium-low and simmer for 10 minutes, or until syrupy. Remove from the heat and set aside until the cake is ready. Pour over the hot cake.

Preparation time: 20 minutes
Cooking time: 10 minutes
Baking time: 25 minutes

Per serving: 235 calories, 6 g. fat (22% of calories), 2.2 g. dietary fiber, no cholesterol, 148 mg. sodium.

E A S Y   M E A L S
F O R   F A M I L Y
A N D   F R I E N D S

*L*OW-FAT MENUS

*I*f you're like most people, your job, family responsibilities

and leisure commitments leave little time for lengthy

meal preparation. But if you're concerned about your family's

health, you aren't willing to settle for a steady diet of high-fat,

high-sodium take-out meals. To show you how to plan

nutritious—but delicious—meals for both everyday dinners and

special company's-coming occasions, we've drawn up these menu

plans. We've combined recipes from the book with simple

accompaniments you can buy or whip up without a formal recipe.

And we've mixed dishes that you can make ahead with those that

need last-minute work so you needn't do everything at once.

SUNDAY BREAKFAST

Orange juice
Cinnamon-Scented French Toast*

Mixed Berry Sauce*
Low-fat turkey bacon

WEEKEND BRUNCH

Mint Eye-Openers*
Tomato juice
Fig and Oat Muffins*

Turkey-Apple Canapés*
Broccoli Quiche*
Fruit and reduced-fat cheese platter

LADIES' TEA

Iced herb tea
Strawberry Tea Sandwiches*
French Duck Salad*

Lemon Poppy Scones*
Orange marmalade
Creamy Apricot Mousse*

WINTER HOLIDAY PARTY

Rubyburst Warm-Ups*
Spinach Dip with Pita Wedges*
Artichoke Mini Pizzas*
Sweet Potato, Sausage and
  Apple Stew*

Platter of grapes, oranges, kumquats
  and other winter fruits
Poached Pears with Raspberry
  Yogurt Sauce*

SUMMER OUTING

Strawberry and Peach Coolers*
Rouille* with crisp raw vegetables
  and bread sticks
Grilled chicken breasts
Marinated Mushroom Brochettes*

Corn on the cob
Green salad with low-fat
  French dressing
Patriotic Parfaits*

ELEGANT CHICKEN DINNER
FOR COMPANY

Scalloped Oysters*
Piccata-Style Chicken with Rice*
Steamed snap peas
Poppy seed dinner rolls

Tossed salad
Creamy Parmesan-Pepper Dressing*
Cheesecake Tart*

EASY LASAGNA DINNER

Lasagna Swirls*
Low-fat whole-grain rolls

Cooked asparagus
Blackberry Crisp*

*See recipe.

THANKSGIVING ANYTIME

Green salad
Creamy Buttermilk Dressing*
Turkey Tenderloin au Poivre*
Mashed potatoes with low-fat gravy

Simply Tomatoes*
Bake-and-serve dinner rolls
Pumpkin Pie* with low-fat
   whipped topping

ITALIAN DINNER FOR COMPANY

Arugula-Stuffed Calzones*
Eggplant Parmesan*
Italian bread

Salad with creamy low-fat
   Italian dressing
Strawberry Fluff Desserts*

EXOTIC ENTERTAINING

Mango Smoothies*
Grilled Chicken with Spinach*
Cucumber Salad*

Pear Chutney*
Lemon Icebox Pie*

CHICKEN FOR THE FAMILY

Lemon-Mustard Chicken Breasts*
Baked Sweet Potatoes with Ginger
   and Honey*

Steamed cauliflower with butter-
   flavored sprinkles
Oriental Rice Pudding*

TURKEY FAMILY DINNER

Turkey and Pear Sauté*
Broad noodles

Steamed carrots
Apple Cake with Orange Syrup*

PIZZA AT HOME

Turkey-Sausage Pan Pizza*
Broccoli and Mushroom Salad*

Oranges Supreme*

QUICK FISH DINNER FOR THE FAMILY

Sautéed Mahimahi*
Yogurt and Mustard Sauce*
Microwave-baked potatoes

Balsamic Broccoli Rabe*
Pear and Raspberry Clafouti*

AN EVENING IN SPAIN

Spanish Pepper Shrimp*
Quick-cooking brown rice
Tossed salad

Raspberry Dressing
Herb Dinner Rolls*
Lime sherbet

*See recipe.

EASTERN SHORE FAMILY DINNER

Crab Patties*
Tartar Sauce*
Peanut Slaw*

Corn and Parmesan Spoon Bread*
Low-fat marble pound cake

SALMON DINNER FOR GUESTS

Creamy Potato and Squash Soup*
*Grilled Salmon with Cucumber
  Relish**
Rice
Steamed broccoli

*Bitter Greens with Hot Vinaigrette
  Dressing**
Angel food cake
Strawberry Sauce*

MEXICAN FAMILY DINNER

Spinach Enchiladas*
Chunky salsa
Rice

Spicy Cornbread*
Fruit Salad with Lime Dressing*

FAMILY DINNER IN ITALY

Matthew's Last-Minute Pasta*
*Green salad with low-fat
  Italian dressing*

Olive Focaccia*
Apricot, Fig and Yogurt Swirl*

MEATLESS FAMILY DINNER

Colorful Stuffed Peppers*
*French bread with reduced-fat
  butter or margarine*

Green Beans with Rosemary*
Chocolate frozen yogurt
Orange and Blueberry Sauce*

*See recipe.

Index

Note: Page references in **boldface** indicate photographs.